Divine Traces of the Daoist Sisterhood

"Records of the Assembled Transcendents
of the Fortified Walled City"

by Du Guangting (850 - 933)

Translated and annotated
with an introduction by

Suzanne E. Cahill

Three Pines Press
P.O. Box 207
Magdalena, NM 87825
www.threepinespress.com

9   8 7 6 5 4 3 2 1

Printed in the United States of America
⊗ This edition is printed on acid-free paper that meets
the American National Standard Institute Z39.48 Standard.
Distributed in the United States by Three Pines Press.

Cover art: Color plates from *Jinci songso*, edited by Jia Lili (Shanxi Ren-
min chubanshe, 2000), pp. 29, 54. Used by permission.

Library of Congress Cataloging-in-Publication Data

Du, Guangting, 850-933.
Divine traces of the Daoist sisterhood: records of the assembled transcendents of the fortified walled city / by Du Guangting; translated and
annotated with an Introduction by Suzanne E. Cahill.
        p. cm.
Includes bibliographical references and index.
        ISBN 1-931483-04-3 (alk. paper)
1. Taoist women--China. 2. Feminism--Religious aspects--Taoism.
I. Cahill, Suzanne Elizabeth. II. Title. III. Title: Records of the
assembled transcendents of the fortified walled city.
        BL1923.D82 2006
        299.5'14082--dc22
        2005035610

To my parents:

Helen Hughes Cahill (1924 - 1992)

Edward James Cahill (1920 - 2002)

And to my sisters:

Alison Cahill Sawyer

Peg Cahill Brotherton

I Pay a Visit to Refined Master Zhao without Meeting Her

Yu Xuanji (844-868)

Where are you and your transcendent companions?
Your green-clothed servant rests alone in the household.
On the warm stove: remains of your steeped herbs,
In the adjoining courtyard: boiling tea.
Painted walls grow dim in the lamps' radiance;
Shadows from banners' poles slant.
Anxiously I turn my head back again and again,
At numerous branches of blossoms outside your walls.

Contents

List of Illustrations

Part 1: The Queen Mother of the West. Source: Han lithograph.

Part 2: A matriarch on her way to the immortals. Source: *Liexian quanzhuan*.

Part 3: The Chart of the True Shape of the Sourthern Marchmount. Source: *Wuyue zhenxing tu*.

Part 4: Portrait of a woman in white, purported to be Lu Meiniang (# 25). Yuan dynasty hanging scroll. Source: Freer Gallery of Art, Washington, D.C. (F1917.114).

Page 152: A divine lady busy at her loom. Source: *Liexian quanzhuan*.

Acknowledgments

I first encountered Du Guangting's "Records of the Assembled Transcendents of the Fortified Walled City" in 1977, while leafing through the Daoist canon in search of a text about women in medieval China. It was a fortuitous discovery. Du's hagiographical collection is one of the rare books from pre-modern China devoted exclusively to female figures. I became fascinated with the first account in the text, a lengthy biography of the goddess Xiwangmu, Queen Mother of the West, and ended up writing a dissertation and then a book on her. Later, wanting to turn away from eternally perfect deities to investigate actual historical women, I remembered that "Records of the Assembled Transcendents of the Fortified Walled City" included human as well as divine women and revisited the text. The current work results from over ten years of study of the whole work.

Du Guangting's accounts of Daoist holy women are among the most detailed and complete records of medieval Chinese women's lives to be found anywhere. Tang dynastic histories and poetry written by Tang men mostly repeat standard images of women as evil empresses, bewitching concubines, or faceless victims of Confucian patriarchy. The references are mostly brief, and the women do not grow or develop. After reading a few biographies of female saints in Du Guangting's collection, I realized that they tell compelling and entertaining stories. These accounts counteract simple stereotypes of medieval women to reveal a rich and complicated reality. The biographies introduce distinctly individual women of diverse regional and class backgrounds. These people change over time, negotiate solutions to conflicts between personal goals and traditional roles, and act creatively within the limitations imposed upon them by the medieval Chinese social context.

The topic of medieval Chinese Daoist women is timely because it relates to issues in the field of critical gender studies that are currently subject to intense debate. These include cultural constructions of gender, body modification, and discipline, as well as women's agency, inner life, voice, self-expression, and place in family and society. Studies of Daoist female saints also contribute to the contemporary discussion about the ability of traditional religions all over the world to accommodate changing roles of women without altering the basic essences and core values of those religions.

This book will question several of our assumptions about medieval Chinese life and thought. For example, is Daoism as good to women as some modern Daoists claim? Was the Tang dynasty really the golden age for women's rights in China? I will also challenge the received scholarship about the relationships between Daoism, Confucianism, and Buddhism during the Tang dynasty. I argue that Tang Daoist writers like Du Guangting supported Confucian officials and values, and considered Buddhists their main rivals.

I believe that religious sources should not be discarded as non-objective, but rather welcomed as rich storehouses of information and ideas. Since Daoism was so central to medieval Chinese life, Daoist texts are essential for an understanding of that life. Texts such as Daoist Master Du's set of biographies, read with elementary caution, have a great deal to tell the modern reader about women, religion, and society in the Tang.

In the realm of theory, I am trying to leave behind both victim feminism—in which women are treated as a-historical, passive recipients of male domination—and the orientalist image of unchanging China. I am looking for creations of culture, control, self-definition, and agency in limiting circumstances. I want to include but also go beyond ideas of women's resistance or contestation and acquiescence or negotiation in relation to normative social roles, to investigate both the dark and light side of creating culture and control within limiting structures. As active participants in their own lives, women can be agents of their own self-destruction and death, as well as of transformation and liberation. Although Du Guangting's accounts concern heroines with happy outcomes, we must not forget the darker side. Shadows give definition to the lives Du highlights. Among choices, I want to include negative choices. I hope to shed light on Daoism, gender, and life in Tang China, and also on the darker side of these subjects.

The works of several authors have influenced this one. In the field of Daoist history, I have profited from the scholarship of Steve Bokenkamp, Judith M. Boltz, Robert Campany, Catherine Despeux, Stephen Eskildsen, Paul Katz, Livia Kohn, Luo Zhengming, Peter Nickerson, Isabelle Robinet, Kristofer Schipper, Franciscus Verellen, and Yang Li. The works of Francesca Bray, Patricia Ebrey, Charlotte Furth, Dorothy Ko, Susan

Mann, and Ann Waltner have helped me understand the place of women in Chinese history and culture. Beata Grant, Li Yuzhen, Diana Paul, Kathryn Tsai, and Chun-fang Yu provided valuable comparative material on women in Buddhism. In the area of women and saints in western medieval religion and society, which I have studied for comparative purposes, I have benefited enormously from the works of Peter Brown, Carolyn Walker Bynum, Georges Duby, Jo Ann Kay McNamara, and Andre Vauchez. Writing by Kay Redfield Jamison, Walker Percy, Marilee Strong, and William Styron has helped me connect conflict, religious practice, and healing. The research and models of Richard Mather, Edward Schafer, and Anna Seidel continue to influence all my sinological works.

In particular, I want to acknowledge assistance graciously given me over the long time that I have been working on this project. I have received invaluable criticism and support from Stephen Bokenkamp, Sue Fernsebner, Russell Kirkland, Terry Kleeman, Dorothy Ko, Livia Kohn, Richard van Glahn, Susan Mann, Cecily McCaffrey, Hal Roth, Audrey Spiro, Christena Turner, Ann Waltner, Yao Ping, Ye Wa, and three anonymous readers for Three Pines Press. I would like to acknowledge Ye Wa for her assistance in identifying and compiling the Chinese characters. Last, but very much not least, I also wish to thank my husband, John McNeece, and son, Sean McNeece, for their patience and support. Sean merits special thanks for help with computers. And John deserves additional credit for carrying my reference books all over China and serving as my first critical editor.

Map of China

Dynastic Chart*

B.C.E.

Xia	ca. 2100-1600
Shang	ca. 1600-1028
Zhou	ca. 1027-256
Western Zhou	ca. 1027-771
Eastern Zhou	ca. 770-256
Spring and Autumn	722-468
Warring States	403-221
Qin	221-207
Han	206 B.C.E.-220 C.E.
Former Han	206-8 C.E.

C.E.

Xin	9-25
Latter Han	25-220
Three Kingdoms	220-265
Wei	220-265
Shu	221-263
Wu	222-280
Jin	265-420
Western Jin	265-317
Eastern Jin	317-420
Six Dynasties	420-589
SOUTHERN	
Liu Song	420-479
Southern Qi	479-502
Southern Liang	502-557
Southern Chen	557-589

---

* These dates are based on William H. Nienhauser, *The Indiana Companion to Traditional Chinese Literature* (Bloomington: Indiana University Press, 1986).

NORTHERN		
Northern Wei	386-534	
Eastern Wei	534-550	
Western Wei	535-577	
Northern Qi	550-577	
Northern Zhou	557-581	
Sui	581-618	
Tang	618-907	
Zhou	690-705	
Five Dynasties	907-960	
Liao	916-1125	
Song	960-1279	
Northern Song	960-1126	
Southern Song	1127-1279	
Jin (Jurchen)	1115-1234	
Yuan (Mongols)	1260-1368	
Ming	1368-1644	
Qing	1644-1911	
Republic (Taiwan)	1911-	
People's Republic	1949-	

Introduction

I address this book both to specialists and non-specialists. I want my students and my non-sinologist sisters as well as my colleagues to be able to read it. The introduction is meant to provide the reader with the background needed to understand the translations and place them in their cultural context. Experts may want to skip some sections.

Aims and Issues

My main aims are simply stated. I want to put women back into the historical picture and come to understand medieval Daoism a little better. Du Guangting's collection of biographies gives me the opportunity to do both. Women are not ahistorical, as Du clearly recognized. Women may live on the borders or inner frontiers of Chinese society, constrained by law and custom, with limited access to means of self-expression, and with limited recognition in Chinese literature, society, and religion. But they are there, creating their lives with the resources available to them.

The present work is part of a long-term project to find women wherever they are and return them to Tang history. Biographies of women, often depicted as marginal or oppositional figures, can provide the historian with information about contradictions in social systems, and arguments or disputes about those systems including attacks on them and justifications for them. I want to look at what women do to create culture in limited spaces with restricted financial security, political or familial power, materials, and skills. I want to examine both positive and negative consequences of women's working in this limited cultural space. Here I look at women's participation in Tang society through the window of their participation in the full religious life of Daoism, the major native religion of the time. In particular I examine issues of family relationships, education, control and self-control, body and gender, literary and religious expression, and the results of religious practices such as asceticism and meditation. I investigate both the bright and dark sides: social empow-

1

erment and religious transformation on the one hand, physical danger and commodification on the other.[1]

What can we find out about medieval Chinese women and their experiences, thoughts, and emotions? Where can we find it? The significant limitations of religious biographies, including the partisan viewpoint of the writer, and the mixing of matters of fact and faith, have led many scholars to neglect them as primary sources. The presentation of miraculous occurrences, such as flying to heaven in broad daylight or conversing with animals, next to mundane details of everyday life, such as birthplace, work, or family relations, can be disorienting for the modern reader, to say the least. Hagiography makes a different claim than historical biography about the truthfulness of its narrative. Daoist hagiography claims to be truthful in the sense that individual saints' lives are genuine or authentic (zhen 真) embodiments of the doctrines of the Daoist religion. In fact the term for one kind of Daoist transcendent is zhenren 真人, literally a "realized" or "perfected" person. In most cases, critical readers of holy biographies have few problems separating reliable historical or social evidence from matters of faith. I would argue that hagiography provides a rich and underutilized resource—especially if read carefully, alongside other texts and material remains of the period.

Texts like Du Guangting's collection help us understand how ascetic physical practices (discipline) lead to Daoist religious goals (transformation) for women. We can examine the links between asceticism, sacrifice, and self-destruction. We can shed light on how medieval Chinese Daoists conceive of the body and self. These texts illuminate the differences in belief and practice between Daoists and their non-Daoist contemporaries and between women and men. We can see how women religious practitioners fit into Chinese society, including the family and the state. We can determine what kind of models these were, and in what sense they represent women of their time, or women in other times and places. Most importantly, we gain insight on what they thought they were doing, and what problems they were solving.

---

[1] My approach to the study of women in Chinese history has been deeply influenced by several thinkers. Dorothy Ko (1994) argues against victim feminism and for a more nuanced approach to women's history. Patricia Ebrey (1993) gives the practical advice that we should study women where we find them: in her case within marriage, in my case in the Daoist church. She also makes useful contrasts between women's situations in the Tang and Song dynasties. Francesca Bray (1997) reminds us to include material culture and technology, and to locate women in the context of their dwelling spaces, work, and relationship to motherhood. And Charlotte Furth (1999) shows the importance and complexity of cultural constructions of the gendered body.

This is a work of exemplary literature rather than a statistically meaningful sample. Du Guangting's accounts provide cases to consider regarding their implications for Chinese society. It has both the rewards (good stories) and the limitations (uncertainty as to how broadly to apply the conclusions the material suggests) of case studies everywhere.[2]

My methodology has been a patchwork of systems worked out to deal with this specific text and the issues it raises. I have drawn upon my training in text criticism, medieval Chinese literature, history, art history, religion, and gender studies. I have also borrowed from the works of anthropologists, archaeologists, and historians of medieval European religion. I believe that the best way to study Du Guangting's rich and complex text is to apply an interdisciplinary approach. I try to make observations and draw conclusions that will be useful to readers in several fields. I relegate discussions of specific disciplinary questions and theories to endnotes.

The Context: Tang Dynasty (618-907)

During the Tang dynasty, when the Daoist master and courtier Du Guangting 杜光庭 (850-933) wrote most of his book and when many of his subjects lived, Chinese wealth, territory, and civilization had reached fabulous heights. The Tang represents a high point in Asian culture, a period in which Chinese people still take great pride. With a succession of effective emperors on the throne, a huge economy, and vast territory, China experienced a great age of prosperity and international prestige. For the first half of this era, government power rested on a secure tax base in agriculture and trade; a well-organized bureaucracy ran the country; a mighty and well-equipped army kept peace along ever-expanding borders; and ordinary subjects of the emperor enjoyed a relatively high quality of life. The Tang dynasty is considered the golden age of poetry, arts, and sciences. The principal capital city of Chang'an, home to the imperial family and center of government and commercial activity, was the biggest city of the medieval world with over a million people.

---

[2] For the courage to consider meaningful a study of medieval culture that relies on models rather than statistics, I rely upon works such as Georges Duby's *Medieval Marriage* (1978). He reconstructs the social history and practice of marriage in one European country during the middle ages, using a small amount of surviving material. He also presents useful information for comparison with China.

Chang'an was also the most cosmopolitan city of its time, the location of a sophisticated international culture.

But in 755, everything changed. A dissatisfied general from the northwestern frontier, An Lushan 安錄山, led a rebellion that shook the country to its roots. Although his army was defeated and he was killed, the country never fully recovered, and many changes took place. The transformations in the Chinese government, economy, and society were so profound that many scholars now locate the transition from medieval to pre-modern China in this mid-Tang rebellion and its aftermath.[3]

Du Guangting lived at court during the waning years of the Tang and witnessed events leading to the downfall of the dynasty and to the subsequent establishment of a smaller kingdom called Former Shu (907-925) with its capital in Chengdu, Sichuan. Du's work is influenced by the circumstances of chaos and crisis, and by the prevailing mood of anxiety and depression that characterized his era.

According to the somewhat idealizing constructions of later Chinese thinkers, Tang society was divided into four main social classes. On top were the bureaucrats or literati officials, who monopolized government and education. Most Tang authors were officials originating in this class. Du Guangting, an official as well as a Daoist master, lived at court with the imperial family and associated with literati officials while he was writing his biographies of Daoist women. Beneath the small, literate official class were the farmers, honored for their essential role in producing food and the economic surplus that allowed Chinese civilization to flourish, but rarely rewarded in any way commensurate with their contributions.

In the Tang dynasty, farmers made up the vast majority of the population. Next were the craftsmen, providers of essential services, also respected for their important contributions to material culture and the economy, but not necessarily well compensated. Last were the merchants, who the Chinese traditionally viewed as parasites living off the labor of others. The government was suspicious of merchants, fearing their ability to accumulate wealth and possibly pose a threat to the central power of the Chinese imperium. Outside the traditional class system, and organized in a hierarchical system that paralleled the relations of bureaucrats and farmers, were the military leadership and the soldiers.

---

[3] For history of the Tang dynasty, see Twitchett 1979. See also Adshead 2004; Benn 2002. On the capital city, see Xiong 2000. On Tang society and history, see the ongoing series edited *Tang Yanjiu* (Tang Studies), from Beijing University Press.

Struggles between the civil (*wen* 文) and military (*wu* 武) sides of government were a constant and characteristic contradiction of the imperial bureaucratic system.

The actual picture of social classes in medieval China, according to contemporary Tang sources, was more fluid and complex. Merchants along the Silk Road contributed substantially to government coffers, officials participated in commerce, and the early Tang emperors were proud of their own military origins and prowess. Du Guangting's subjects, representing the diversity of Tang society, come from all social classes.

Geographers divide China into two great regions: the northern one centered on the Yellow river and its plains, and the southern one centered on the Yangzi River and its surroundings. But a cultural geography would divide the Tang world most prominently into the areas around the capital cities on the one hand, and, on the other, everywhere else. The two capitals of Chang'an and Luoyang, seats of government and centers of culture and commerce, both located in the north on tributaries of the Yellow River, were considered the most central and desirable locations. Another important city for our story is Chengdu in mountainous Sichuan province to the southwest of the capital cities. Du Guangting accompanied the Tang emperor and court to Chengdu when they were forced to flee the capital in 881. Du also lived there as a courtier in the subsequent Former Shu dynasty. Several of our subjects were also active there. The women in Du's biographies come from all over the Tang empire, with a strong preference for south.

Along with the official world of government administration and tax registers, there was a world of holy mountains and waterways. The most prominent of the holy mountains and the oldest were the marchmounts or sacred mountains of the five directions: Mount Tai 泰山 in the East, Hua 華山 in the West, Song 嵩山 in the Center, Heng 衡山 in the North, and another, different Heng 恆山 in the South. There were also famous Buddhist mountains such as Mounts Emei in Sichuan and Tiantai in Zhejiang, still pilgrimage sites today. And there were Daoist holy mountains. One of the most famous was Mount Qingcheng in Sichuan, where the Celestial Masters school of Daoism began. Du Guangting probably lived there while compiling his text. Another eminent mountain was Mount Mao, residence of the three Mao brothers, deities associated with the beginnings of the Supreme Clarity school of Daoism in the fourth century C.E.

In addition to actual places that we can locate on a map, there were imaginary sites, such as the heaven of the Queen Mother of the West on Mount Kunlun far beyond the borders of the known world in the exotic occident, and Penglai and other Isles of the Blessed far away in the Eastern Sea. Above the earth there were many Daoist heavens, and tribunals or courts for the dead beneath the earth. And for Daoists, there were grotto heavens, cave worlds beneath holy mountains where the faithful could go to survive the chaos and destruction that arrived at the end of each world age. All of these otherworldly places were inhabited by divine beings such as creators, heavenly honored ones, and transcendents. Du Guangting was a student of holy cosmography—the mapping of the religious world—and wrote several works on numinous and lucky places. His subjects often travel to or ultimately reside in such places.[4]

Daoist Religion in the Tang

By the time the Tang dynasty ruled China, Daoism already had a long history as China's native major religion. Since the second century of the Common Era, Daoists had revered a host of deities, engaged in numerous rituals, and practiced individual self-cultivation, all in order to attain perfection, which included eternal life and residence in the Daoist heavens. The two earliest traditions of Daoism that could be considered religious institutions began in the late Han dynasty, one in Sichuan province and one in the capital city of Luoyang. In Sichuan the school known as the Celestial Masters (Tianshi 天師) began with visions of the deified Laozi by the first Celestial Master Zhang Daoling 張道陵 in 142 C.E. The group grew into a great organized community, producing scriptures, precepts, methods of organization, and ritual practices that continue in some form down to the present. The Great Peace (Taiping 太平) School that began in Luoyang was utopian, messianic, and apocalyptic. They also created scriptures and practices that survive today.

During the fourth and fifth centuries, two great schools arose which continued into the Tang. These are the Supreme Clarity (Shangqing 上清) and the Numinous Treasure (Lingbao 靈寶) schools. The Shangqing tradition emphasized perfection through individual practices such as meditation and asceticism; it found adherents among the imperial family and

---

[4] On mountains and caves in Daoist cosmology and practice, see Hahn 1988; 2000.More detailed studies of specific mountains are found in Chavannes 1910 on Mount Tai; Robson 1995a, 1995b, 1995c on the southern Mount Heng.

elite of the Tang. The Lingbao school favored collective ritual and community worship and provided many rites for the state and people of the Tang. The main Daoist schools were religious institutions, with clergy organized in a hierarchical fashion that echoed both the imperial and the divine bureaucracy. Texts and rituals were handed down through lineages. There was always considerable overlap and borrowing between different schools. For most lay people, distinctions between schools made little difference in daily belief and practice. More important for the average believer would be local and official cults along with family and regional traditions. But for clergy like Du Guangting, we can assume that school and lineage did have meaning. Du Guangting was a Shangqing master, the pre-eminent member of the Shangqing lineage in his generation. In his writings, Du tried to unite the two main traditions of his time under the leadership of his own Shangqing school. All his works, including the present one, are intended to glorify both Daoism and his school.[5]

Daoist adepts worked to achieve perfection by means of religious practices that were organized in a hierarchical order leading from the simplest stages to the most difficult. They began with faith and good works, progressed to ascetic practices such as fasting and sexual abstinence, and finally reached meditation and visualization. Mature and successful religious practice led to fruits of the faith, such as youthfulness and superpowers. In the end, the successful adept departed from this world and ascended to heaven to become part of the celestial bureaucracy.[6]

A perfected or realized person in Daoism is comparable to a saint in the Catholic Church. Saints in most religions are made by assignment of titles by imperial or religious authorities or by popular acclaim, and defined as receivers of cult, creators of community, and conduits to the divine. A Catholic saint is verified by investigation under canon law and legitimated by the church, one of the most powerful institutions of medieval Europe. In contrast, Daoist saints prove their transcendence by the manner of their departure: their perfection is verified when they do not die and decompose, but instead ascend to heaven leaving either no corpse at all or a light and fragrant shell. And Daoist saints are legitimated by their ties to two of the most important social systems of medieval China: lineage and bureaucracy. They are placed within a school lineage and granted a posthumous position in the celestial bureaucracy.

---

[5] For Daoism, its history and texts, see Kohn 2000, 2001; Bokenkamp 1997; Robinet 1997); and Kirkland 2004. On Tang-dynasty Daoism, see Barrett 1996; Kirkland 1997; Kohn and Kirkland 2000.

[6] For relevant studies, see Kohn 1989; Robinet 1993; Eskildsen 1998.

Thus verification is linked to proof of body's incorruptibility, while legitimization is linked to inclusion in a Daoist fictive family and lineage, and assignment of heavenly office.[7]

Gender Roles in the Tang

Gender roles during the Tang dynasty were heir to the ideas and customs of earlier eras. Concepts still governing understanding of women's roles in the Tang include *neiwai* 內外 (literally, "inside and outside"). This is the Chinese version of the model of gender relations sometimes called "separate spheres" in which the men work and operate outside the household in the worlds of agriculture and public life, while the women live and work within the household, taking charge of child-raising and the domestic economy. While separate spheres denotes distinctions in location, the Chinese folk expression "men till and women weave" expresses the difference in terms of economic function. Another concept informing female and male roles is that of yin and yang. Yin, originally the shady bank of the river or side of the hill, represents the dark, wet, passive, responsive female force. Yang represents the bright, hot, active, creative male force.

By the Han dynasty, yin and yang come to represent equal and opposite forces in the universe, constantly acting upon one another to create and maintain the world. This implies a certain equality in the value of male and female; yin-yang duality has often been used by Chinese feminists to find something positive and worth keeping in past traditions. Later more negative connotations attach to yin, and the term comes to imply something inferior or even harmful. Another model, suggesting the lower position of women compared to men in the social hierarchy, is that of *san-zong* 三從, literally: "the three follows." This suggests that a woman follows, that is: takes her status from and obeys, men in her family at all stages of her life. As a child, she follows her father, as a young wife, she

---

[7] On the process of sanctification in the Catholic church, see Woodward 1990. On sainthood in the western middle ages, see Brown 1981; Vauchez 1997. All three follow a long tradition of scholarship that assumes the importance of saints and hagiographies in medieval western history. This contrasts with the attitudes of several great early twentieth century historians of China, such as Hu Shih (1891-1962), who scorned Daoism and Buddhism as products of a backward era that posed obstacles in the path of China's modernization and strength. Chinese scholars in general, from the second half of the twentieth century on, have started to recognize the importance of religion in Chinese history. On the process of making Daoist female saints in China, see Cahill 1999.

follows her husband, and as an elderly widow, she follows her oldest son. One final expression important in understanding gender roles in early China is *nannü zhi bie* 男女之別, literally: "distinctions between men and women." This implies that men and women are and should be different. Taken together, these ideas and expressions assume that men and women are distinguishable, that certain activities and places are appropriate for each, and that women follow men in the gender hierarchy.

Women in early Chinese society were expected to conform to norms that later came to be called "Confucian ideals." According to classical literature, medical texts, and books on appropriate behavior written especially for women, women were to be virtuous, hard working, and filial. Their greatest duty as loyal subjects and filial daughters-in-law was to bear and raise sons for the patriline into which they married. Their own interests were subordinated to or identified with the interests of their family.[8]

The Tang dynasty has the reputation of being a good time for women. Several famous women of the period, such as the empress Wu Zetian 吳則天 (d. 705) and the beauty Yang Guifei 楊貴妃 (d. 756), are well known even today. Bound feet were still in the future. Women could inherit property and widows could remarry. Many factors account for women's relative power and prestige during this time. The Tang ruling family derived partly from nomadic tribes in Central Asia, generally referred to as *hu* 胡 (Turkish or barbarian) in classical literature. They had different and more relaxed notions of the proper roles and work of women. In addition, intermarriage between powerful clans intensified during the Tang dynasty, with women from prominent families becoming highly desirable as wives.

The positions of women from the great clans in their husbands' families depended to some extent on the political clout their original families maintained in society.[9] Women had more political power, personal freedom, and chances for social prominence than in the following period, when Li-school thinkers (known in the West as Neo-Confucians) were to assert that a virtuous woman could not be talented. Still, we must not lose sight of the many significant restrictions placed on Tang women by patriarchal law, custom, and social ideals. As our biographies show, this was not exactly a golden age for the liberation of Chinese women, although it was a time in which some women found great opportunities for leadership and accomplishment.

---

[8] For studies of this aspect of Chinese women, see Raphals 1998; Hinsch 2002.
[9] See Tung 2000; Deng 2003; Yao 2004.

Women and Daoism in the Tang

Religion was a source of both power and constraint for medieval Chinese women. The belief that yin force was equal and opposite to the yang force in Daoist cosmology was extended, however unevenly, to women's power and prestige in the Daoist church. Women played important roles in the Daoist religion from its earliest beginnings in the Celestial Masters and Great Peace schools of the Later Han dynasty. Even before the Tang, women contributed to Daoist ritual, practice, teachings, and institutional life, both as leaders and followers. Along with nuns, priestesses, and laywomen, there were prominent female Daoist saints, hermits, and wonderworkers. Daoist scriptures, like those of the Buddhists, show a range of attitudes towards women.

The attitudes displayed by Daoist and Buddhist texts alike concerning women's social and family roles reflect the surrounding culture more than any fundamental teachings of the faith. The Daoist church provided both female clergy and laywomen with opportunities to acquire education and play leadership roles in society and politics. And the Daoist church, much like the Buddhist, provided a social and economic safety net for women in need. Daoist female deities and saints provided women with devotional foci and models for their spiritual lives. Famous and infamous Daoist women of the Tang, including princesses such as Jade Verity (Yuzhen 玉真, ordained 711), imperial consorts such as Yang Guifei (d. 756), and nun-poets such as Yu Xuanji 魚玄機 (d. 868) served as examples of female agency.[10]

While many accounts of Daoist female figures are found scattered throughout the Daoist canon, Du Guangting's collection is the first and only text to present exclusively the lives of female Daoists. In Du's day, there were already well-known collections devoted to the lives of Buddhist nuns and exemplary Confucian women. Perhaps the author intended to supply a set of Daoist biographies to rival those. In addition, the textual record suggests that through the end of the Tang dynasty, Daoist women and men engaged in roughly the same practices and rituals. After the Tang, special Daoist practices for women appear, clearly intended to separate them and distinguish their activities from those of

---

[10] On women and Daoism, see Despeux and Kohn 2003. On Daoist nuns, see Zhou 2004. On equality between men and women in Daoism, see Anderson 1994. To compare the history of nuns in the West, see McNamara 1996. On fasting and women in medieval Europe, see Bynum 1987.

men. Du Guangting's sequestering of women's biographies in his collection prefigures the segregation between men and women in Daoist life and practice that occurs in the following period.

Women and Buddhism in the Tang

Du Guangting considered Chinese Buddhism his most important competition. Du frequently compared Daoism and Buddhism, arguing that Daoism was superior to Buddhism as a religious choice for women in particular, as well as for society as a whole. While there are distinctions between women's roles in the Buddhist and Daoist religions, there are also similarities.

Buddhism, originally imported from India along the Silk Road, was transformed and domesticated by the beginning of the Tang dynasty. The Buddhist religion was a rich, prestigious, and powerful institution, supported by people and rulers alike. Buddhist scriptures show a broad range of attitudes towards women, from the most misogynistic writings of early celibate monks portraying women as lewd temptresses, to later Mahayana scriptures arguing that women as well as men possessed a buddha nature and could be enlightened.

The Chinese had translated the *Vinaya* or monastic rules for nuns, and nuns lived in convents in the capital and elsewhere throughout the realm. A great early sixth century work, the *Biqiuni zhuan* 比丘尼傳 (Biographies of Nuns),[11] detailing their heroic contributions to society and to the faith, was an important model for Du Guangting in writing his biographies of Daoist female figures. Eminent women Buddhists, such as Sui Wendi's mother and Empress Wu Zetian, provided models of women wielding power. Inscriptions in cave temples near Luoyang and Dunhuang show the prominence of nuns as patrons of religious art. The same inscriptions reveal that many laywomen devotees also controlled wealth and used it to make donations to the Buddhist church. The Buddhist order for women provided great opportunities for women to gain an education, live independently of the patriarchal family system, and exercise social leadership and influence.

Most women, however, did not take holy orders. For laywomen, Buddhism offered social and religious support. The Buddhist deity known as Guanyin, often depicted as female after the Tang dynasty, personified

---

[11] This important collection is translated in Tsai 1994.

the virtue of compassion, and was a figure of devotion believed to bring women children and salvation from all kinds of disasters. Chinese lay-women living in the family also had to cope with the Buddhist version of ritual impurity adhering to childbirth. The Chinese family system required that they bear sons. Yet popular Buddhist belief held that women who had given birth had to atone for a sea of blood released by child-bearing. Unless the proper religious rituals performed by their filial children rescued them, they would live forever in the lowest hells after death. Tang Buddhism provided a broad and often contradictory range of attitudes towards women and models for them to follow.[12]

The Author

Du Guangting (850-933) was a native of Guacang in Chuzhou (modern Zhejiang). As a young man, he failed the imperial exam in the classics, then moved to Mount Tiantai. Better known in the Tang as a Buddhist than a Daoist holy place, Mount Tiantai was sacred to both religions. There Du prepared himself for the Daoist priesthood. He became one of the greatest masters of the Shangqing school, the Daoist tradition that emphasized self-cultivation. This school appealed especially to the official class and royal family. Du joined the court of the Tang emperor Xizong (r. 874-888) as an official and as a Daoist master.

In 881, during the rebellion of Huang Chao 黃巢 (d. 884), Du followed Xizong into exile in Chengdu, Sichuan. He returned to the capital with the emperor and his entourage in 885. The last date specifically named in Du Guangting's text is 886. Emperor Xizong died in 888. In the meantime his military commander, Wang Jian 王建 (847-918), was taking control of Sichuan. He was ruler there by 891, founding a kingdom known as Former Shu. Du Guangting was honored at the new court and awarded high positions and grand titles, including his best known honorific title "Prior-Born of Broad Completion," bestowed upon him in 913. Du signs off his introduction to the collection with that honorific, suggesting he completed the book shortly after 913, unless the epithet was added later. During Wang Jian's reign, Du was tutor to the heir apparent. When his student took the throne as the second Former Shu sovereign, Wang Yan 王衍 (r. 919-925), Du received further honors and titles, including that of

---

[12] For women in Buddhism in general, see Paul 1980. A comprehensive study of Guanyin is found in Yü 2001. On gender politics in traditional China, see Lai 1999.

Celestial Master who Transmits Truth, before retiring to Mount Qing-cheng at the summit of the Mingshan range.

Du Guangting was a prolific editor and author, many of whose works survive today in the *Zhengtong Daozang* 正通道藏 ("Daoist Canon of the Rectified Unity Reign Period; 1445). Of his numerous works, in addition to the present text, those most relevant to this study concern ritual pro-cedures, holy places, and relations of the Daoist church with the Chinese imperium. Du Guangting tried in his writings to unite the two main teachings of his time, Shangqing and Lingbao, under the leadership of his own school. All of Du's works, including the present one, glorify both Daoism and his school.[13]

Du Guangting's book of holy women has several expressed purposes. In his introduction to the text, Du states his desire to record the lives of women saints neglected by other sources, to link his female subjects in a religious lineage that joins past and present, and to show the great vari-ety of valid paths to the Way. He recommends these saints as authentic and worthy of veneration. He also intends to demonstrate that adepts can and must seek their own salvation through religious practice. And he praises the Tang dynasty for producing such auspicious signs of heaven's approval as living saints.

A careful reading of the whole text also suggests some motivations that Du Guangting does not state directly. His hidden agendas are not di-rectly related to gender, but include concerns that pervade most of his writings. Du wants to clarify points of Daoist doctrine. He argues for the superiority of Daoism over Buddhism, for the unification of the Daoist church, and for the exaltation of his school over others. He wants to ex-plain local cults to individual saints in a way that will bring these cults into his school and make them acceptable to his audience of literati offi-cials and Daoist leaders. He wishes to save Daoist records from the chaos attendant upon the end of the Tang dynasty, encourage imperial and literati patronage of the Daoist church, and promote the Daoist religion as a means of salvation in troubled times. He wants to ally the Daoist church with the imperial bureaucracy and with Confucian values such as loyalty and filial piety. He supports the legitimacy of the Tang court in

---

[13] On the life and works of Du Guangting, see Verellen 1989. I have generally fol-lowed Verellen in matters of dating Du Guangting's career and works. See also Bell 1987; Yang 2000; Luo 2003a; 2003b. Luo cites the many worthwhile studies undertaken by Chi-nese scholars in recent decades, and raises several fascinating questions on the biographical study of Du Guangting, including the possibility that there existed two authors named Du Guangting, some of whose works may have been conflated by modern scholars.

exile in Chengdu, laying the groundwork for his own future service in the subsequent Former Shu court there. Intentional or not, by separating women's biographies, Du reinforced the separation of men and women in all aspects of life that was to increase in severity and momentum during the subsequent Song dynasty.

The Text

Song imperial bibliographers list Du Guangting's hagiographical account of Daoist holy women, the *Yongcheng jixian lu* 墉城集仙錄 (Records of the Assembled Transcendents of the Fortified Walled City) and state that it was ten scrolls in length and contained 109 separate accounts. Today a work of this title is preserved in two different versions in the *Daozang* of the Ming dynasty. One recension (DZ 783)[14] contains thirty-seven separate accounts; the other consists of twenty-seven accounts, collected in the authoritative Song-dynasty encyclopedia *Yunji qiqian* 雲笈七籤 (Seven Slips from a Bookbag of Clouds, DZ 1032), chs. 114-16. Du Guangting's preface says that his collection is ten scrolls in length, but the longest version extant today is only six scrolls long. Perhaps at some point editors divided the original work and added additional material. Also, a further twenty-six lives derived from Du Guangting's original work appear in the Song imperial encyclopedia *Taiping guangji* 太平廣記 (Broad Records from the Era of Great Peace), chs. 56-70. If we eliminate biographies that are repeated, a total of seventy-nine of Du's original accounts are preserved today.

Of the twenty-six lives in the *Taiping guangji*, nine tell the stories of figures also recounted in one of the *Daozang* editions, but they are shorter and less detailed. They also contain significant differences in plot and characterization. I conclude that these accounts may retain the outline of Du Guangting's original work, but they have been abbreviated and altered too much to be counted as authentic examples of his hagiographical corpus.

The two versions preserved in the *Daozang* deserve further study as works by Du Guangting. They have only two biographies in common: those of the Queen Mother of the West and the Mysterious Woman of

---

14 "DZ" stands for *Daozang* (Daoist Canon). Texts in this collection are referred to according to numbers in Komjathy 2002; Schipper and Verellen 2004. The *Yongcheng jixian lu* is found in 30: 24154-207 of the reduced 60-volume edition (Taipei: Yiwen, 1977).

the Nine Heavens. The two overlapping biographies are virtually identical in both versions. But other than these two shared accounts, the two editions of Du Guangting's records differ in subject matter and purpose. The first text mentioned above (DZ 783) narrates the lives of major and minor celestial goddesses and spells out their ranks and duties. This text could help a Daoist adept to visualize the goddesses as part of meditative practice, or let a believer know the appropriate deity to call upon for help in a specific situation.[15]

In contrast, the second version in the *Yunji qiqian* (hereafter abbreviated YJQQ) begins with the lives of two heavenly goddesses, but then devotes the majority of its entries to biographies of women who started out as mortal human beings. It is this second version that I translate below. It interests me more than the first for several reasons. For one, most of its subjects started life as human women living on this earth in identifiable historical periods. As we will see, the biographies have wildly varying degrees of historical plausibility, but they have the potential to reveal more information about real women in Chinese history than goddess narratives.

This version also seems more authoritative on a number of counts. First, it includes Du Guangting's own preface. Secondly, the Song dynasty editors of the YJQQ found this recension the most convincing and included it in their work. Thirdly, I believe that this version of the text hangs together as a whole, forming a lineage register recording the transmission of Daoist teachings from deities in the heavens to human women on earth.

The term *lu* 錄 in the title of Du's text, which I generally translate "records," is also used to designate Daoist registers of deities and lineages. This religious genealogy begins with the Queen Mother of the West, an eternal goddess whose special task was bestowing techniques and texts on humans, and proceeds in roughly chronological order through various Daoist female figures from the earliest times to Du Guangting's own era. Du Guangting himself suggests he has written a lineage document when he says, at the end of his preface, that he "gathered this flock of

---

[15] While I do not pursue the study of DZ 783 here, I do not mean to disparage it. Organizing the gods according to identity and rank is a great service. The gods and goddesses of Daoism are numerous and complex, many of them with multiple names and appearances. Du Guangting follows the example of the earlier Shangqing master Tao Hongjing (456-536), whose work he certainly knew. Tao clarified the roles and ranks of both gods and goddesses in his *Zhenling weiye tu* (Chart of the Ranks and Functions of Realized Ones and Numina, DZ 167).

explanations [biographies] and collected them as the records of a single household." The term for household or family, *jia* 家, is commonly used for religious lineages. The Queen Mother appears at the beginning of the text as the ancestress of the women whose lives follow as well as the ultimate source of their texts and arts. Part of her name, *wangmu* 王母, which I usually translate "Queen Mother," is glossed in Han dynasty dictionaries as "ancestress." In this way, Du provides his subjects, even the unmarried and childless ones, with an ancestral lineage to care for them in the next world and bring them status in this one. He also combines accounts of women representing different traditions, to create a unified lineage. Du is both inclusive, pulling women into the history of Daoism, and exclusive, separating female from male figures.

Du Guangting's compilation covers twenty-seven biographies of varying lengths, including three goddesses and twenty-six women. (Two of the biographies have more than one subject.) They span the period from before creation up to Du's own lifetime. The author narrates the lives of the nine saints who lived closest to his era in the richest detail. His hagiographical accounts all follow a similar structure, which derives from numerous sources. Official biographies in the dynastic histories rank first among Du's sources. These are called *zhuan* 傳 or "transmissions," a term that includes but is not limited to biographies. The organization and literary style have also been influenced by earlier "exemplary women's" biographies and by hagiographical accounts of Chinese Buddhist nuns. In addition, earlier Daoist hagiographical works and collections of "strange tales" (*zhiguai* 志怪) certainly influenced the author. And the miscellaneous short stories later called fiction (*xiaoshuo* 小說), so popular among Tang literati, must have been in Du's mind as he wrote his biographies. These fictional works also frequently covered narratives of the lives of extraordinary individuals and their trials, conflicts, and accomplishments. Du must also have competed with the powerful and popularizing example of Buddhist transformation tales such as those found at Dunhuang on the Silk Road. Finally, family and religious genealogies or lineage registers provided a model for Du's "Records."[16]

Du Guangting's style is dense and allusive, combining material from many works available to him that are no longer extant. He also weaves miracles and wonders together with observations on social institutions and everyday life in Tang China. These complexities can make transla-

---

[16] On official biographies, see Cutler and Crowell 1999; Mou 1999, 2004. For studies of strange tales, see Campany 1996; DeWoskin and Crump 1996. A study of Dunhuang transformation tales is found in Mair 1989.

tion and interpretation challenging, but the work repays the effort. The "Records of the Assembled Transcendents" is a primary source unequalled in its richness for investigating the social and religious history of medieval Chinese women.

Form of a Typical Biography: The Life Cycle of a Daoist Female Saint

The biographies vary in length from one paragraph to many pages, but they all follow a similar and predictable format, covering the life and times of the subject in chronological order and addressing certain key questions. They combine the formal structure of a dynastic biography with the religious concerns of a Daoist master. They proceed through certain important stages in the religious development of the subjects. The typical life cycle of a female Daoist practitioner found in Du Guangting's accounts fits into what we might call a quest narrative or pilgrim's progress, following a journey or path of life that includes obstacles, ordeals, and tests. The subject faces struggles, contests, and challenges that lead her to discipline, transformation, and liberation. She assumes such roles as teacher, warrior, magician, or leader. Each saint models a path to Daoist salvation; the individual details of each one's life make her unique.

Du Guangting's accounts open with information about the saint's ancestors, immediate family, and place of origin. This locates her in time, space, and social class. Du may also include her family's religious background. Here we see great diversity, as though Du was trying to be as inclusive as possible.

Next Du turns to the childhood experiences of his subject, including the presence or absence of family support for the individual's Daoist practice.[17] Childhood is often the time for the saint's first experience of contradictions in values between filial piety and her religious vocation. Du may describe her appearance and health, her material life and circumstances. In covering her childhood, Du also reports on his subject's education, providing valuable evidence about female literacy in medieval times. Early evidence of her vocation, such as devotion, precocity, and virtue, along with evidence of her special selection, such as magical powers or visits from divinities, may also appear during her childhood.

---

[17] Childhood in Tang China is an understudied subject. See Kinney 1995; 2004.

She begins her religious practice, expressing faith, and performing good works (especially *yin'gong* 陰功 or "hidden good works"). She may even begin ascetic practices.

Childhood ends with her second big struggle: the marriage crisis. Around puberty, conflict may arise between a subject and her family over whether or not she is to marry. As Du Guangting says in his introduction, marriage or "the Way of one yin and one yang" can be a religious vocation for some Daoists. Cases of companionate marriages occur among Du's subjects. And traditional Chinese social and familial values demand marriage. To be a filial daughter and a loyal subject, a woman must marry. But for some, religious vocation demands celibacy. Celibacy in this context has a range of meanings from temporary abstinence from sexual intercourse to lifelong virginity. In social terms, it means refusal to reproduce; asceticism denies offspring to her husband's ancestral line. Ritual purity may at times, or even for a lifetime, demand abstinence from sexual activity. And Daoist texts often regard sexual intercourse as a drain of *jing* 精 (essence) and *qi* 氣 (breath or vital energy) that the practitioner needs to save for religious practices. For such female adepts, marriage is an obstacle. Some go so far as to mutilate themselves so that they become unmarriageable, or even to commit suicide to avoid marriage. And some married women claim sickness as a pretext to avoid intercourse.

Some women who do not marry may become hermits, wanderers, or wonderworkers. Others enter the convent. Along with professed religious vocation, we can identify several reasons women enter convents. They may be given to the convent by their parents to honor a vow or save the child from illness or want. They may become nuns to escape a life of poverty, in response to a charismatic or healing master, or to avoid marriage and childbirth. Members of the imperial harem may enter holy orders after retiring, at the death of the emperor, or as a temporary measure intended to purify themselves between marriage to one royal family member and another. On the positive side, they may join to attain freedom and literacy or the opportunity to become social or political leaders. When a woman enters a convent, the convent then becomes her family, according to Tang law as well as to her own self-concept.[18]

---

[18] The law code of the Tang dynasty is the first Chinese law code surviving in its entirety. In the section on general principles, chapter six, article fifty-seven concerns Daoist priests and nuns. Article 57.2a states:"The relationship of Daoist and Buddhist priests and nuns to their masters is the same as for paternal uncles and aunts." Article 57.2b continues:

After figuring out where and how she is to live, the subject enters the stage of mature religious practice. In a household, convent, or hermitage, in sickness or in health, most subjects make the contributions that earn them transcendence during this phase of life. The saint may engage in good works, the more secretly the better, such as feeding starving people and animals or burying abandoned corpses. She may act explicitly on behalf of the Daoist church by restoring shrines, relics, and holy places. She may strike blows for Daoism against the rival faith, Buddhism. Some subjects defend their bodies against the evil intentions of libidinous Buddhist monks, or protect shrines from Buddhist vandals. Others argue forcefully with Buddhist thinkers. They may weave or embroider industriously and skillfully, putting women's work in the service of devotion to the deities or financial support of the convent. They may teach and lead people in the convent or outside it, contributing to the wellbeing of others and the transmission of the Dao.

Several of Du's subjects involve themselves with Daoist rites. They receive and promulgate new ceremonies. They perform, lead, and teach rituals. They read, chant, and copy ritual texts, and transmit them to others. Along with rituals that benefit the human community, Du's subjects engage in Daoist religious practices intended to lead to individual transcendence. These include techniques of ascetic self-cultivation such as calisthenics, fasting, and celibacy. After perfecting asceticism, they may progress to meditation practices including breathing exercises, visualization, inner alchemy, and ingesting divine vapors.

The good works, asceticism, and meditative practices lead to rewards for the subject. She will be free from social and physical constraints. She may gain supernatural skills such as flight, communication with animals, the ability to disappear, and multiplying foods. She will retain youthfulness, beauty, and good health in old age. She may live centuries. These fruits of the faith provide evidence of her perfection.

Finally, at the end of her earthly life, each subject undergoes her ultimate transformation, from this world to the next. Often a deity gives the saint a prediction of her time for departure. She thus knows and controls her own end. There are two main methods by which she can take leave. The first, also the rarest and most prestigious, is ascension to heaven in broad daylight in the presence of witnesses. The second is liberation by means of the corpse (*shijie* 尸解), in which the subject appears to die and to leave

---

"The master's relationship to his [or her] disciples is the same as for nephews and nieces in the male line." See Johnson 1979; 1997.

a corpse behind for burial. But the body she leaves is in fact just an empty husk, light as a beetle's carapace, and the adept has escaped secretly to the heavens.[19] Either of these forms of departure is sufficient evidence to affirm her transcendence. Additionally, in both cases the subject's corpse does not decay. Her body remains beautiful and youthful; her hair might even keep growing. She emits a miraculous fragrance rather than the stench of rotting flesh. This odor of sanctity is another proof of her perfection. Her departure reveals her perfection and is an important moment in the formation of her cult.[20]

Also important to cult formation is the subject's afterlife. After her career in this world among humans, she takes up a post in the heavenly bureaucracy. Whereas a regular dynastic biography ends with posthumous official positions awarded by the emperor to the subject as an honor, a Daoist hagiography often closes with bestowal of celestial positions that Daoists take literally. Entering a Daoist lineage and the celestial bureaucracy, she is legitimized as a saint. Her afterlife will continue in cult, ritual, images, and in Du Guangting's account. Her ascension provides hope for other believers, both male and female.

Other Sources

Several types of text supply valuable comparative information on women in Tang China to help us understand Du Guangting's "Records of the Assembled Transcendents." One is Buddhist writings, including both hagio-graphical writingssuch as the *Biqiuni zhuan* and Buddhist canonical literature found in the *Vinaya* (Monastic Rules) and *Sutra* (Sermons of the Buddha) sections of the *Taishō Tripitaka* or Chinese/Japanese Buddhist canon in its 1910 edition. Another important type of source is found in Daoist hagio-graphies such as the *Liexian zhuan* 列仙傳 (Transmissions Concerning Arrayed Transcendents, DZ 294) of the Han dynasty and the *Shenxian zhuan* 神仙傳 (Transmissions Concerning Divine Transcendents),[21] contained in the *Daozang jiyao* 道藏輯要 (Collected Es-

---

[19] On this form of ascension, see Robinet 1976a; Cedzich 2001.

[20] This life cycle has remained classical for female Daoist saints as can be seen from the legend of He Xiangu, one of the Eight Immortals. See Jordan and Overmyer 1986, 56-57; Grant 1995, 37-38. It is, moreover, also typical for Buddhist saints and female saviors. See Levering 1989; Grant 1995.

[21] The *Liexian zhuan* is translated in Kaltenmark 1953, and the *Shenxian zhuan* in Campany 2002.

sentials of the Daoist Canon), a supplement to the Daoist Canon. Other Daoist canonical literature includes texts on ritual and meditation.

Then there are imperial encyclopedias, such as the *Taiping guangji*, and official dynastic histories, especially the *Jiu Tangshu* 舊唐書 (Old Book of the Tang), and *Xin Tangshu* 新唐書 (New Book of the Tang). In addition, poetry collections such as the *Quan Tangshi* 全唐詩 (Complete Tang Poetry), *Tang caizi zhuan* 唐才子傳 (Transmissions Concerning Talented Tang [People]), and *Tangshi jishi* 唐詩記事 (Recorded Anecdotes Concerning Tang Poetry), provide insight into women's inner lives. Exemplary and prescriptive literature for women, such as the *Lienü zhuan* 列女傳 (Transmissions Concerning Arrayed Women), attributed to the Han scholar Liu Xiang 劉向 (ca. 79-8 B.C.E.); Lady Ban Zhao's 班照 *Nüjie* 女戒 (Precepts for Women); the *Nü Lunyu* 女論語 (Analects for Women); and the *Nü Xiaojing* 女孝經 (Classic of Filial Piety for Women), reveal contemporaneous perceptions of women's virtues.[22] Fictional prose accounts of women by Tang and later literati such as Huangfu Mei, Mori Ogai, and Robert van Gulik, show how these women have been understood then and later, in China and elsewhere.[23]

Important Terms

Chen 辰, "chronograms," refers to the asterisms recognized by Chinese astronomers along the paths of the moon and planets across the sky. They include the twelve stations of Jupiter on the ecliptic, analogous to the twelve signs of our zodiac, and the twenty-eight lunar lodgings. They are used in many scales of keeping time, from the hours of the day to the sixty year cycles of the almanac and the official Chinese calendar. "Chrono-" comes from the time-keeping function of these asterisms, and "-gram" from the idea that they make a pattern.[24]

Guan 觀, "belvedere," refers to a Daoist temple or sometimes a convent or monastery. The Chinese term indicates a good view or a place for

---

[22] On the Han Dynasty courtier, historian, and essayist Ban Zhao, see Swann 2001. On exemplary women's biographies, see Lee 2003; Mou 1999. For women's moral precepts and filial piety, see Wang 2003; Ebrey 2003.

[23] See Kelly 1978; Mori 1951; Van Gulik 1968. These three sources shed light on Yu Xuanji, a Tang-dynasty Daoist nun who does not appear in Du Guangting's account, but whose life provides insights and comparative materials. For a study, see Cahill 2002.

[24] The translations for *chen*, *jing*, and *wuyue* were devised by Edward H. Schafer (1977a, 5-6).

viewing the heavens, and so belvedere with its root meaning of beautiful vista seems suitable. The institution matches the Buddhist *si* 寺, originally the name of a government office, that refers to a temple or monastery compound.

Jing 景, "phosphors," refers to heavenly bodies of exceptional brightness, suggesting a divine message, being, or purpose. The sun and moon are referred to as *erjing* 二景, "the two phosphors."

Sanshi 三尸, "three corpses, "also known as the "three worms," form part of Daoist psycho-physiology. They represent hostile forces within the adept's own body that conspire to thwart the adept's efforts to achieve perfection through Daoist practices, even if that means killing the adept . They must be destroyed or at least brought under control for a person to make progress in spiritual cultivation.[25]

Shijie 尸解, "liberation by means of the corpse," refers to a process of attaining transcendence. The adept who has perfected himself or herself appears to die, leaving behind a corpse suitable for burial, but in fact the dead body is an illusion, and the adept has already departed for the heavens. Sometimes this method of transformation is compared to the shedding of a cicada's carapace.

Wuyue 五岳, "Five Marchmounts," refers to five sacred mountains that in ancient times were believed to stand at the four outposts and the center of the habitable world. Ancient kings, such as Mu of the Zhou Dynasty and the Martial Thearch of the Han dynasty, would periodically tour their realms on horseback, with these holy mountains marking the boundaries of their marches. Important in ancient China, the marchmounts are deeply embedded in Daoist ritual and imagination. During the Tang dynasty, as noted earlier, the Five Marchmounts included Mount Tai located in modern Shandong in the east, Mount Heng in Hunan in the south, Mount Song in Henan in the center, Mount Hua in Shanxi in the west, and Mount Heng in Shaanxi in the north.

Xian 仙, also written 僊, "transcendent" or "immortal," refers to a Daoist ideal being, who has transcended the human condition, including mortality. Daoist adepts were believed to ascend to transcendence after a life of religious practice. The translation "transcendent" comes from the root meaning of the word: "to leap over."

---

[25] For a study of these divine parasites, see Kohn 1995b.

Yinde 陰德, "hidden virtue," refers to good works that are performed secretly with no expectation of reward or fame. The term especially applies to acts of compassion such as feeding starving animals or people, caring for the sick and needy, and burying abandoned corpses. *Yin'gong* 陰功, "hidden good works," is a synonym for *yinde*. Good works in general, and especially hidden good works, were the Daoist answer to the popular Buddhist idea of karma. The notion of karma developed in India in the sixth century B.C.E., in response to persistent questions about reincarnation. Karma is a system of accounting for good and bad deeds; when an individual dies, the good and bad karma is measured. If good prevails, the individual gets a fortunate rebirth. If bad prevails, the person may be reborn as an animal, hungry ghost, or even as a denizen of hell. Karma, in combination with rebirth, explains social injustice while promoting social stability. The Daoists took over this useful and comforting notion, and renamed it "good works," *de* 德 or *gong* 功.

Zhenren 真人, "perfected," or "realized person" refers to a person who has achieved the Daoist ideal of perfection, including immortality, through religious self-cultivation. These perfected beings reside for the most part in the Daoist heavens; they may teach or transmit texts to mortals.

Zhuan 傳, "transmissions," refers to texts or teachings that have been transmitted from one person (or deity) to another. Such transmissions include biographies, such as those included in the dynastic histories. But *zhuan* is not limited to biographies; in the dynastic histories it can refer to essays on important groups, such as the essay on the border people known as Xiongnu in the *Shiji* 史記 (Records of the Historian) of Sima Qian 司馬遷 (ca. 145–85 B.C.E.). In Daoist contexts, *zhuan* can refer to a teaching or indeed to the Dao itself that is being transmitted.

Format and Conventions

In the chapters that follow, I introduce, translate, and annotate the "Records of the Assembled Transcendents of the Fortified Walled City." I begin with Du Guangting's own preface to the work, and continue through the entries in the order in which they appear in the YJQQ version of the text. The biographies are grouped in four sections, according to types of subject, in the following order: goddesses, matriarchs, inhabitants of the grotto heavens, and Tang saints and transcendents. In most cases, an individual introduction precedes each translation, and notes follow. (The exception is the inhabitants of the grotto heavens, who receive a collective introduction.) The individual introductions set the context, clarify specific issues, and link the particular sections of text with themes outlined in this chapter.[26]

The Chinese text of the YJQQ version of Du Guangting's "Record" is included below as an appendix. References to the page numbers in the Chinese text are inserted where appropriate in my translations.

Tang emperors and their reign titles — official mottos given to signify the relevance of the age — are mentioned on occasion, especially in the biographies of Tang saints (Part 4). The dates of rule and the exact dates of the reign titles that occur in the text are as follows:[27]

Taizong	626-649	Honorable Outlook	23 Jan. 627 — 7 Feb. 650
Ruizong	684-690	Cultured Illumination	27 Feb. 684 — 19 Oct. 684
	710-712	Spectacular Cloud	19 Aug. 710 — 1 Mar. 712
Wu Zetian	690- 705	Prolonged Longevity	23 Oct. 692 — 9 June 694
Xuanzong	712-756	Opened Prime	22 Dec. 713 — 9 Feb. 742
		Heavenly Treasure	9 Feb. 742 — 12 Aug. 756
Daizong	762- 779	Great Calendar	18 Dec. 766 — 12 Feb. 780
Shunzong	Feb.-Sept., 805		
		Eternal Probity	1 Sept. 805 — 25 Jan. 806
Xianzong	805- 820	Primal Accord	25 Jan. 806 — 9 Feb. 821
Yizong	859-873	Total Comprehension	17 Dec. 860 — 17Dec. 874

---

[26] I use *pinyin* romanization throughout, except when quoting or citing sources that use Wade-Giles or other systems. Tang reign periods follow Kroll 1984. Dates in the Chinese sixty-unit cycle are romanized in *pinyin*, then translated by a letter A – J for the ten stems followed by one of the twelve animals of the Chinese zodiac for the twelve stems. For example: a *wuchen*, "E-Dragon" year.

[27] The dates and translations follow Kroll 1984.

Translation

"Records of
the Assembled Transcendents
of the Fortified Walled City"

by

Du Guangting (850 - 933)

Du Guangting's Introduction to His Text

The "Records of the Assembled Transcendents of the Fortified Walled City" begins with an introduction that Du Guangting calls a "discussion"(*xu* 序).[28] There he explains that the title of his book derives from "Fortified Walled City" (*yongcheng* 墉城), the name of the capital city of the Queen Mother of the West, located according to some sources on the mythical western mountain Kunlun. Since the Queen Mother leads the female transcendents and appears first in the book, Du names his collection of biographies after her home, where all his subjects are registered in the scrolls of the immortals.

The introduction discloses the author's intentions in compiling this collection, arguing that information on the lives of female transcendents is important and worth reading. His book provides evidence of the power and diversity of the Way. His intended audience includes his royal patron Wang Jian (r. 907-919), ruler of the Former Shu kingdom in Sichuan (907-925), along with other potential literati and Daoist readers. Du states some of his motivations in a straightforward manner; to discern others we must read between the lines. I will begin with Du's overtly expressed goals. His book is clearly commemorative and didactic. He aims to remember women of the past and present who obtained the Way and became transcendents, that is: realized beings or deities. He claims that such figures have lived in every era, including his own. Transcendents existed before the world was created; they continue into the present. Some are famous, others are obscure, and many surviving books narrate their stories.

Du Guangting begins in his introduction and continues in the biographies that follow to clarify matters of Daoist doctrine, often interrupting his narrative to give a short sermon on correct beliefs. Du affirms that the Way is one but there are many paths to reach it. Some saints become per-

---

[28] I have benefited from previous Chinese studies of this text, most notably Yang 2000; Luo 2003a; 2003b.

fected by associating with Daoist deities, others by obtaining texts that teach them Daoist practices, still others by ingesting elixirs or by proving their determination and devotion. In his introduction, Du outlines a variety of paths; he goes into detail about these paths in individual biographies. He states that there are many methods to prove that one has achieved transcendence, aside from the most famous: ascending to heaven in broad daylight before a large audience. He even asserts that believing you must ascend bodily to achieve perfection is ignorant blindness. In individual entries, Du explains some methods of verifying and legitimizing an individual's transcendence. Du also cautions the reader that perfected beings are not always obvious to the mortal eye; they might look like ancient crones or mendicant medicine sellers, so we should treat everyone we encounter with respect.

Du distinguishes several classes of transcendents, from great deities through lesser celestial bureaucrats to earthly transcendents and even ghost transcendents. Ghost transcendents are sincere practitioners who die before achieving their goals. Protected by the great deities of Daoism, after a certain number of years of acquiring merit among the ghosts, without ever having their names inscribed on the registers of the dead, they return to the heavens. This must have been a comforting thought for believers who did not live long enough to see their practice come to fruition, and also to the relatives of such people.

Du asserts that resolute efforts to attain the Dao, even if they do not seem to bear fruit in this life, always gain recognition and are never wasted. Du strongly believes that humans can achieve transcendence through their own efforts. He repeatedly states that we must seek the Way through our own individual work. Transcendence can be learned, so he urges the reader to work hard. Not only full-time Daoist practitioners, but also rulers have the potential to ascend the steps to the Dao, so their good deeds in this world help them gain merit. Thus Du encourages rulers (part of his intended audience) to be benevolent for their own sake as well as the sake of their subjects.

Du Guangting's aims are less obvious when it comes to connections with gender roles, his royal family patrons, Daoists of the past, and Buddhism. Du's discussion reflects his inconsistency and ambivalence about roles of women in Daoism. His introduction explicitly refers to gender only in its opening and closing remarks. Most of the introduction is gender-neutral or gendered male. The general instructions apply to any practitioner, but those Du refers to are all male, except in the concluding section. Du's first words tell the reader that this book chronicles women. Towards the end, Du remarks that the positions of men and women are clear and distinct, but that they have been mixed together in transmitted texts. In the present work, he separates out the women to analyze and explain their contributions. Devoting a whole text exclusively to women honors them but also follows a convention of separating male and female biographies that appears earlier in both Buddhist and Confucian traditions. This separation prefigures the strict distinction between men and women that becomes so pronounced in China in the centuries to come. Separate does not mean equal. Du grants important ranks and duties to female celestials, but the female scale starts below its male counterpart. He posits a ranking system that mirrors the patrilineal and generational hierarchies of Chinese society. In this he resembles his great forefather, the fifth century Shangqing Daoist master and editor Tao Hongjing 陶弘景 (456-536).[29]

Throughout his work, Du Guangting praises the Chinese family values of filial piety and loyalty in his subjects. He states that the female adept need not extricate herself from family life in order to achieve transcendence. Human marriage, he claims, the "Way of one yin and one yang" is a religious vocation, bringing each partner to completion. Its divine patrons are the Queen Mother of the West and Lord King of the East. And yet Du's subjects repeatedly refuse marriage, sometimes by extreme means such as flight, self-starvation, or suicide. Even those who do not openly reject marriage mostly manage to avoid it. This suggests that Du shares the opinion of earlier Shangqing masters that marriage, sexual intercourse, and domestic life are impediments to spiritual growth and accomplishment for both male and female adepts. Married women adepts must expect to face the additional obstacle of childbearing. In place of a human household, Du locates his subjects in the family of Daoist practitioners. Instead of the genealogy of an earthly clan, he relates his female transcendents within a divine lineage register.

Elsewhere in his text, Du seems to suggest that male/female distinctions are not significant. In individual biographies, he depicts women performing the same rituals and practices and reading the same texts as their male counterparts. Early texts on Daoist religious ceremonies and practices rarely specify the gender of the actors. And he even goes so far

---

[29] A study of Tao Hongjing's life and work is found in Strickmann 1979.

in one case (the joint biography of Liu Chunlong and Guo Shuxiang, #9) as to assert that celestial positions are earned by merit, regardless of gender differences.

To Du Guangting and other literati Daoists, as to many Mahayana Buddhist thinkers of his time, distinctions such as male and female were fundamentally meaningless and empty when it came to questions of salvation. Everyone, male or female, could find transcendence through individual effort. And yet the practices and concepts of the social institutions of his day shaped his worldview. Equality was not a social ideal governing human relations in medieval China. Hierarchies based on class, age, and gender were the norm. In Du's scheme of things, the standard adept was male. He valued the female practitioner but probably regarded her as a somewhat deficient male. In fact, he emphasizes the efficacy of Daoism as a path to perfection by demonstrating that *even* women can attain it.

Mentioning human rulers in his introduction both flatters and warns his intended audience: the Former Shu rulers of the Wang family. They bestowed honors and a court position upon Du Guangting. He presented this book to the throne of Former Shu in Chengdu, probably sometime after 913 when he received the title of Prior-Born of Broad Completion from the Former Shu king. The last date in the text is 886, so it could have been finished any time after that and before his death in 933. Du's discussion specifically mentions that kings may become transcendents. Therefore what they do has consequences. By implication, the gods are watching and keeping score. As the appearance of Tang emperors and imperial family in several of his entries suggests, Du wants to flatter Former Shu rulers by offering evidence of their legitimacy as successors to the Tang.

Some of Du's other works, tracing the honors bestowed upon the Dao by successive emperors of the past, and recording auspicious omens propitious for the Wang family rulers, suggest that he was interested in securing imperial patronage for the Daoist church and for himself. For example, Du states directly that some subjects of his records are living proof that the current rulers have received the mandate of heaven.

Early on in his discussion, Du Guangting cites famous literary images associated with Daoists of the past. In this way he links himself as Daoist master and writer with great thinkers and schools that went before. He

alludes to Zhuangzi, the Warring States sage whose parables and arguments paved the way to understanding the Dao and freeing humans
from the fear of death. He mentions a story about Zhang Daoling, second-century visionary and founder of the Celestial Masters school. He
refers to a story about Xu Xun 許遜, a third-century master who ascended to heaven together with his entire household, including dogs and
chickens.[30] Du mentions practices associated with both Lingbao and
Shangqing schools. Along with promoting female saints, his introduction
also supports his broad project of uniting all the important schools and
traditions of Daoism under the single banner of his own tradition.

A ghost at the banquet, rarely acknowledged but present and influential,
is Buddhism.[31] Although Du Guangting and other Daoists borrowed lib-
erally from Buddhism, they also competed fiercely with that foreign religion. They competed for the faith and donations of the people, for imperial and official patronage, and for influence in government and society. Competition and syncretism between the two religions is present at
every level of society. Names, doctrines, practices: all were mixed. For
example, the origins of the title *tianzun* 天尊, "heavenly-honored one,"
an honorific reserved for Daoist high gods and for the Buddha, are still
debated. Chinese Daoists and Buddhists both claim to have invented the
term.

And Daoists had to match or improve upon attractive Buddhist ideas.
Through Buddhism, Daoists appropriated older Indian notions such as
karma, reincarnation, and kalpa (world age). Karma is the sum of good
and bad deeds people carry from one life to the next, a moral accounting
that determines the fate of each individual in the next life and helps explain social injustice in the current life. Daoists absorbed karma in their
idea of merit or good works. Accumulation of merit led to spiritual progress; particularly worthy Daoists could pass along some of their merit
to their descendents. The idea of reincarnation, endless passage from one
life to the next until the individual gains salvation, does not exist in
China before the advent of Buddhism. Thereafter it coexists uneasily
with older Chinese notions of ancestor worship and filial piety. The
Buddhist kalpa was assimilated into the Daoist cycle of world creation

---

[30] On Xu Xun, see Boltz 1987, 70-78.
[31] On Buddhist history and doctrine, see Robinson and. Johnson 1982. On Buddhism
in China , see Wright 1959; Ch'en 1964; Zürcher 1959. For translations of the Buddhist
sutras discussed in this introduction, see Thich 1988, 1992; Gomez 1996; Watson 1993. On
Buddhist influence on Daoism, see Zürcher 1980.

and destruction, marked by alternations of mulberry groves with the Eastern Sea.

Daoist texts, competing with Buddhist cosmologies that featured grand paradises and terrible underworlds, described their own heavens and hells, combining old native lore with bits of appropriated Buddhism. Buddhists had the Triple Refuge or Three Treasures: the Buddha, the Dharma (the teachings of the Buddha), and the Sangha (Buddhist monastic community, or more broadly, the whole Buddhist community). Daoists had their own triple refuge. To compete with the Buddha himself, they offered the deified Laozi. To compete with the Dharma, Daoists put forth the Dao or the Way. And to rival the Sangha, they put forth the Daoist monastic or lay community. The Buddhists had their *Tripitaka* or "Three Baskets;" the Daoists had their own canon, the *Daozang* or "Treasurehouse of the Way."

Daoists also laid prior claim to core teachings of Buddhism. They claimed to have originated the notion of *sunyatā* or emptiness, the central teaching of a whole class of Mahayana Buddhist scriptures known as the *prajñāparamitā* (Perfection of Wisdom) sutras on "the wisdom that ferries us across (from ignorance to enlightenment)." These sutras include some of the best known Buddhist texts of all times, such as the *Heart Sutra* and *Diamond Sutra*. Buddhist Madhyāmika logic uses the concept of emptiness to reconcile important philosophical contradictions such as that between infinite and limited, the Buddha and me, enlightenment and ignorance.

Mahayana Buddhists believed that all beings, as taught in the *Lotus Sutra*, have buddha nature and can achieve enlightenment. Daoists such as Du Guangting taught that all people could become transcendents through our own efforts. The *Lotus Sutra* also explains that bodhisattvas use *upaya* or "skill-in-means" to teach Buddhist doctrine in a manner appropriate to each listener's level of understanding. And compassionate bodhisattvas such as Guanyin or Avalokiteśvara rescued beings in distress and granted people their greatest desires.[32] Compassionate Daoist deities and saints, including several of Du's subjects, also taught and saved people. Buddhists accumulated merit to gain good karma and ultimately enlightenment and escape. Daoists performed good works, especially secret good works, to move along the path to transcendence.

---

[32] The *Lotus sutra* is translated in Hurvitz 1976; Watson 1993.

Some holy sites, including Mount Tiantai in modern Zhejiang where Du studied as a young man and several places he mentions in the records, were sacred to both religions. Both traditions treated several of Du's subjects as saints. For example, Buddhists and Daoists both revered Huang Guanfu and Wang Fengxian (#23, 26). Du naturally asserts the superiority of the Daoist claim.

Du Guangting not only appropriated attractive aspects of Buddhism, he argued against the rival faith. The lives of several of his subjects reflect vigorous competition between the two religions. Du does not shrink from a little character assassination. Buddhist monks are portrayed as libidinous and violent in the biographies of Hua Gu and Gou Xiangu (#17, 19). The virtuous Daoist maidens evade attempted vandalism, rape, and murder at their hands. These stories, regardless of their merit as historical fact, must be recognized as anti-Buddhist propaganda. And Du reports that some saints, brought up in pious Buddhist households, or having access only to Buddhist places of worship, nonetheless instinctively chose Daoism. The implication is that the reader should make the same choice.

In the middle of a biography, Du often digresses to deliver a sermon. In the case of Wang Fengxian (#26), he explains that Confucianism and Daoism are like the father and elder brother of the people, while Buddhism is like their mother. Since people know their mothers but may not know their fathers or elder brothers, it is no surprise that people honor the Buddha and fail to respect Confucians or Daoists. Here he explicitly allies Daoism and Confucianism against Buddhism. In the same biography, Du explains that the religious icons revered by Buddhists are actually copied from images of the great Daoist deities. He never misses a chance to assert the temporal primacy and doctrinal superiority of Daoism over Buddhism.

Du concludes his introduction with the statement that the present text collects biographies of women who have attained the Dao as the records of one family or lineage. He has arranged them in a hierarchy with the Queen Mother as their head. She is the subject of the first biography.

Translation

[YJQQ 114.1a] "Records of the Assembled Transcendents of the Fortified Walled City" chronicles the affairs of women of ancient and modern times who obtained the Way and ascended to transcendence. Leaving behind the common, they climbed to transcendence; leaping over the ordinary, they provided evidence of the Way. They halted the [swift passage of human life, normally as transitory as a] procession of images seen by the light of a hurricane lantern or from a fast horse passing a crack in the wall. They enjoyed the longevity of Zhuangzi's village oak or of the toad and cinnamon tree in the moon.[33] They transformed shapes made of bubbles and foam into ones as solid as metal and rock. Their prolonged lives passed through several generations. Every era has such people. They continue through kalpas [world ages] of years.

The traces of divine transcendents who obtained the Way are resplendently visible, arranged and edited in scriptures and declarations, mysterious charts, and unsurpassable registers. Some ascended through stages to supreme holiness; others advanced through the ranks to the highest realization. Some govern and rule the various heavens; others preside over and master the arrayed marchmounts. [1b] Some ride the [constellation] Winnowing Basket to float on the Han River [Milky Way]; others eclipse the moon and race the chronograms. Some attend court feasts in the Nine Realms of Clarity; others circle and soar to the eight ends of the world.

[Lives of the transcendents from] before the Opening Illustrious Ones departed and the kalpas began to revolve, are in many cases transmitted and narrated in detail in the precious books in the Three Caverns.[34] [Transcendents who lived] between the era of the Nine Illustrious Ones and Three Ancients[35] and [the era when] humans began to employ oxen and ride horses in all cases returned to earth. They suspended their work in the heavenly bureaus in order to descend and save living spirits. They came from their transcendent offices to govern [the worldly administration] temporarily. They handed down laws, established teachings, and held the state in their hands.

---

[33] *Zhuangzi* 4 contains a story about an oak tree that grew to great old age because people considered it useless. The cinnamon tree in the moon, repeatedly chopped down, grows back again.

[34] The Opening Illustrious Ones (*Kaihuang* 開皇) are great Daoist deities of the beginning of creation. The Three Caverns are the three major divisions of the Daoist canon. See Schipper and Verellen 2004.

[35] That is, after the beginning of human history and historical time.

They assisted contemporary classical scholars and helped court historians, who in turn completely revealed [those transcendents'] deeds.[36]

Then we come to those [transcendents] who hid their light and muddied their traces while they harnessed phosphors and climbed to the chronograms. Some of them had accomplishments that stand out like mountain peaks or forests [alternatively: are known among hermits of the mountains and forests], yet they escaped into mist and smoke, rising lightly with auroral clouds. Others left the hubbub and stirred-up mud of this world in their own bodies to seize the reins of [divine birds such as] simurghs or cranes and mount to the void. Some of them personally assisted thearchs and kings. Still others delighted in dwelling among the common people. They accomplished hidden merits, so that their mysterious virtues became known on high. They could even cause chickens and dogs to fly, plucking up the whole courtyard so that everyone was all lifted up together. [The deeds of even these hidden transcendents] shine forth in slips and fascicles [of the Daoist written record].

Indeed, no generation lacks such [records of transcendents]. Formerly the Qin dynasty great minister Ruan Cang and then the Han chief editor Liu Xiang [79-8 B.C.E.] recorded the transcendents' doings, and their works have circulated in the world.[37] [2a] Next we have "Documents from the Grotto Underworlds," "Transmissions Concerning the Divine Transcendents," "Transmissions Concerning The Study of the Way," "Transmissions Concerning the Assembled Transcendents," "Sequel to Transmissions Concerning the Divine Transcendents," "Transmissions Concerning Transcendents of the Grottos," and all the records and compilations of the Supreme Perfected. We have records and registers such as these by no less than ten authors.[38] In addition there are chapters in books on "Famous Mountains and Beneficent Places," discourses in texts on "Embracing the Earth" or "Moun-

---

[36] That is, they dwelt among humans and were recognized. The next group, although unrecognized when they lived in the world, are nonetheless made known in Daoist texts.

[37] Ruan Cang was a Qin dynasty official whose lost work on transcendents was supposed to have been the basis of Liu Xiang's *Liexian zhuan*. For a discussion, see Campany 2002, 104, and *Ge Hong neipian*, 2.22. Liu Xiang (79- 8 B.C.E.) was a member of the Han royal family. He was a great statesman and imperial librarian as well as bibliographer and biographer. Works attributed to him include the *Lienü zhuan* and *Liexian zhuan*.

[38] These texts include well-known records of transcendents, such as the *Shenxien zhuan* of Ge Hong (283-345), also attributive author of the *Baopuzi* (Book of the Master Who Embraces the Uncarved Block; Ware 1966); the *Daoxue zhuan*, a text of the sixth century that survives in fragments and citations (Bumbacher 2000); and the *Xu xianzhuan* of the mid-Tang (DZ 295). Hagiographies and records of the Shangqing school concerning the perfected, including the *Zhen'gao* (Declarations of the Perfected, DZ 1016). For a survey of this literature, see Penny 2000; Schipper and Verellen 2004.

tains and Seas."[39] And there are records like those of "Searching for Deities" and "Broad Phenomena,"[40] and the literature on transcendent recipes and classes of drugs. [All of these texts] cite the surnames and given names [of the transcendents] and transcribe traces of their affairs to bring them to our attention. How could I ever succeed in even naming them all? Therefore I conclude that the affairs of the divine transcendents shine forth resplendently and are not hidden.

Among the constant drift of popular lore, some say that a divine transcendent must wait until the bodily form is abandoned and left behind and until the cloud-soul experiences complete perfection before he or she may be properly called a divine transcendent. This is not so. To believe that bones and flesh *must* ascend and soar is certainly an extreme case of ignorant blindness that has not yet penetrated the truth. So what is it really like? The classics of the perfected say that when they obtain the Way and leave the world, some are hidden while others are obvious. Although verifying the Way is the single goal,[41] its practice shows distinctions. That is why we say that the Ways of the transcendents number in the hundreds. We are not limited by a single route; there is not just one single method to grasp. [2b]

Some [transcendents acquire their immortality by] becoming friends of realized people, some the guests of heavenly thearchs. For some, dragons in harness come suddenly to welcome them; mixed and blended teams of clouds accompany them on far journeys. Examples of this include [Daoist masters like] Gu Xi, Chang Li, Qing Guang, and Chisongzi.[42]

Others, receiving texts and obtaining registers, learn to conceal phosphors and refine their shapes. Their numina and flesh having been born repeatedly, their prior accomplishments and victories increase. Examples include the Five Old Ones, the Supreme Thearchs, and the Realized Kings of the Four

---

[39] The *Fudi mingshan fu* (DZ 599) is a geographical record by Du Guangting. The *Shedi lun* is a lost Tang geographical text purported to be fifty-five *juan* in length, and compiled by Su Deyan and Kuang Yin. The "Mountains and Seas" is the *Shanhai jing*, a work of fantastic geography and ethnography of ancient China and surrounding lands. It contains parts of varying dates and was edited in the Han dynasty by Liu Xin. See Yuan 1980; Mathieu 1983; Birrell 1999; Strasberg 2002.

[40] These two are Gan Bao's *Soushen ji* (DZ 1476) of the early fourth century (De-Woskin and Crump 1996) and the *Bowu zhi* by Zhang Hua (232-300)..

[41] Or it might be translated "climbing to the way," reading *deng* 登, "climb," for *zheng*, 證, "verify."

[42] The only one of this list I can identify is Chisongzi (Master Redpine) a famous elixir taker and embodiment of hard individual work at religious practices. See Kaltenmark 1953.

Poles.[43] Still others possess an essence that is sincere and unchangeable, so that tests and difficulties do not move them. Their eyes fixed on Kunlun Hill, in their hearts they attend morning audience with the Great Thearch and then they obtain the Way. Examples include the Lords of the Yellow Belvedere, Majestic Way, and Ineffable and Broad [Way].[44]

Then in addition there are [elixirs whose recipes are revealed in texts known as] the "Great Grottos," "Seven Transformations," "Eight Reports," and "Three Charts." [And there are elixirs known as] the mottled talisman of sperm in the womb, concealed fungus of the crooked and plain varieties, jade sperm and gold fluid, the secret talisman of Yellow [River] water, blue blossoms from the red tree, round and hard scarlet seeds, illustrious images of white feathers, and nine-times recycled eight-fold rose gems. One ingests these and transforms into a phoenix or transforms into a dragon. Eating just a tidbit of one of them, one becomes [unchangeable] like gold or like jade.[45]

And again there are [astronomical elixirs known] from secret texts such as "Golden Earrings" and "Jade Pendants," illustrated texts such as "The Three Illustrious Ones"[46] and "Eight Phosphors," [3a] numinous [recipes like those for] like the "Floriate Cinnabar" and "Plain White Memorial," and essentials such as "Metal Verity" and "Divine Tiger." [Transcendents who ingest these elixirs] fly along with feathered wings, able to leap over the void and stamp around in empty space. With the radiance of fluid gold, they can conjure up deities and restrain rebels. When gliding and soaring upwards, their king-fisher-colored feathers and dark pinions flap. Controlling and drawing the reins [of divine chariots], they fly up through the canopy of the sky to the curving chronograms. Having practiced the seventy-four [alchemical] reci-

---

43 The Five Old Ones are deities extant before creation, the Supreme Thearchs are the highest Daoist deities of the three heavens, and the Realized Kings are gods of the four directions. These generic titles stand for all the high gods of Heaven and Earth, before and after creation.

44 Kunlun Hill is Mount Kunlun, where the paradise of the Queen Mother of the West is located. It corresponds to the Buddhist Mount Sumeru as a holy mountain and pillar connecting Heaven and Earth, and also to the Western Paradise of Amitabha Buddha in Pure Land Buddhism as a celestial realm of complete perfection and beauty. I have not been able to identify the three lords.

45 No texts with these exact names survive today and I have not been able to link each ingredient with a modern material substance. The author is speaking in generalities here and not giving away any secrets. Du lived at a time when both outer, operative alchemy and inner, meditative alchemy were practiced and he includes elements of both, while at times claiming that inner alchemy is superior.

46 I am not able to identify each text and substance. The Three Illustrious Ones refers to the *Sanhuang wen* (Writs of the Three Illustrious Ones), ordination texts handed down in both the Shangqing and Lingbao traditions.

pes without missing a single hair's breadth of detail, and having received the thirty-seven forms [of celestial vapors],[47] they gradually become equipped with a perfectly feathered appearance [i.e., they grow wings or, alternatively, wear imposing court regalia]. Some have received the Nine Royal Gifts so that they can mount and skim [the void].[48]

[Transcendents] fulfill the seven tests, proving themselves honorable and resolute.[49] They draw upon the unsurpassable teachings of the masters, verifying them within their own hearts. Successive semblances cannot change their resolve. Lightning and thunder cannot startle their attention. Riches and high position cannot move their intentions. Sound and appearance [music and beauty] cannot seduce their inner person [literally, the lining of their garments]. They exemplify the sayings: "My fate rests with me" and "We obtain prolonged life ourselves." [That is: longevity is a matter of individual will or achievement.]

Therefore, how could all the ancients and moderns who obtained [the Way] ever be comprehensively discussed? The Southern Realized One[50] once said: "Once your merits reach three thousand, you can ascend to heaven in broad daylight. The liberal Way has no end, and you can learn to achieve deathlessness on your own." This [all the self-taught transcendents mentioned above] is what she meant.

In the case of the highest [class of] transcendent, both spirit and form fly up together in a cloud chariot with a feathered canopy. The next [class of transcendent] transforms covertly by means of concealed phosphors in a deep valley or dark forest. [3b] The next release their form and lodge it in semblances, just as snakes shed their skins or cicadas their shells. Flying up to mount the heavens is best, while deliverance by means of the corpse is the inferior method.

---

[47] Seventy-four recipes may refer to techniques handed down to humans by the seventy-four great celestial deities of Shangqing Daoism. The thirty-seven forms could be thirty-seven forms or colors of celestial vapors. Alternatively, the thirty-seven forms (se 色) might be a borrowing from rival Buddhist teachings that laid out thirty-seven conditions (pin 品; bodhipakṣika dharma) leading to bodhi or enlightenment.

[48] "Nine Royal Gifts" is an inclusive reference to ancient ceremonial gifts bestowed by the emperor upon a vassal in recognition of great service. The gifts include such things as chariots and horses, clothing, foods and ceremonial vessels.

[49] The "seven tests" are seven trials given by the first Celestial Master Zhang Daoling to his student Zhao Sheng to test his earnestness and devotion. After Zhao passed all seven tests, Zhang Daoling transmitted elixir texts to him.

[50] The Southern Realized One is Lady Wei Huacun (251-334), a Libationer of the Celestial Masters church and a major figure in the Shangqing revelations. The *Taiping guangji* contains an account of her (57.256-59).

There are also those who accumulate merit without finishing, and those who pile up virtue without display. Some reach the ultimate in filial piety, the ultimate in loyalty, the ultimate in uprightness, or the ultimate in heroic fervor. Others set their hearts on the Way and never forget it, and yet all their merit may never reach them. They roost in the bitter cold, refining their practice alone within their own bodies, and do good deeds without regard to whether [their good works] are obscure or revealed. The Grand Supreme considers them determined, and the Grand Ultimate places confidence in them.[51] They die only when their limits are reached and their spirits have received blessings, so that they obtain the ability to act as good and happy ghosts. Earth-governing deities do not regulate them, not do ghost registers inscribe their names. They may wander footloose and fancy-free to beneficent villages with untrammeled pleasure, following their own intentions. After a sufficient number of years [acting as beneficent ghosts] they are able to become what we call ghost transcendents. Then they can return, ascending to the midst of concealed phosphors.

Those who dwell among the ranks of rulers, accumulating merit and piling up virtue, also enter the steps to transcendence. This being the case, doing good deeds is never wasted effort [for a ruler].

Transcendence may be learned. Merits cannot be categorized as great or minute, nor can actions be considered broad or slender. [4a] Everything depends on establishing merit without resting, acting for the best without wearying. Those of you who refine and practice the Way, shouldn't you work hard?!

Furthermore, there is the Way of one yin and one yang, the marvelous use of which regulates and completes categories and creations, giving birth to the flock of forms. From birth to birth they never stop, renewal after renewal mutually continuing. Therefore, covered by Heaven and supported by Earth, clear and turbid join their contributions. The sun illuminates and moon presides, so daytime and night are equally blessed in their functions. Depending

---

[51] Grand Supreme refers to the Grand Supreme Lord of the Way (Taishang daojun), one of the highest Shangqing deities. The term Grand Ultimate (Taiji), comes from the *Yijing* (Book of Changes) divination tradition and is used by Daoists to designate the state of existence prior to the division of yin and yang. Its best-known form (a diagram of a circle divided into black and white sections) was first recorded in a Daoist context by the inner alchemist and theoretician Chen Tuan (906-989). Precursors are found in the works of the Buddhist author Zongmi (780-841) and Robinet demonstrates a connection between the two (1997, 221; 1990.) Later, Song masters of the Li-school, known in the Wes as Neo-Confucians adopted it, starting with Zhou Dunyi (1017-1073). Here it is personified as a deity.

upon these two semblances [yin and yang], the three forces [of heaven, earth, and human beings] become complete in us. Thus the Wood Lord presides over the east, while the Metal Mother is revered in the west.[52]

The positions governed by male realized ones and female transcendents are very distinct [clear]. However, in my reading of declarations and classics, as well as what is narrated in illustrated biographies, [male and female transcendents] are mixed together in entries and registers. And some have not previously been analyzed in full. Now I have examined the classic(s) of seven sections from Supreme Clarity [Daoist canonical literature] as references that preserve and comment upon matters of practice. In essays on constantly flying and pacing the inner void of the sun and moon and five stars [planets], the primal father and mysterious mother go along as equals, completing each other like a yang epithet and yin given name. So here the author has gathered that flock of explanations and collected them as records of a single household.

Women transcendents take Metal Mother as most honored, and Metal Mother takes the Fortified Walled City as her base for governing. [4b] Having edited and chronicled the affairs of women transcendents of ancient and modern times who obtained the Way, I give it the title "Records of the Assembled Transcendents of the Fortified Walled City." Our supreme classics say that the ultimate position for a man who obtains the Way is Realized Lord, and the ultimate position for a woman who obtains the Way is Primal Ruler. This transmission takes Metal Mother as head. The primal rulers follow her. There are altogether ten scrolls [of biographies of transcendents]. The Prior-Born of Broad Completion, Du Guangting, selected and edited the texts.

---

[52] Mugong (Wood Lord) is another name for Lord King of the East (Dongwanggong), and Jinmu (Metal Mother) is another name for Queen Mother of the West (Xiwangmu). The terms for the quadrants where each of them presides, translated here as "east" and "west," are actually *zhen* and *dui*, two of the eight trigrams of the *Yijing* that correspond to the eastern and western directions.

Part 1

Goddesses

1. The Queen Mother of the West

The Queen Mother of the West (Xiwangmu 西王母) was the highest goddess of Daoism. As her name suggests, she was both ruler and royal ancestress. In addition, she governed the west, the region of death and eternal life. The west is the direction associated with yin, the dark female force. The Queen Mother had the authority to grant or withhold individual immortality, the goal of Daoist believers. She also governed relations between gods and humans. And she was the patron of women in Daoism, especially women outside the family such as prostitutes and nuns.

Du Guangting places the Queen Mother first in his "Records," to honor her as the founder and patron of the lineage of women transcendents and adepts that is the subject of his entire book. She is the first ancestress and ultimate teacher of all the figures in the book, as well as the origin of all their saving rites, texts, and elixirs, and techniques. One derivation of part of her name, *wangmu*, is used in ancestral ceremonies as an honorific to address paternal grandmothers and female ancestors further back in the patriline. The heading of her entry, "The Queen Mother of the West Transmits the Transcendent Way," underlines her importance as the founder of a religious lineage. All other entries, except that of a second goddess whose biography immediately follows the Queen Mother's, are titled simply with the name of the subject. This biography is one of two that have been preserved in both versions of Du's collection in the Daoist canon. The present translation relies mainly on the recension found in the YJQQ, drawing only upon the Ming version when it provides clarification or fills in a gap.

Du's hagiographical account of the Queen Mother is one of the most complete biographies in his collection and one of only three entries on deities who were never human beings. In the case of such a supernatural being, Du's adherence to the form of biography found in the official dynastic histories is striking. Like the official biographer of an important person, Du includes his subject's name, rank, lineage, place of origin, and significant deeds. Like an official historian, Du also makes editorial comments intended to edify his readers. This form of writing had legitimacy and familiarity among his literati audience, lending credibility to accounts of often mysterious and otherworldly events. The biography

43

form also suggests parallels between divine and human official hierarchies that Du explicitly states elsewhere. In writing this account, Du's intentions were to preserve information about the goddess's acts among humans, recommend her as a subject of devotion, and give the faithful a precise and correct picture of her appearance for their visualization exercises.

The biography of such a powerful being affords the author an opportunity to make several authoritative doctrinal pronouncements. He borrows the Queen Mother's eminence to clarify Daoist teachings, unite various Daoist traditions, and at the same time glorify his own tradition: the Shangqing or Supreme Clarity school of Daoism. He intended her splendor and power to show the superiority of Daoist deities and teachings over those of the rival Buddhists. The biography contains several accounts of the special relations the Queen Mother had with great Chinese rulers of the past. Submitting his collection to the emperor Wang Jian, Du flattered the Former Shu court and supported the ruler's legitimacy. He also promoted Daoism as an effective means of salvation in times of peril. In doing so, he certainly hoped to inspire the government to support the Daoist church.

In keeping with her eminence, the Queen Mother's biography is unusually long. It contains material from several earlier sources, both literary and canonical. Du begins by listing several titles by which she is known, identifying them as diverse expressions of a single being who represents the ultimate yin. Some of these titles may have originally named separate deities of ancient and Han times who are brought together in the Tang Daoist cult of the Queen Mother. Knowledge of the correct titles is important to believers and clergy who want to address her correctly in ritual, and to promoters of Daoism, such as Du Guangting, who want to include and tame her earlier manifestations.

Next we read of the goddess's origin along with her consort, the Eastern King or Wood Lord (Dongwang 東王, Mugong 木公), from the primordial Dao at the beginning of creation. Her birth and her mandate to nourish living beings and protect all women verify her primacy as a deity. Du then turns to a description of her paradise on Mount Kunlun, a mythical mountain far to the west, in the exotic occident. In his descriptions, the Queen Mother's paradise competes with the lavish scenes of Western Paradise of Amitabha Buddha depicted in the Pure Land sutras and with the settings of the historical Buddha's lectures so extravagantly described in the *Lotus Sutra*. Du lists a number of places linked to her cult, attempting to be as inclusive as possible.

Du Guangting describes the Queen Mother's appearance as a beautiful, mature woman of the upper classes. Reminding us of her powers of creation as well as her performance of the womanly work of textile production, she wears a headdress shaped like the brakewheel of a loom (*sheng* 勝). This refers to the celestial loom upon which she weaves the universe into being. Du's vivid portrayal of the goddess competes with descriptions of Buddhist deities such as the bodhisattva Guanyin 觀音 in the *Lotus Sutra* and *Pure Land Sutra*. Du also attempts to delineate a standard icon of the goddess. Devotees need a precise and correct image of the goddess for purposes of visualization exercises. Details of clothing and hairdo must be specified as identifiers. With a vague or incorrect image as prompt to their meditations, they might invite a demon into their minds.

And yet, Du cannot simply reject older canonical images of her that disagree with his own. So he resorts to some pretty dubious logic. He reconciles contradictory images of her preserved in diverse sources, such as the *Shanhai jing* 山海經 (Classic of Mountains and Seas),[53] Han-dynasty classical dictionaries, and literary accounts of famous Chinese emperors of antiquity. Responding to venerable portrayals of the goddess as a ferocious creature who is part human and part tiger, for example, Du explains that these must be mistaken references to her feline messenger. Du removes references to the goddess as bestial or monstrous, bringing her more in line with the literati sensibilities of the Shangqing Daoists. She could be the teacher or older sister of the beautiful goddesses who reveal sacred texts to mortal adepts in the 360s, later collected by Tao Hongjing in the *Zhen'gao* 真誥 (Declarations of the Perfected, DZ 1016).[54]

The Queen Mother's teacher, the Celestial King of the Primordial Commencement (Yuanshi tianwang 元始天王), is one of a triad of primal Daoist deities; the goddess's position in the lineage of such an important teacher underscores her legitimacy and power. She presides over other divinities at Daoist rituals, and she decides who can receive ordination and transmission of sacred texts.

---

[53] This text is translated in Birrell 1999; Mathieu 1983.
[54] Studies of the *Zhen'gao* appear in Strickmann 1981; Hyland 1984; Robinet 1984.

Introductory matters explained, Du moves to his own deepest interest: the Queen Mother's encounters with human heroes and her transmission of the Way. In these meetings she plays diverse roles, such as master, lover, mother, and go-between. The first human she meets is the Yellow Thearch (Huangdi 黃帝), legendary first Chinese ruler and first Daoist immortal, founder of the Chinese imperial bureaucracy and of traditional Chinese medicine. She sends her envoys, including the Mysterious Woman of the Nine Heavens, ancient goddess of sex and war and subject of the second biography in Du's collection, to visit the Yellow Thearch. Through the Mysterious Woman, the Queen Mother grants the emperor a magical talisman that guarantees him victory in the cosmic battle between chaos and order, the struggle that results in the founding of China. The Queen Mother's later gifts verify his legitimacy, teach him the means to become an immortal, and place him first in the human lineage of adepts who receive Daoist scriptures from the goddess. The transmitted scripture Du quotes stresses the Shangqing beliefs that individual asceticism and meditation lead to the transcendent Way. Du's account makes the goddess the Yellow Thearch's master, in this manner claiming responsibility for the first emperor's military, governmental, and cultural contributions.

By honoring the Yellow Thearch, Du includes the traditions of the Huang-Lao school of Daoism, which revered him together with Laozi. That school flourished in the second century B.C.E. It joined concerns of political legitimacy and military strategy with the pursuit of personal immortality, and made notable contributions to early cosmology and imperial theory.

Next the Queen Mother bestows seminal gifts upon another early sage emperor, Shun 舜. Shun was a legendary paragon of virtue to Confucian thinkers, and Du's inclusion of him here strengthens his argument that Confucian and Daoist values were originally close. When she encounters Shun, the Queen Mother gives him maps and jade tokens that affirm his political and cosmic power. According to Du, she has the power to bestow symbols of the mandate of heaven upon human rulers. She enacts the will of heaven.

Later, the Queen Mother meets Laozi 老子, the attributive founder of Daoism and one of its highest deities, in a story that survives only in the Ming dynasty version of the biography. Du refers to Laozi as Lord Lao, his title as a Daoist deity. Du places this meeting in ancient historical times, in the year 1028 B.C.E., during the reign of the Zhou King Zhao (1052-1001 B.C.E.). Also present at the time is the gatekeeper Yin Xi 尹喜, who according to legend encouraged an unwilling Laozi to transcribe a foundational text of Daoism, the *Daode jing* 道德經 (Scripture of the Way and its Power, DZ 664). Daoists revered Yin Xi as a heroic transmitter of scriptures from the divine realms to this world. Again, Du asserts the Queen Mother's central role in transmission of one of the most sacred and universally revered texts of Daoism.

The Queen Mother explains the *Chang qingjing jing* 常清靜經 (Scripture of Constant Purity and Quiet, DZ 620) to them. By describing her as the teacher of Lord Lao and Yin Xi, Du Guangting again puts her in the senior and superior position. The text in question is one of several short Daoist scriptures composed in the eighth to ninth centuries, of which the most important is the *Qingjing xinjing* 清靜心經 (Heart Scripture of Purity and Quiet, DZ 1169). Du also wrote a commentary upon one version of this text that became prominent in the Song and evolved into a central scripture of the Complete Perfection (Quanzhen 全真) school. It may be the same as the work mentioned here. Perhaps a later editor, recognizing Du's connection with the text, inserted this incident.

To explain why the "Scripture of Constant Purity and Quiet" did not appear in earlier collections of Daoist texts, Du quotes a preface he attributes to the third century Daoist patriarch Ge Xuan 葛玄. Ge Xuan claims that these teachings had been passed down orally until he himself wrote it down. Once again the original source is the Queen Mother. As the Mahayana Buddhists had to explain the origin of sutras that appeared long after the Buddha's death, the Daoists also had to explain revelations from Laozi that suddenly turned up many centuries after his departure.

These scriptures promote the practice of inner observation (*neiguan* 內觀), a Daoist version of the Buddhist practice known as insight meditation, a technique of making the world and one's place in it the subject of spiritual cultivation, in which the mind is empty and calm and observes all sensory data with complete impartiality. As a Shangqing master, Du believed inner observation was a crucial step towards attainment of the Dao. The scriptures in this class combine the idea and practice of inner observation with the structure of Buddhist mantra texts such as the *Heart Sutra*, the shortest of the Perfection of Wisdom sutras. In both content and form, the "purity and quiet" texts compete with and are deeply in-debted to Buddhist practice and scripture.

In a passage recorded only in the YJQQ, the Queen Mother next meets heroic figures in the founding of early Daoist schools. This passage is out of chronological sequence, sandwiched between events that occurred during the early Zhou dynasty. At least two of the characters flourished during the Han dynasty (206 B.C.E.–220 C.E.). Zhang Daoling was the first patriarch of the Celestial Masters school and Mao Ying 茅嬰 was a lead-ing deity of Shangqing Daoism. They visit the Grand Supreme Lord of the Way, a major deity and transmitter of scriptures in the Lingbao Dao-ist tradition. They travel with others across the heavens to the Queen Mother's palace on Mount Kunlun to receive sacred texts. The Queen Mother takes credit for transmitting texts in revelations to the founding masters of the major schools. She bestows her greatest favors on Mao Ying, giving him the "Scripture of the Mysterious Realized Ones," that is: the Shangqing Daoist written corpus. This narrative links the Shangqing and Lingbao traditions, and pushes the association far back in time.

Du next turns his attention to the adventures of an actual historical ruler. The Queen Mother of the West meets the Zhou King Mu (r. 1001–946 B.C.E.) by the Turquoise Pond on Mount Kunlun. This story, a favorite of Tang dynasty poets and artists, existed in Du's time in several independ-ent versions. Most likely as sources for his account are the *Mu Tianzi zhuan* 穆天子傳 (Transmissions Concerning Mu, the Son of Heaven, DZ 291) and the *Liezi* 列子 (Book of Master Lie, DZ 730), both of disputed date but certainly extant by the fourth century C.E..[55]

As the story goes, King Mu traveled with his eight exquisite steeds to the paradise of the Queen Mother of the West on Mount Kunlun. King and goddess toasted each other, exchanged sad poems, and parted. A love affair is implied. King Mu wanted to learn her secrets of immortality, but duty to his people called him home. He returned to his capital and sub-sequently died there. Medieval Chinese readers interpreted this story as a noble and touching tragedy. The king was a tragic hero who almost earned immortality and the love of a goddess, but in the end failed to do so because of his concern for his subjects and his attachment to this world.

---

[55] For translations of these two texts, see Mathieu 1978; Graham 1990.

After relating King Mu's story, Du takes the opportunity to give his readers a lesson on the various classes of immortals. He defines nine classes of heavenly transcendents, explaining that they must all pay a ritual visit to the Queen Mother and receive transmissions before they can ascend. Du also notes that only transcendents can unfailingly identify other transcendents.

About a thousand years later (as long as some accounts say it takes the peaches of immortality on her tree to ripen), the Queen Mother descends from the heavens with an elaborate entourage to visit the Han dynasty capital city of Chang'an. Here Du draws upon a textual tradition about this famous meeting that included the fifth-century *Han Wudi neizhuan* 漢武帝內傳 (Inner Transmissions Concerning the Martial Thearch of the Han Dynasty, DZ 292),[56] and the *Hanwu gushi* 漢武故事 (Old Stories about the Martial [Thearch of] the Han). She sweeps into the palace of the Martial Thearch of the Han (r. 140-87 B.C.E.).

The year is 110 B.C.E. The date is the seventh day of the seventh month, the festival of the herd boy and the weaver girl, the night *par excellence* for an encounter between deity and humans. Du describes the goddess's physical appearance in meticulous detail. The verbal image stresses her majestic beauty and also provides Daoist practitioners with a precise picture for use in visualization. The emperor, himself a devout Daoist, receives her with great ceremony, and requests her teaching. She provides him with a feast including peaches of immortality, a performance of divine music and dance, and transmission of her teachings. Peaches are an old medicine and symbol of health and longevity, joined to the Queen Mother's cult sometime during the Han dynasty.

In her long lecture, the goddess voices some of Du's most strongly held beliefs. She encourages the emperor to practice asceticism, purify himself, and meditate in order to become immortal. She stresses that he can find salvation within his own body and only through his own efforts. After perfecting himself through physical and mental austerities, he may ingest elixir drugs, of which she then recites a long list. The drugs, like the peaches, show the link between Daoist practices and traditional Chinese medicine. The Martial Thearch vows to become her disciple. Again, we see the Queen Mother assuming the superior position of teacher in relation to a Chinese emperor. In the end, the emperor, unable to stop mak-

---

[56] Translations of this text include Schipper 1965; Smith 1992.

ing war and behaving licentiously, dies, and his precious texts go up in flames.

At the end of Du's account the Daoist texts that the Queen Mother had transmitted to the Martial Thearch, along with a jade casket and jade staff, are recovered, while the emperor's grave remains undisturbed. Du rather unconvincingly claims that the miraculous appearance of these items without any sign of grave robbing, may be evidence of the emperor's achievement of Daoist immortality through deliverance by means of the corpse. No other account holds out such hope for the ruler. In other versions of the story, as in the rest of Du's account, the Martial Thearch, like King Mu before him, was a flawed but admirable human hero who held immortality in his grasp and then lost it. The reader can easily identify with their struggles. Their stories, favorites of later Chinese writers and artists, have both tragic and erotic resonance.

One last encounter of the goddess and a human recorded by Du Guangting takes place in 1 B.C.E. This passage only appears in the Ming version of the text. It describes at some length the Queen Mother's transmission of texts and technologies to Mao Ying, a story the other version of the text sketchily notes in an anachronistic sequence about her bestowals on several founders of Daoist schools. The Queen Mother successfully gives teachings—along with a divine wife—to Mao Ying, who becomes a god of Mount Mao and a patron deity of Shangqing Daoism. The divine wife is Lady Wei Huacun, herself a leader of the Celestial Masters who becomes a major deity and teacher of the Shangqing school. After investing Mao Ying and his two younger brothers, the Queen Mother of the West returns with her attendants to her holy mountain. This account recapitulates much of the story of the Martial Thearch and the Queen Mother, and probably is based on a now lost biography that was formerly part of the *Maoshan zhi* 茅山志 (Essay on Mount Mao, DZ 304).

The final part of Du's account repeats the goddess's main functions as a teacher, transmitter of sacred scriptures, and keeper of the keys to immortality. He leaves the door open for further visits from the Queen Mother to our world by closing with the statement: "This is not a complete account." And, in fact, the goddess has continued to appear throughout Chinese history, most recently to groups of women in Taiwan today who write down and publish texts they say she transmits to them while possessing their spirits.

Translation: The Queen Mother of the West Transmits the Transcendent Way

[114.4b] The Queen Mother of the West is the Metal Mother of the Nine Numina, the Grand Marvel, and Tortoise Mountain.[57] One source calls her Metal Mother of Tortoise Terrace, She of the Grand Numina and the Nine Radiances. Another source calls her The Primordial Ruler, Metal Mother. She is, in fact, the Perfected Marvel of the Western Florescence and the Ultimate Worthy of the Grotto Yin.[58]

At the time of the Former Way, the breaths were congealed and quiescent, deeply imbued with and embodying nonaction. About to disclose and lead to the mysterious accomplishment of creation, and to produce and transform the myriad phenomena, first the Way produced [the Queen Mother's consort] Wood Lord by transformations from the breath of the perfected realization of the eastern florescence. Wood Lord was born beside the Cyan Sea, in the Barrens of the Gray-Green Numen, where he governs the breaths of yang harmonies, and arranges the internal structure of the eastern quadrant. [5a] He is also called Lord King.

Then the Way produced Metal Mother by transformation from the breath of the perfected marvel of the western florescence. The Queen Mother was born at the Yi River [near Luoyang] in Divine Island [China]. Her surname is Gou. As soon as she was born, she soared up in flight. She governs the breaths of the yin numina and arranges the internal structure of the western quadrant. She is also called the Queen Mother.

In all respects, she derives her substance from the great non-existent; she nurtures her spirit with the mysterious enigma. In the midst of impenetrable clouds in the western quadrant, the unmixed seminal breaths of the great Way were divided, and the breaths were bound together to make her shape.

---

[57] An earlier translation of parts of this text appears in Cahill 1993. For the whole text, based mainly on the *Daozang* edition, see Wang 2003, 346-365. A short account of the Queen Mother of the West is also found in *Taiping guangji* 260. Its brevity in comparison to the text translated here suggests that the *Taiping guangji* versions of Du Guangting's biography may all be similarly reduced. Thus they have value, but only limited value, in reconstructing the complete original text of Du's "Records."

[58] Du lists her various names. The names and titles express her lineage, essence, functions, and individual identity. Tortoise Mountain or Terrace is in the Kunlun range. On her various names and possible early identities, as well as her emergence in the Han and later periods as a figure of both popular and imperial worship who had origins in several earlier deities, see Cahill 1993.

Together with the Eastern King, Wood Lord, through structuring of the two primal breaths, she nourishes and raises Heaven and Earth, firing and casting the myriad phenomena [creating the world]. She embodies the basis of the pliant and yielding, functioning as the origin of the ultimate yin. From her location corresponding to the western quadrant, she mothers and nourishes all classes and categories of beings. In heaven, beneath heaven, in the Three Worlds and the ten directions, all women who ascend to transcendence and attain the Way are her dependents.

The palaces with watchtowers where she lives are located west of the Western Pestle Peak in the Tortoise Mountain range. That is her capital city. In the hunting parks of Mysterious Orchard and Vacant Wind [peaks] at Mount Kunlun, there are metal city walls [fortress walls] of a thousand layers, [5b] surrounding twelve jade storied buildings, with watchtowers of rose-gem florescence, halls of radiant cyan, nine-storied mysterious terraces, and purple kingfisher cinnabar chambers. On the left, the palace compound is girded by the Turquoise Pond; on the right, it is ringed by the Kingfisher River. Beneath the mountains, the Weak River, in nine layers of swells and rolling waves, rushes along for one hundred thousand feet. Unless one has a whirlwind cart with feathered wheels, he can never reach this place. The jade watchtowers mentioned above stick up into the heavens; their green terraces receive the empyrean [that is: hold up the heavens.] Under azure blue-gem eaves, inside vermilion purple chambers joined blue-gems make variegated curtains, and the bright moon shines distinctly on all four sides.

She wears a flowered *sheng* headdress.[59] She carries at her belt numinous emblems. Her attendants on the left are transcendent girls; her attendants on the right are feathered lads. Precious canopies match reflections, while feathered banners shade the courtyard. Beneath the balustrade and steps of her shaded courtyard, the grounds are planted with white jade bracelet trees and a cinnabar diamond [ruby?] forest. There are a myriad stalks of "hollow blue" mineral, and a thousand lengths of turquoise tree trunks. Even when there is no wind, divine reeds spontaneously harmonize sounds, clinking like jade belt pendants. In all cases, they play the sounds of the nine performances [of Emperor Shun's music] at the [seasonal festivals of the] Eight Unions.

---

[59] The *sheng* headdress is a crown in the shape of a brakewheel from the celestial loom with which she weaves the universe into being. See Loewe 1979, Kominami 1974, and Liang 1999.

The divine isle-land [China] is southeast of Mount Kunlun. As the *Erya* says, "This is the Queen Mother's land where the sun sets."[60] Another text says, "The Queen Mother has disheveled hair and wears a *sheng* headdress. She has tiger's teeth and is good at whistling."[61] [6a] Now this statement actually refers to the Queen Mother's envoy, the spirit of the white tiger from the metal quadrant. It is not the Queen Mother's veritable shape.

The Heavenly King of the Primordial Commencement bestowed upon her the Register of the Ninefold Radiance of Tortoise Mountain, from the Primordial Unification of the Myriad Heavens. With it he commissioned her to control and summon the myriad numina, to unify and gather the realized ones and the paragons, to oversee oaths and to verify faith, and generally to take charge of the ceremonies of feathered beings [alternatively, of the honor guards] of the various heavens. Therefore, at meetings of celestial worthies and supreme paragons, such as court appearances or feasts, and at places for examining and editing texts, the Queen Mother in all cases presides, reflecting divine light on the proceedings. The precious scriptures from the Realm of Supreme Clarity, jade writs of the Three Caverns, and in general whatever is bestowed at ordination: all these are either obstructed or given by her.[62]

The Yellow Thearch.[63] Formerly the Yellow Thearch punished the Wormy Rebel [Chiyou] for his violence.[64] But before his aggression was completely checked, the Wormy Rebel performed illusionistic transformations. He raised the wind and summoned the rain in all directions; he blew smoke and spat mist. The leaders and masses of the Yellow Thearch's army grew

---

[60] The *Erya* is a Han dynasty glossary for reading the classics. In the section on geography in that text, "where the sun sets" is identified one of the Four Wildernesses (21.9.7, 14.4.1).

[61] A similar passage appears in Guo Pu's commentary to the *Shanhai jing* (2.23b, 16.7b).

[62] The Heavenly King of the Primordial Commencement, also known as the Heavenly Honored One, one of the high gods of Daoism, is the Queen Mother's teacher. For Daoists of the Lingbao school, the Heavenly King of Primordial Commencement is the only high god to emerge from primordial chaos, and is the source of scriptures. The precious scriptures from the Realm of Supreme Clarity are the holy texts of Shangqing Daoism. Jade writs of the Three Caverns are Daoist canonical texts in general. The Three Caverns are the three main divisions of the Daoist canon (see Schipper and Verellen 2004).

[63] Section headings are added by the translator.

[64] The Yellow Thearch is the legendary first emperor of China, and also, according to Daoists, the first human to become immortal. He is a major deity in Huang-Lao Daoism which rose to prominence during the Han dynasty. The Wormy Rebel is a storm god who is transformed into a war god by the Han dynasty (see Lewis 1990). A descendent of the god of agriculture, Shen Nong, he is the Daoist parallel to Māra, the Buddhist embodiment of the forces of nature who tries to stop Shakyamuni Buddha from attaining enlightenment under the bodhi tree.

greatly confused. The Thearch returned home to rest in a fold of Mount Tai [in Shandong]. Bewildered, he went to bed depressed.

The Queen Mother sent an envoy wearing a dark fox cloak to bestow a talisman upon the Thearch, saying "Grand Unity is located [written] on its front, Heavenly Unity on its back. [Alternatively: 'Grand Unity comes before; Heavenly Unity comes afterward]. Whoever obtains it will conquer; when he attacks, he will overcome." [6b] The talisman was three inches wide and a foot long, with a blue luster like jade. Cinnabar-colored drops of blood formed the text upon it. The Thearch hung it at his waist.

Once he had done this, the Queen Mother commanded a woman with a human head and bird's body to come to him. She told the Thearch, "I am the Mysterious Woman of the Nine Heavens," and bestowed [sacred arts] upon the Thearch.[65] [These included] Plans of Yin and Yang for Five Intentions from the Three Palaces, [divination] Techniques from the Grand Unity for Hiding the *Jia* and Calculating the Six *Ren* Cyclicals, [and instructions for] Pacing the Dipper. In addition [she gave him] the key to [or mechanism of] the Yin Talisman and texts of the Five Talismans of Numinous Treasure and Fivefold Victory. Consequently, he subdued the Wormy Rebel at Zhongji. After he had exterminated this descendent of Shen Nong and executed the rebel Yu Gang at Banquan, the empire was greatly settled. Then he built his capital at [Mount] Zhuolu on the Upper Valley [in Hebei].

After a number of years, the Queen Mother sent her envoy, the white tiger spirit. Then, riding a white tiger, she perched in the Thearch's courtyard and bestowed upon him some territorial maps. In later years, she further bestowed upon the Thearch a [scripture called] "The Rectified and Realized Way of Pure Quietude and Nonaction." The words to it went:

> If drinking and pecking [eating grains] do not cease, your body
> will not become light. If thinking and worrying do not cease, your
> spirits will not become pure. If sounds and forms do not cease,
> your heart will not become tranquil. If your heart is not tranquil,
> then your spirits will not become numinous. If your spirits are not
> numinous, then the Way cannot accomplish its requisite marvels.
> [This Way] does not depend on paying homage to the stars and
> treating the Dipper with ceremony, thereby causing yourself to suf-
> fer bitterly, exhausting your frame and wealth. It all depends on

---

65 The Mysterious Woman of the Nine Heavens, an old goddess of sex and war, is brought into the Shangqing pantheon as the Yellow Thearch's teacher. Her biography is the next entry in Du Guangting's "Records."

remaining unwavering deep in your heart. [This is] the Way of the divine transcendents. It certainly can extend your life.[66]

Further Bestowals. After that, Shun of Yu took the throne. The Queen Mother sent an envoy to bestow a white jade bracelet upon Shun. He also benefited from territorial maps [she gave him]. Consequently, Shun extended the Yellow Thearch's territory of nine isle-lands [provinces] to twelve isle-lands. The Queen Mother also sent her envoy to bestow an illustrious tube upon Shun, which he blew to harmonize the eight winds [musical tones].

In the twenty-fifth year of King Zhao of the Zhou dynasty [1028 B.C.E.], when the planet Jupiter was in B-hare [*yimao*], Lord Lao and the realized person Yin Xi went traveling to look around the eight cords.[67] They wandered west to the Tortoise Terrace. On their behalf, the Queen Mother explicated the "Scripture of Constant Purity and Quiet." Then later the Transcendent Lord Ge Xuan of the Left Palace of the Grand Ultimate, in his preface to that scripture, states:

> Formerly I received [this text] from the Thearchic Lord of the Eastern Florescence. The Thearchic Lord of the Eastern Florescence received it from the Thearchic Lord of the Golden Watchtowers. The Thearchic Lord of the Golden Watchtowers received it from the Queen Mother of the West. In every case it was transmitted orally from one to the next, without recording worlds or graphs. At this time, I am writing it down and making a record for the generations [that is: finally transmitting it to humans].[68]

The "Examination and Chronology of the Official Texts for Thearchs" says: "The Queen Mother's country is located in the wildest part of the four wildernesses."[69] [7a] Formerly, Mao Ying (courtesy name Shushen), Wang Xiu,

---

[66] This section is only found in the Ming *Daozang* version of the Queen Mother's biography (DZ 783).

[67] Yin Xi was the legendary guardian of the western passes who forced Laozi to write down the Daode jing before allowing him to wander off west. The eight cords are the eight longitudinal markers of the night sky. See Kohn 1997.

[68] Ge Xuan was a Daoist patriarch of the third century C.E. and an uncle of Ge Hong. The two masters are claimed as ancestors by both the Lingbao and Shangqing schools. The incident with Laozi and the "Scripture of Constant Purity and Quiet" is also not found in the YJQQ version of Du's biography, but appears in DZ 783.

[69] The *Shangshu dijianqi* was presumably a commentary on the *Shangshu* or *Shujing* (Book of Documents), the first collection of Chinese historical documents and, as one of the five classics, a part of the Confucian canon.

(courtesy name Zideng), and Zhang Daoling (courtesy name Puhan), along with the nine paragons and seven realized ones were all able to receive [sacred] texts. In every case, this came about because they went to formal court audience with the Queen Mother at the Watchtowers of Kunlun [although it was so far away].[70]

[Mao] Shushen and [Zhang Daoling] attended the Grand Supreme Lord of the Way. Then, riding nine-canopied vehicles, and reining in chariots pulled by flying dragonlets, they passed over the peaks of the Heaped Stones [Mountain Range], crossed the ford of the Weak Flow [River], and leaped over the ripples of the White Water [River] and the Black Waves [River] [on Mount Kunlun]. In the blink of an eye, they were suddenly paying a formal visit to the Queen Mother beneath her watchtowers. As for [Wang] Zideng, on the pure fast of the fifth month the Queen Mother bestowed upon her the "Rose-gem Floriate Pure Classic of the Treasured Brilliants and Seven Chronograms [sun, moon, and five planets]."

Lord Mao followed the Royal Lord of the Western Walled City to the White Jade Tortoise Platform. There he paid a formal court visit to the Queen Mother, seeking her Way of extending life. He said: "This extremely unworthy one, Ying, longs for the years of a dragon or phoenix. By means of [my body, as transient as] tidbits of morning mushroom, I want to amass years full of new moons." The Queen Mother sympathized with his diligence and ambition. She told him: "My former master, the Heavenly Honored One of the Primordial Commencement, [7b] together with the Illustrious Thearch of the Heaven-Striking Mulberry Tree, bestowed upon me jade belt pendants, golden earrings, and the Way of the two phosphors [sun and moon] for binding [deities] and refining [practice]. Above it sets in motion the Grand Ultimate; below it creates the ten directions. It pours out the moon and sucks on the sun in order to enter the gates of heaven. [The text is] named the "Scripture of the Mysterious Realized Ones." Now I bestow it upon you. It is proper to be diligent in refining it." Thereupon she appointed the Royal Lord of the Western Walled City to analyze and explain it one point after another as she bestowed it upon him. She also gave him [other] precious texts. [Then her] four lads all scattered to the [four] directions.

---

[70] This account is found only in the YQQJ version. Mao Ying or Lord Mao, putative founder of the Shangqing school of Daoism, was the oldest of three brothers who lived during the Han dynasty on Mount Mao, also known as Bucklebent Mountain, in modern Jiangsu province. Wang Zideng is a goddess who is a musician, messenger, and companion to the Queen Mother. Wang Zideng can appear as female or male, depending on the needs of the situation. Zhang Daoling is the founder of the Celestial Masters, one of the first institutionalized schools of the Daoist religion.

King Mu of Zhou. A long time later, King Mu [of Zhou, r. 1001–946 B.C.E..] gave the command to harness his eight fine steeds in two teams of four, together with seven floriate officials [driving].[71] In the team drawing the imperial chariot, the inside pair of horses consisted of Flowery Bay on the right and Green Ears on the left. The outside pair of horses were Red Thoroughbred on the right and White Sacrifice on the left. In the main chariot, Father Zao was holding the reins and Shang was to the right. In the team of the next vehicle, the inside horses were Big Yellow on the right and Faster-than-Wheels on the left, while the outside horses were Robber Black on the left and Son of the Mountain on the right. Bo Yao was in charge of the chariot, Can Bai acted as rein holder, and Pai Wu was to the right.

Riding full speed ahead for a thousand *li*, they reached the nation of the Great Sou Clan [or Jusou clan]. The Great Sou Clan head then offered as tribute the blood of white swans for the king to drink; he set out ox and horse milk to use for washing the king's feet. After the men from the two vehicles drank, they proceeded along the road. They spent the night in a fold of Mount Kunlun on the sunny side of the Red Water River. The next day, they ascended Kunlun Hill in order to inspect the palace of the Yellow Thearch. They heaped up dirt on it to make a sacrificial mound, in order to hand down knowledge of [their visit] to later generations.

Subsequently, King Mu was a guest of the Queen Mother of the West. As they toasted each other with drinks at the side of the Turquoise Pond, the Queen Mother of the West composed poems for the king. The king matched them. Their lyrics were sad. Then he observed where the sun set: in a single day, he had gone ten thousand *li*. The king sighed and said, "I, the Unique Person, am not overabounding with virtue. Later generations will certainly trace back and count my excesses!" It is also said that the king grasped a white jade tablet and heavy multi-colored tabby-weave silk, offering them in order [to acquire the secrets of] the Queen Mother's longevity. [8a] She sang the "Poem of the White Clouds." On top of Cover Mountain, he carved stone to record the traces [of this event], then returned home [to the Middle Kingdom].

Heavenly Ranks. Now, as for the transcendents in the world who have ascended to heaven; in general they fall into nine classes. The first supreme transcendents are called Realized Rulers of the Nine Heavens. The next tran-

---

[71] For the story of King Mu of the Zhou dynasty, I rely mostly on the fuller version found in DZ 783. On the account of King Mu in the *Mu Tianzi zhuan* (DZ 291), see Mathieu 1978. Guo Pu's commentary to the *Shanhai jing* contains his versions of the text of the poems the Queen Mother and King Mu exchange.

scendents are the Realized Illustrious of the Three Heavens. The third are called Grand Supreme Realized People. The fourth are called Realized People Who Fly Through the Heavens. The fifth are called Numinous Transcendents. The sixth are called Realized People. The seventh are called Numinous People. The eighth are called Flying Transcendents. The ninth are called Transcendent People. All these class ranks may not be skipped or superceded.

So it is that at the time one ascends to heaven, first one must salute the Wood Lord, and afterwards pay a ceremonial visit to the Metal Mother. Only when the business of receiving transmissions and ordinations is finished can one ascend to the Nine Heavens. One enters the Three Realms of Clarity, salutes the Grand Supreme, and receives an audience with the Heavenly Honored One of the Primordial Commencement.

Thus it is that at the beginning of the Han dynasty there were four or five children playing in the road. One child sang: "Wearing a blue apron, I enter heaven's gate; I bow to Metal Mother and salute Wood Lord." Among the people of the time, no one recognized him. Only [the second century B.C.E. transcendent] Zhang Zifang recognized him. Zhang went over to salute him, saying: [8b]

> This is none other than a jade lad of the Lord King of the East. A transcendent person who attains the Way and ascends to heaven must bow to the Metal Mother and salute the Wood Lord. Anyone who is not himself a master who skims the void and climbs to realization cannot recognize the ferrying over [liberation of a transcendent].

The Martial Thearch. The Filial and Martial Illustrious Thearch of the Han, Liu Che, was fond of the Way of extending life.[72] During the original year of the Primordial Enfeoffment reign period [110 B.C.E.], he climbed the heights of Marchmount Song [near Luoyang] and there built a terrace for seeking realized ones. He fasted, observed abstinence, and made his thoughts seminal. On an E-dragon (*wuchen*) day in the fourth month, the Queen Mother sent Wang Zideng, the Jade Girl from the Fortified Walled City, to come and talk with the thearch for her. She said:

> I have heard that you are willing to slight the emoluments of the four seas and keep at a distance the noble rank of a myriad

---

[72] For the story of the Han emperor Wu, see Schipper 1965; Smith 1992. Du bases his account on several versions of the story of the Martial Thearch.

vehicles in order to seek the veritable Way of extended life. How diligent! On the seventh day of the seventh month, I will certainly come for a little while.

The thearch inquired of Dongfang Shuo to find the proper ritual response to this divinity.[73] Then he purified himself and fasted for one hundred days, burning incense in the palace.

On the night in question, after the second watch [9-11 p.m.], white clouds arose in the southwest. Dense and thick, they came directly towards the courtyard of the palace and gradually drew near. Then came auroral clouds of nine colors. Pipes and drums shook empty space [the sky]. [9a] There were hosts of dragons, phoenixes, men, horses, and a group of guards mounted on *qilin* [mythical feline-equine-avian mounts] and harnessing deer. There were open chariots [of transcendents] and heavenly horses, with rainbow banners and feathered streamers. The radiance from a thousand vehicles and myriad outriders illuminated the palace watchtowers. Celestial transcendents, followed by their officials, majestic and severe, numbered one hundred thousand multitudes. All were ten feet or more tall. Once they had arrived, both the followers and officials disappeared.

The Queen Mother rode an imperial carriage of purple clouds, harnessed with nine-colored, dappled dragons. Tied around her waist, she held the tablets of the celestial realized ones; as a pendant she had a diamond numinous seal. In her clothing of multi-colored tabby-weave silk with a yellow background, the patterns and variegated colors were bright and fresh. Metallic radiance made a shimmering gleam. At her waist was a double-bladed sword for dividing phosphors. Knotted flying clouds made a great cord. On top of her head was a great floriate topknot. She wore the crown of the realized ones with hanging beaded strings of daybreak. She stepped forth on shoes with squared, phoenix-patterned soles of rose-gem. Her age might have been about twenty. Her celestial appearance, full beauty and numinous face were utterly unique. She was certainly a realized numinous being.

She descended from her chariot supported by two serving girls, ascended the dais, and sat down facing east. The thearch saluted her, kneeled, and inquired how she fared. Then he stood in attendance. After a good long while, she called the thearch and allowed him to be seated. She laid out a celestial fast consisting of fragrant flowers, a hundred fruits, purple mushrooms, and

---

[73] Dongfang Shuo was a courtier of the Martial Thearch of the Han who was believed later to have been an immortal in disguise. He has a biography in *Hanshu* 65 (Watson 1974, 79-10). On elixirs, see Sivin 1968; 1980.

magic mushrooms—as variegated as prismatic shellfish. Their seminal essences were rare and odd; they were not what regularly exists in this world. The thearch could not even name them. [9b]

She also ordered a serving girl to fetch peaches. A jade basin was filled with seven of the fruits. They were as large as bustards' eggs. She took four and gave them to the thearch. Mother herself ate three of them. When the thearch had eaten his peaches, he hastily put away the pits. Mother asked him why he was doing this. He said, "I just want to plant them." Mother told him, "These peaches only bear fruit once in three thousand years. The land in the Middle Kingdom is poor; even if you plant them, they will not grow. So what is the point?"

Thereupon the Queen Mother commanded her serving girls: Wang Zideng to play the eight-orbed chimes, Dong Shuangcheng to blow the Cloud Harmony Mount Organ, Shi Gongzi to strike the jade sounding stones from the courtyard of Mount Kunlun, Xu Feiqiong to sound the Thunder Numen Flute, Wan Linghua to hit the musical stone of Wuling, Fan Chengjun to strike the Lithophone of the Grotto Yin, Duan Anxiang to play the harmonies of the Nine Heavens, and [An] Faying to sing tunes of the Mysterious Numina. The whole ensemble of sounds was exciting and distinct; their numinous timbres startled empty space.

When the song was finished, the thearch got down from his mat, kowtowed, and asked about the Way of extending life. The Queen Mother told him: [10a]

> If you could consider glory cheap and delight in humble living quarters, if you could become addicted to the void and acquire a taste for the Way, then you would naturally revert to excellence. However, your passions are licentious and your body desirous, your lewd behavior is unbalanced and your excesses extreme, you kill and attack in battle without the right to do so, and thus you waste and squander your vital energies. Excessive licentiousness becomes the means [literally, chariot] to rip open your body, and lust becomes an ax to smash your body. Killing produces an echo in response; profligacy corrupts the heart. If you store up desire, your spirits will fail. If you accumulate all these pollutions, your lifespan will be cut short. With your own unworthy body, you provide lodging for thieves who will annihilate your frame. It is just as if you took a piece of wood a little over a foot long, and attacked it with a hundred knives. If you wanted to sever and cast off the three

corpses and to make your body whole and permanently enduring in this manner, it could never be done. It would be the
same as a wingless quail wanting to drum its wings on the
Heavenly Pond, or a mushroom born in the morning wanting
to enjoy whole springs and autumns.

Cleanse yourself of this whole multitude of disorders; reject
annihilation and change your intentions. Protect your spirits
and vital energies in the scarlet archives; lock up the palace of
debauchery and do not open it. Still your profligacy and ex-
travagance in a quiet room. Cherish all living beings and do
not endanger them. Observe compassion, devote yourself to
charity, refine your vital energies, and hoard your seminal essence. If you behave in this fashion, you will be close to ideal.
[10b] If you do not act like this, [seeking the Way of extending life] would be like trying to cross the Yangzi River carrying rocks.

The thearch received the Queen Mother's admonitions on his knees, then
said:

I, Che, the untalented one, am plunged into a capricious mode
of life. Having inherited the work of my predecessors, I am
impeded by earthly ties. My punishments and government
[law codes] are full of error and falsehood. My sins pile up,
making hills and mountains. After today, please allow me to
practice your words of instruction.

The Queen Mother told him:

As for the Way of nourishing your nature and the essential re-
quirements of regulating the internal order of your body, by
now you already have a solid understanding of these. But you
must practice diligently without being remiss. Formerly on the
Lofty Empyrean Terrace, my master, the Heavenly Honored
One of the Primordial Commencement, bestowed on me his
essential words [on breathing and visualization]:

If you want prolonged life, you must first obtain it within
your body. Make firm and preserve the three ones, and
protect the numinous root [tongue]. Take the floriate vin-
tage of the mysterious vale [saliva] and force it into the
deep treasure passage [throat]. Irrigate and extend the
pure seminal essence; have it enter the celestial gate

[mouth]. At the golden apartment, have it turn and enter the central barrier [nose]. Then divide the bright light into blue and white, and have it reach the mud ball [in the center of your brain].

Nourish the fluids and lock up the seminal essence and you will make the body and spirits whole. Keep the spirits of the three palaces in good order and well defended; then you will preserve the scarlet palace. The unflowing source of the E-snake [*wusi*] organ from the yellow courtyard [spleen] will penetrate and pass through the five viscera and twelve threads. It will be exhaled from and inhaled into the six archives [lesser viscera], and then the cloud-souls and earth-souls will be delighted. [11a] You can drop the hundred afflictions of the present place and block extremes of heat and cold. You will protect your seminal essence, retain your lifespan, and permanently extend and preserve your life.

This is what is called exhaling and inhaling the grand harmonies to preserve and protect the spontaneous. It is the authentic and essential Way. Even when ordinary people do it, all of them automatically extend their lives. They can also control and make servants of ghosts and divinities, and can wander and play on the Five Marchmounts. All they cannot do is fly through empty space or ascend into the void. If you can practice this, it will be adequate to allow you to live long enough in this world [to accomplish transcendence]. Of those who have studied transcendence, there has never been one who did not start with this.

Now when we come to things like numinous drugs of the Grand Supreme, rare phenomena of the Supreme Thearchs, [drugs] produced in concealment beneath the earth, and marvelous grasses from the multi-layered clouds: these are all drugs of the divine transcendents. One who obtains drugs of the supreme class will not grow old until the age of Latter Heaven. These are what beings of the Grand Supreme ingest. They are not treasured by middle transcendents.

Some drugs of the middle category, if obtained and ingested, will allow one not to pass away until the age of Latter Heaven. These are in fact what celestial realized beings ingest. They are not pursued by lower transcendents. Among this next class of drugs are: ninefold cinnabar elixir and gold fluid, purple floriate rainbow blossoms, nine times recycled elixir of the

Realm of Grand Clarity, liqueur of five clouds, [11b] mysterious frost and scarlet snow, three ascending and prancing yellows, white incense from Ying Isle-land in the eastern [ocean], [drugs] born in flight from the Mysterious Isle-land, eight minerals and a thousand fungi, *weixi* plant and ninefold radiance, stone gall from Western Flow, blue-green cash from Watchet-wave River, left over grain rations from High Hill, [produce of] Piled-Stone Mountain and Rose-gem Field, recycled cinnabar elixir from the Grand Barrens. They are increased with golden orchids, scarlet grasses with extended radiance, and cloud lads' flying bucklers. If one obtains and ingests these, he will ascend to heaven in broad daylight. They are what flying transcendents ingest. They are not anything heard of by earthly transcendents.

Among the lowest class of drugs are: pine and cedar resins, mountain ginger and sinking seeds, chrysanthemum flowers and water plantain, boxthorn and pachyma fungus, acorus rush and gate-winter [asparagus], great victory and yellow seeds [Solomon's seal], numinous flyer and red arrow, the gum, wood, and blossoms of the peach tree, climbing hemp and connector-of-the-broken [teasel], *weirui* and golden thread.

Such are the lesser drugs. I have only enumerated a fraction of them. The botanicals are exceedingly numerous, their names numbering in the thousands. If you obtain and ingest them, you can thereby prolong your years. Although you cannot extend your enjoyment without any limits or ascend on high to the blue heavens, still they may be used to make your body radiant and glossy and return a youth's complexion to you. They allow you to control flocks of ghosts and use them as servants, and to become an earth transcendent. [12a]

Those who seek the Way must first follow these steps, and then gradually they can reach distant victories. If you can inhale and exhale, and rein in the seminal essence, you will protect and make firm the spirits and breaths. When the seminal essence is not cast off, then you will permanently endure. If the breaths are extended and preserved, then you will not die. This method does not require expenditures for drugs and minerals, or the hard work of scheming to lay hands on them. Just grasp it in your own body. The common folk of a hundred surnames use this method daily, without recognizing it. This is therefore the Way of the supreme class, the requisite essential of spontaneity.

Furthermore, as for a person's single body: heaven stores it with spirits, the earth stores it with a shape, and the Way stores it with breaths. If the breaths are preserved, you live. If the breaths depart, you die. The myriad creatures as well as woody and herbaceous plants are all also like this. The body takes the Way as its basis. So how could you not nourish its spirits and make firm its breaths in order to complete your frame? For a person's corporeal frame and spirits together to be whole: that is what the supreme paragons valued. If the frame is annihilated, the spirits are cut off. How could this not be painful? Once you lose your present body, for a myriad kalpas [world ages] it will not return. Don't you think you should treasure it? What I have been saying is in fact the words bestowed upon me by my master, the Heavenly Honored One of the Primordial Commencement. [12b] Afterward I will command the jade girl, Li Qingsun, to write it out and grant it to you. You are to put it skillfully into practice.

The Queen Mother, having commanded that her vehicles be harnessed, was on the point of departing, when the thearch got down from his mat, kowtowed, and requested that she stay. The Queen Mother then commanded her serving girl to summon the [scriptural transmitter] Lady of the Supreme Primordial to descend and join them at the thearch's palace. After a good long while, the Lady of the Supreme Primordial arrived. Again they sat. She provided a celestial feast. After a long time, the Queen Mother of the West ordered the Lady to bring out the Writ of the Eight Unions, the [Talisman of the] Veritable Shape of the Five Marchmounts, the Talismans of the Six Cyclicals of the Five Thearchs, and the [Talisman of the] Numinous Flying Beings: altogether twelve items. She said: "The texts may be transmitted from above the heavens only once in four myriad kalpas. Once they are among humans, every forty years they may be bestowed upon a gentleman who possesses the Way."

The Queen Mother then commanded the serving girl Song Lingbin to open the cloud-patterned multi-colored tabby-weave silk bag and take out a fascicle to bestow on the thearch. The Queen Mother stood up holding the text. With her own hands, she granted it to the thearch. As she did so, the Queen Mother recited an incantation:

Heaven is high and earth low;
The Five Marchmounts fix their configurations.
Spurting breaths of the Primordial Ford,
Mysterious seminal essences of the Great Conduits, [13a]
Nine paths encircling the heavens;
Extended peace of the six harmonies,

Eight Unions of the Grand Supreme,
Accomplishments of the flying celestials:
All are credentials of realized transcendents.
On the basis of these you communicate with numinous beings.
Leak them and you will fall into annihilation and putrescence;
Treasure them and you return home to long-toothed old age.
You, Che, be careful of them!
I'm telling you, disciple Liu!

When the incantation was finished the thearch saluted and bowed to receive the Queen Mother's words:

> Now that you are beginning to study the Way and have re-
> ceived talismans, it would be appropriate for you to perform
> special sacrifices to various veritable numina of the rivers and
> marchmounts and to purify yourself and fast before hanging
> the talismans on your belt. After forty years, if you are going
> to transmit and hand down what you possess, then Dong
> Zhongshu and Li Shaojun may be bestowed with it.[74] Since
> you are thearchic king, you should be all the more diligent in
> your sacrifices to the rivers and marchmounts in order to pac-
> ify the state and households. Cast tallies to the veritable nu-
> mina to pray for the black-haired masses [the Chinese people].

Her words finished, she commanded the chariots, giving the word to depart, together with the Lady of the Supreme Primordial. Their followers and officials collected together. When they were about to ascend to heaven, she laughed and pointed at Dongfang Shuo, saying:

> This is a little boy from my neighbor's household. His nature
> is very mischievous. Three times he has come and stolen my
> peaches. Formerly he was a transcendent official of Mount Tai,
> but because he sank into drunkenness on jade wine and caused
> a loss of harmony among the bureaucrats, [13b] he was ban-
> ished to serve you. He is not of the common run of men.

After that the Martial Thearch could not make use of the Queen Mother's admonitions. He abandoned himself to strong drink and good looks. He killed and attacked without respite. He invaded the Eastern Liao [Liao Peninsula] to strike Korea, and opened communications with the southwestern

---

[74] Dong Zhongshu (179-104 B.C.E.) was a courtier and Confucian thinker of the early Han dynasty. His works present the most complete embodiment of the synthetic system of thought known as Han cosmology or the Han synthesis. For translations of his work, see DeBary and Bloom 1999, 292-310. On Li Shaojun, a Daoist magician of the same era, see Campany 2002, 222-28.

barbarians. He constructed terraces and kiosks, raising them out of earth and wood. Inside the realm bounded by the four seas, the people were depressed and angry. From this time on, he lost the Way. He made an imperial visit to Huizhong and presided over the Eastern Sea. He made sacrifices to the Queen Mother three times, but she did not come again. The texts he had received he arranged on the Cedar Beam Terrace, where they were burned by a celestial fire. Li Shaojun discarded his form and departed. Dongfang Shuo soared up in flight and did not return. The affair of the shamans and their dangerous potions arose.[75] The thearch grew more and more regretful and resentful.

In the second year of the Primordial Commencement reign period [87 B.C.E.], he died at Five Oaks Palace and was buried at the Fertile Tumulus [near modern Xi'an]. Later the Daoist texts that had been deposited in the Fertile Tumulus—fifty or more scrolls filling a golden box—came out one day at Mount Baodu. There was also a jade casket and jade staff that emerged in Fufeng market town. When [officials] examined the Fertile Tumulus, they found it undisturbed as of old, and yet [the emperor's] casket and staff had come out among people. This might be evidence of liberation of the corpse by entrusting it to shapes [i.e., evidence of Han Wudi's transcendence]. [14a]

Mao Ying. Again there was the Great Lord Mao Ying who ruled over Bucklebent Mountain in the south.[76] In the second year of the Primordial Longevity reign period [1 B.C.E.], in the eighth month, on the F-rooster (*yiyou*) day, the Realized Person of the Southern Marchmount [Lady Wei Huacun], Lord Chi, and Wang Junfang of the Western Walled City, along with various blue lads, followed the Queen Mother and descended together to Mao Ying's chambers.[77] In an instant, the Celestial Illustrious Great Thearch sent his messenger in embroidered clothing, Ling Guangzi Qi, to present Ying with a divine seal and jade writing tablets. The Lord Thearch of Grand Tenuity sent the Autocrat's Notary of the Left Palace of the Three Heavens, Guan Xiutiao, to present Ying with an eight-dragon multi-colored tabby-weave silk car-

---

75 On shamans in the Han dynasty, see Twitchett and Fairbank 1986: 671-73.

76 This part of the translation makes also use of the *Daozang* edition. Its text may rely on a now lost biography that was formerly part of the *Maoshan zhi* (see Schafer 1980). The Queen Mother gives Mao Ying texts, powers, and a divine bride, Lady Wei Huacun (see Schipper 1965).

77 Lord Chi is Chisongzi, Master Redpine. Wang Junfang is Mao Ying's teacher. Below he is called Wang Fangping. Elsewhere he is called Wang Yuan. He is an immortal who started as a master of esoterica at court and then obtained the Dao after a period of practice as a hermit in the mountains. He is connected in legend with the goddess Magu. The four great thearchs and lords, Sida dijun, are high celestial deities. Wang Ziqiao is a famous immortal who was supposed to have lived during the Zhou dynasty. He could summon phoenixes with his pipes. For all these figures, see Campany 2002, 259-265.

riage and purple feathered floriate clothing. The Grand Supreme Lord of the Way sent the Dawn Assisting Grandee, Shi Shumen, to present Ying with the Veritable Talisman of the Metal Tiger and a folly bell of flowing metal. The Incomparable Lord of the Golden Watchtower commanded the Realized Person of the Grand Ultimate to send the Jade Squires of Rectified Unity and Supreme Mystery—Zhong, Bao Qiu and others—to present Ying with swallow wombs of the four junctions and divine fungi of flowing brightness. [14b]

When the messengers from the four deities had finished their bestowals, they had Ying eat the fungi, hang the seal at his belt, don the clothing, straighten his cap, tie the talismans at his waist, grip the folly bell, and stand up. The messengers from the four told Ying:

> He who eats concealed fungi from the four junctures will take up the position of Steward of the Realized Ones. He who eats jade fungi of the Golden Watchtowers will take up the position of Director of Destiny. He who eats metal blossoms of flowing brightness will take up the position of Director Responsible for Transcendent Salaries and Promotions. And he who eats the paired flying plants of extended luminosity will take up the position of Realized Lord. He who eats the grotto grasses of night radiance will always have the responsibility of governing the autocrat's notaries of the left and right. You have eaten all of these. Your longevity will be coequal with Heaven and Earth. Your place will be situated as the Supreme Realized Person who is Director of Destiny and Supreme Steward of the Eastern Marchmount [Mount Tai]. You will control all divine transcendents of the former kingdoms of Wu and Yue [in southeastern China], and all the mountains and water sources left of the Yangzi River.

Their words finished, all the messengers departed together. [Next] the Five Thearchic Lords [deities of the four directions and the center], each in a square-faced [four-sided] chariot, descended in submission to [Mao Ying's] courtyard. They carried out the commands of the Grand Thearch, presenting to Ying a purple jade plaque, writs carved in yellow gold, and a text inventory of the nine gifts. They saluted Ying as Supreme Steward of the Eastern Marchmount, Realized Lord Who is Director of Destiny, and Realized Person of the Grand Primordial. Their business finished, they all departed.

The Queen Mother and Ying's master, Royal Lord of the Western Walled City, set forth drinks and a feast from the celestial kitchen for Ying. They sang songs about the Mysterious Numina. [15a] When the feast was over, the Queen Mother took the Royal Lord and Ying to examine and inspect

Ying's two younger brothers, and bestowed upon each of them the requisite essentials of the Way. The Queen Mother commanded the Lady of the Supreme Primordial to bestow on Mao Gu and Mao Zhong the Hidden Writs of the Supreme Empyrean, the Seminal Essence of the Way of Cinnabar Elixir and the Phosphors, and the like, comprising the precious scriptures of the Daoist Canon in four sections. The Queen Mother held the Hidden Writs of the Grand Empyrean and commanded her serving girl Zhang Lingzi to hold the oath of exchanging faith, while she bestowed [the texts] on Ying, Gu, and Zhong. The affair concluded, the Queen Mother of the West departed by ascending to heaven.

Wei Huacun. After this, the Primordial Ruler of the Purple Void, Lady Wei Huacun, purified herself by fasting on the Hidden Primordial Terrace located in the mountains on the sunny side of the Luo River. The Queen Mother of the West and the Incomparable Lord of the Golden Watchtower descended to the terrace. They were riding an eight-phosphor carriage. Together they had visited the Supreme Palace of the Pure Void and had received by transmission the Hidden Writs of the Realm of Jade Clarity in four scrolls in order to bestow them upon Huacun. At this time the Lady of the Three Primes, Fengshuang Li, along with the Left Transcendent Lord of the Purple Yang, Shi Lucheng, the Lofty Transcendent Lord of the Grand Ultimate, Yan'gai Gongzi, the Realized Person of the Western Walled City, Wang Fangping, the Realized Person of the Grand Void, [15b] Chisongzi of the Southern Marchmount, and the Realized Person of Paulownia-Cedar Mountain, Wang Ziqiao—over thirty realized beings in all—each sang to the tune of the yang songs and yin songs of the Grand Ultimate.

Then the Queen Mother sang a song for them:

> I harness my eight-phosphor carriage;
> Like thunder! I enter the Realm of Jade Clarity.
> Dragon pennants brush the top of the empyrean;
> Tiger banners lead vermilion-clad men-at-arms!
> When I wander footloose and fancy-free, at the corners of the
> Mysterious Ford,
> The myriad flows do not stop for even a little while.
> Grievous—this alternate departing and lingering of unions;
> When a kalpa is exhausted, Heaven and Earth are overturned.
> She must seek a phosphor with no center,
> Not dying and also not born,
> Embodying the spontaneous Way,
> Quietly contemplating, harmonizing the great stygian realm.
> At Southern Marchmount she displays her veritable trunk,
> Jade reflections shining on her accumulated essences.
> Having the responsibility of office is not your affair;

Empty your heart and you will naturally receive numina.
This "Scarlet River Tune" [narrates] your auspicious meeting;
The joy you give each other is never-ending.[78]

The Queen Mother finished her song, and the answering song from the Lady of the Three Primes also reached an end. Then the Queen Mother, along with the Lady of the Three Primes, the Left Transcendent Lord of the Purple Yang, and the Transcendent Lord of the Grand Ultimate, as well as Lord Wang of the Pure Void, departed together with Wei Huacun of the Southern Marchmount. They went southeast and all visited Mount Huo in the Heavenly Terrace Mountains. [16a] When they passed the Golden Altar on Bucklebent Mountain, they gave a feast for the Grand Primordial Realized Person Mao at the Grotto-heaven of the Floriate Yang. Leaving Huacun behind, beneath the jade eaves of the grotto palace at Mount Huo, the whole flock of realized beings ascended following the Queen Mother of the West and returned to Tortoise Terrace.

The Grand Realized Metal Mother is master and maker of the myriad classes of beings, teacher and leader of the whole flock of realized ones and paragons. Her position is honored and lofty; she holds central control of registration in both the hidden and revealed [esoteric and mundane worlds]. For example, there are cases like Bian Dongxuan who came in person to her court and received the Way, and Xie Ziran who attended the phosphors and then ascended to transcendence.[79] In the transmissions concerning [Bian] Dongxuan and [Xie] Ziran, when they refer to Master Metal Mother, they mean the Queen Mother. In affairs for which evidence is given in the mysterious scriptures, her traces are certainly numerous. This is not a complete account.

---

[78] This song is attributed to the Tang poet Meng Jiao (751-814) in *Quan Tangshi* 2253, but is attested in the *Han Wudi neizhuan* long before Meng's time.

[79] Bian Dongxuan is a Tang-dynasty female ascetic (# 22 below). Xie Ziran is a female realized one whose biography is recorded in the *Xu xianzhuan* (DZ 295). She received transmissions of texts and practices from the Queen Mother and other deities. Xie ascended to heaven in broad daylight in the middle of the Honorable Prime reign period (785-805). Her absence from present versions of Du Guangting's collection provides further evidence that the text has not been transmitted in its entirety.

2. The Mysterious Woman of the Nine Heavens

The second entry in Du Guangting's "Records" concerns another goddess with ancient origins. The Mysterious Woman of the Nine Heavens (Jiutian xuannü 九天玄女) is the only subject, aside from the Queen Mother, who has entries in both editions of Du's collection. She is also the only one, except for the Queen Mother, whose biography is titled with more than just her name. In her case, the word "transmissions" is added. The title can be read in two ways: "The Mysterious Women of the Nine Heavens Transmits [the Dao]" and the more conventional "Transmissions Concerning the Mysterious Woman of the Nine Heavens." There is no reason to assume that this play on the double meaning of *zhuan* 傳 (referring to transmitted biographies or to the act of handing over) is unintentional. The prominent position of the Mysterious Woman's biography, the doubling of this section of the text in both recensions, and the expanded title all suggest her importance to Du Guangting and to his project of constructing a female lineage that transmits the Way from deities to people.

During the Han dynasty when her cult first became prominent, the Mysterious Woman of the Nine Heavens ruled war, sexuality, and everlasting life. After the Han dynasty, her worship declined, but her memory did not die. Developing schools of Daoism assimilated her over the next few centuries. Her appearance, personality, and functions changed to accommodate the new demands.

Du Guangting's account of the Mysterious Woman, like that of the Queen Mother, narrates the beginning of Chinese civilization in the Yellow River basin. Here Du repeats the tale of the Yellow Thearch's struggle with the forces of chaos introduced in the previous entry. The Yellow Thearch's triumph allowed the creation of the system of order we know as traditional Chinese civilization. In this entry, Du emphasizes the Mysterious Woman's role, crediting her with giving the Yellow Thearch divine tokens that turned defeat to victory in his primal battle. Afterwards, the thearch settled down to rule China and establish traditional government and social institutions. At the end of his long life, he ascended to heaven riding a yellow dragon, becoming the world's first transcendent. According to Du Guangting's closing statement, the Mysterious Woman made possible both his contributions and his ascent.

The Mysterious Woman of the Nine Heavens was important to Du Guangting as the disciple of the Queen Mother of the West and master of the Yellow Thearch. In hierarchical order in this collection of biographies, she ranks below the Queen Mother and above her student. Du Guangting has enlisted the Mysterious Woman as a mediating ancestress in the female Daoist lineage register he constructs by means of this text. She forms an essential link in the chain of transmission of the Way between the source of sacred texts and the first human adept. Since the Yellow Thearch was the first person to ascend to transcendence, his master was the first to reveal Daoist arts to the human realm. The Mysterious Woman mediates between Heaven and Earth. Her intermediary status and primacy justify Du Guangting's interest in her.[80] His account includes elements of her tale that harmonize the concerns of various schools of Daoism.

Like the Queen Mother of the West, the Mysterious Woman is an old body god, mentioned in the earliest Daoist works on physiological micro-cosmology. Physiological micro-cosmology is a system in which the human body is regarded as a microcosm of the universe and is populated with gods who the adept may visualize, meditate upon, and petition for favors. Some of these gods exist only in the body, but most of them are miniaturized versions of the great deities of the heavens, earth, and underworlds. The Mysterious Woman appears in small scale versions of herself at least three times in the *Huangting jing* 黃庭經 (Scripture of the Yellow Courtyard, DZ 331, 332). There the adept is directed to send down his breath to enter her mouth. The *Huangting jing*, a text favored by Shangqing Daoists also appears in Du's biography of Xue Xuantong (# 27) who chants the scripture as part of her practice.[81]

The Mysterious Woman is also invoked three times in the *Laozi zhongjing* 老子中經 (Central Classic of Laozi, DZ 1168).[82] Written a little earlier

---

[80] On transmission of texts and numinous objects from early Daoist religious movements to the Shangqing school, see Robinet 1979b; 1984, 1:137.

[81] The Mysterious Woman is mentioned three times in commentaries to the inner chapters of the *Huangting jing*: 3:1, 3:1, 15:17 (see Schipper 1975). On physiological micro-cosmology as reflected in the text, see Homann 1971, 1976; Schipper 1978, 1994. The Queen Mother also appears several times in the text.

[82] On this text, see Schipper 1979

than the *Huangting jing* of the fourth century, it describes various body gods in numerical order. The Mysterious Woman appears first under the heading of the nineteenth divine transcendent where she is "located in the space between the kidneys, dressed only in the white of Venus and the brilliant stars. Her pearl of grand brilliance shines to illuminate the inside of the adept's whole body, so that he can extend his years and not die."

Next, under the heading of the twenty-third transcendent, she is described as one of three deities sitting on divine tortoises. The author comments "the Mysterious Woman is the mother of the Way of the void and nothingness." Finally, she appears in the entry on the twenty-fifth divine transcendent, known as the Grand Unity (Taiyi 太一). The text directs the adept as follows: "Close your eyes and meditate on a white breath between your shoulders. In its center is a white tortoise. On top of the tortoise is the Mysterious Woman. The Director of Destiny [life-spans] and the Director of Registers [of immortals] are to her right and left. The adept summons them, saying 'Director of Destiny and Director of Registers, pare so-and-so's name from the Death List and inscribe it on the Life List of the Jade Calendar.'" Long life on earth and immortality in heaven are promised as an automatic result of this procedure.

These early visualizing texts locate the Mysterious Woman along the central meridian of the body and associate her with the circulation of breaths that nourishes the vital spirits and is necessary for longevity. Her identity as a body god and her connection with the Daoist project of prolonging life through nourishing the vital forces may be inferred from Du's list of the talismans and texts she bestows upon the Yellow Thearch, although these also have a clear and primary military connection. Longevity procedures were always central to the Mysterious Woman's cult. Repeating popular beliefs, Du states that the Yellow Thearch's ascent to transcendence was exclusively due to arts he received from her.

The Mysterious Woman also has connections to alchemy, an essential part of the Shangqing Daoists' project of prolonging life. From the third century, she is associated with alchemical experiments and the search for the elixir of immortality. Ge Hong 葛洪 (283-343), one of the patriarchs of Du's school and a great enthusiast of elixirs compounded from heavy metals (who nevertheless avoided ingesting any himself), mentions her in his *Baopuzi* 抱朴子 (Book of the Master Who Embraces the Uncarved

Block, DZ 1185).[83] He asserts that she prepares elixirs together with other deities. When adepts create metal elixirs, they must first erect altars to the Mysterious Woman. Ge Hong links her with other processes for prolonging life, noting that the Yellow Thearch discussed calisthenics and diet with her.

Du preserves a faint reflection of her alchemical connections in the names of some objects and substances the Mysterious Woman gives the Yellow Thearch. But their primary meanings, as in the case of her gifts suggesting processes for nourishing the vital spirits by visualizing body gods, remain military. Later, during the Song dynasty, the Mysterious Woman was closely associated with inner alchemy, and most of the books in the *Daozang* that mention her name are Song alchemical works. Here, as in the previous entry, Du Guangting seems to regard this practice favorably.

But almost as interesting as what Du tells us is what he leaves out. His most glaring omission from the Mysterious Woman's biography concerns her sexuality, the first association any medieval Chinese person would make to her name. From the Han dynasty onwards, she was one of three goddesses who figure in texts on bedchamber arts as the Yellow Thearch's teachers. The other two are the Natural Woman (Sunü 素女) and the Selected Woman (Cainü 采女). Their instructions are recorded in a question and answer format.[84]

There was once a separate *Xuannü jing* 玄女經 (Scripture of the Mysterious Woman), like the Natural Woman's text in dialogue form and composed during the Han dynasty. Fragments of this work are incorporated in Sui-dynasty edition of the *Sunü jing*, the one we use today. This *Xuannü jing* did not concern the arts of war, as did most earlier texts bearing the name of the Mysterious Woman, but like the *Sunü jing* it covered the arts of sexual pleasure and hygiene. Accurate identification of the contents of lost texts on war or sex is complicated by the Chinese ten-

---

[83] This work is translated in Ware 1966. She is mentioned in 4.16a, 16.11a, and 13.3a.

[84] The Natural Woman is prominent in the the *Sunü jing* (Scripture of the Natural Woman; see Van Gulik 1961).Van Gulik translates *Sunü* as "Plain Girl." *Su* originally means the off-white color of undyed silk. I translate it as "natural," following English fashion and decorators' usage, to avoid the connotation of "homely" that "plain" carries. The association of "natural" with "sexual" in most English speakers' minds is appropriate here. For more on Chinese sexual classics, see Wile 1992.

dency to equate sexual intercourse with military action and to give handbooks on sexual techniques names suggesting military strategy.

These handbooks, often illustrated with pictures showing positions for sexual intercourse, were familiar to educated Chinese from the Han dynasty onwards. They were used both by married couples and by courtesans with their clients. They taught men and women how to perform and enjoy sex, and showed men how to increase their health and longevity through the retention of semen. Wang Chong 王充 (27-91), the Han dynasty author of the *Lunheng* 論衡 (Discussions Weighed in the Balance), criticizes sexual arts as "not only harming the body but also infringing on the nature of man and woman."[85] Wang's remarks assume that the practices he condemns were widely known.

During the Six Dynasties period, as the Shangqing school of Daoism gained ascendance among the upper classes, the *Xuannü jing* continued to figure in bibliographies. The sexual practices she taught are compared to alchemical and physiological procedures for prolonging life. In a passage from Ge Hong's *Baopuzi*, the Mysterious Woman tells the Yellow Thearch that sexual techniques are powerful, "like the intermingling of water and fire—they can kill or bring renewed life depending upon whether or not one uses the correct methods" (6.9a). At the same time, the Shangqing and Lingbao schools responded to criticism of earlier sexual practices originating in the Celestial Masters school of Daoism that included ritual intercourse in the "mingling of the breaths" (*heqi* 合氣) ceremonies.[86] Both medieval groups, identifying with Confucian family values, wanted to bring Daoism into harmony with the demands of a patrilineal social order and sexual standards.

During the Sui and Tang dynasties, the *Xuannü jing* remained familiar among the literati. It was noted in the section on medical texts in official bibliographies. The fragments that remain today survived as parts of medical works copied in Japan. A text called *Dongxuanzi fanzghong shu* 洞玄子房中術 (Bedchamber Arts of the Master of Grotto Mysteries), probably written by the Tang poet Liu Zongyuan 柳宗元 (773-819), describes in explicit detail the sexual arts taught by the ancient goddess.[87] During

---

[85] Van Gulik 1961, 79.
[86] See Kohn 1995a, 147-50.
[87] Van Gulik 1961, 125-34.

the Tang as in earlier periods, the name of the Mysterious Woman of the Nine Heavens called up ideas of sexual arts, both secular and sacred.[88]

If Du Guangting's account of the Queen Mother minimizes her monstrous side, his biography of the Mysterious Woman neglects the sexual side of her nature. This accords with his tendency to sanitize deities by removing or explaining away features of popular origin, especially traits offensive to the moral codes of the upper classes. Du excises references to their animal natures, leaving out of his account, for example, depictions of the Mysterious Woman as a human-headed bird. It apparently would not do to have a high goddess of Shangqing Daoism involved in actual physical sex. As described in countless passages in the *Zhen'gao*, metaphysical relations between the sexes were more in their line. Divine women taught human men rather than having corporeal sex with them. Expurgating the goddess's sexual side also casts suspicion on human sexuality and marriage. Du grants in his introduction to this text that the "Way of one yin and one yang" is a valid path to the Dao, but several biographies of this collection cast doubt upon marriage as a worthy religious vocation.

To bring the ancient deity known as the Mysterious Woman of the Nine Heavens into harmony with the great goddesses who taught the patriarchs of Shangqing Daoism through purely mystical unions, Du Guangting expurgated heterodox and crude elements of her popular legend, even those that were very familiar to him. The overt sexuality and violence of her earlier image provided tremendous energy to be sublimated for lofty ideals. The new school absorbed the old deity, with all the attendant appeal and historical depth as well as the problems caused by a less than perfect fit between the personality of the old goddess and the values of the new system.

For his "Records" Du Guangting had to perform a double image transformation on the Mysterious Woman. Not only did he sanitize her violence, bestiality, and sexuality, but he also enlists her as a matriarchal ancestress in the female Daoist lineage he constructs in this text.

For Du Guangting, the Mysterious Woman of the Nine Heavens was a military strategist who won by magical means rather than through

---

[88] Sexual encounters between humans and goddesses are a common theme in ancient China and Tang poetry. For more on the subject, see Hawkes 1974; Schafer 1978; Cahill 1985.

bloodshed, a master who transmitted the arts of immortality, and a crucial figure in the transmission of the Dao from heaven to human women. Most Tang poets who mention her refer to her relationship with the Yellow Thearch. For the average literary gentleman of the Tang, familiar with both her old and new images, the prospect of a divine woman who promised sexual prowess and bliss, victory over one's enemies, and life everlasting, was too attractive to dismember in the interests of Shangqing orthodoxy.

The Mysterious Woman may have been tamed in Du's text, but her original image resonated with people's needs. Surely her face in the Tang dynasty outside Du's account was much wilder and sexier. And there was no need for our literary gentleman to sacrifice her old image and replace it with the new; he could picture the classical goddess when he thought of sexual intimacy, and revere her sublimated twin in contemplation. Tang beliefs about the Mysterious Woman of the Nine Heavens demonstrate the human capacity to hold contradictory views simultaneously.

Translation: Transmissions Concerning the Mysterious Woman of the Nine Heavens

[114.16a] The Mysterious Woman of the Nine Heavens was the teacher of the Yellow Thearch and the disciple of the Primal Ruler known as the Incomparable Mother [Queen Mother of the West].[89]

In former times, when the Yellow Thearch was ruler of the Youxiong kingdom,[90] he assisted the grandson of Shen Nong, Yu Gang. [16b] Later, when [Yu Gang's rule] was in decline, the various feudal lords attacked each other, seeking each other with shields and swords. Based on the color attributed to his direction, each gave himself a title after one of the five phases. Thus the descendent of Tai Hao [Fu Xi] called himself the Blue-Green Thearch, while the descendent of Shen Nong, Yu Gang, called himself the Scarlet Thearch, the descendent of Gong Gong called himself the White Thearch, and the descendent of Ge Tian called himself the Black Thearch. The [legitimate] Thearch, arising from the Barren Wastes of Youxiong, called himself the Yellow Thearch. He restrained himself and respected his nobles. He anxiously [literally: tossing and turning at night = sleeplessly] cultivated virtue.[91]

But after the Thearch had been on the throne twenty-one years, the Wormy Rebel set forth his calamities. [The Rebels'] eighty-one elder and younger brothers had wild animals' bodies and human speech. They had bronze heads with iron foreheads. They relished sand and gobbled rocks, but they did not eat the five grains. They created the shapes of five tigers to harm the

---

[89] An earlier translation of this biography is published in Cahill 1992. Another account of the Mysterious Woman is found in *Taiping guangji* 251.

[90] Youxiong, an ancient name of a region now centered around Xinzheng county in Henan province, in the basin of the Yellow River, is one of several places identified as the home of the Yellow Thearch's clan.

[91] The figures named in this paragraph are all legendary ancient heroes and rulers. Shen Nong, father of Chinese agriculture, figures in genealogies of ancient heroes and kings. Yu Gang is his grandson. Tai Hou, an early ruler associated with spring and the dragon, was believed from Han times to be identical with Fu Xi. The half-man, half-serpent Fu Xi created crafts and writing. He was the brother and husband of the serpentine Nü Wa, who is credited with the creation of humans. Gong Gong, originally a mythic king ruling prior to the Yellow Thearch, appears in ancient tales sometimes as a flood hero and others as a usurper of royal power. By the Han dynasty, Gong Gong was connected to the struggle between order and chaos and the contest for world kingship after the Yellow Thearch. See Birrell 1993b.

black-haired [masses of the Chinese] people, and cast weapons in the mountains of Gelü [Shandong] without employing the Thearch's decree.

The Thearch, wanting to punish them, sought far and wide for talented and capable men to help him. He obtained the Feng Hou [Wind Duke] at a corner of the sea and Li Mu at the Great Marsh. He made an assistant of Da Hong, and took Tianlao [Heavenly Elder] as his teacher. He established the offices of the three common-lords in the image of the Three Platforms [constellation]. [17a] Feng Hou acted as the Supreme Platform [star], the Tianlao as the Middle Platform, and Wu Sheng as the Lower Platform.[92]

First, the Thearch grasped his precious tripods [ritual bronze vessels]. Without being heated on a stove, their sacrificial contents were cooked. Then he welcomed the sun and consulted divining stalks. He made Feng Hou his general and the son of [his wife] Lady Fei Xiu his heir apparent. He employed Zhang Ruo, Xi Peng, Li Mu, Rong Guang, Lung Xing, Cang Ji, Rong Cheng, Dao Nao, and She Long. The flock of his vassals acted as auxiliary wings. But when they fought the Wormy Rebel at [Mount] Zhuolu, the Thearch and his teachers did not triumph. And then the Wormy Rebel created a great mist, so that for three days inside and outside were indistinguishable.[93]

Using the [Big] Dipper's governing mechanism as a model, Feng Hou made a great vehicle with its handle pointing south to distinguish correctly the four

---

[92] Feng Hou, Li Mu, and Da Hong were three of the first officials the Yellow Thearch appointed to help govern his people. Legend tells us that he found Feng and Li by following directions obtained in a dream. Tianlao was his teacher and Wu Sheng another early minister. The three platforms, corresponding to a constellation of stars, represent three great divisions of government, each led by a different feudal lord. Here Du abbreviates and harmonizes diverse accounts of the founding of China's imperial bureaucracy from various classical texts.

[93] This paragraph describes the emperor's attempts to legitimize, consolidate, and stabilize his empire in the face of the Wormy Rebel's challenge. The *ding* tripods are bronze ceremonial vessels used in periodic sacrifices to the imperial ancestor. Their possession constitutes evidence of legitimacy. He designates the son of Lady Fei Xiu as his heir, thus assuring the succession. And he employs several ancient worthies of myth and legend, hailing from different eras: Zhang Ruo is another of the first dignitaries to assist him in government, Cang Jie is his scribe, Hong Cheng another ancient ruler and purported inventor of the calendar (itself an imperial prerogative and instrument of rule), Shen Long an early minister, and Da Nao the emperor's teacher and inventor of the traditional Chinese system for calculating time. Mount Zhuolu, where the emperor first fights the Wormy Rebel without success, and where he eventually conquers the rebel and sets up his capital, is located in modern Hebei province, in the territory of the Warring States Kingdom of Zhao, a region known as the Upper Valley at least since the Qin dynasty. For more, see Lewis 1990; Birrell 1993.

directions [a compass].[94] The Thearch, drawing upon his anxiety and grief, fasted beneath Mount Tai. The Queen Mother sent him an emissary wearing a dark fox-fur cloak. She bestowed talismans upon the Thearch, saying: "If you make your thoughts essential and then report to Heaven, you will definitely receive a response from the [diety known as] Grand Supreme."

After several days there was a great mist, so impenetrable it obscured both daylight and the dark of night. Then the Mysterious Woman descended into it, riding a cinnabar phoenix, holding phosphors and clouds as reins. She wore variegated kingfisher feather garments of nine colors. She perched before the Thearch, who repeatedly saluted her and received her command. [17b] The Mysterious Woman said: "I base myself on the teachings of the Grand Supreme. If you have any concerns, you may question me."

The Thearch kowtowed and said: "The Wormy Rebel is cruelly crossing us. His poison is harming all the black-haired people [i.e. the Chinese people]. The four seas are sobbing. No one can even protect his own nature or life. I want the art of winning a myriad victories in a myriad battles in order to cut off the harm facing my people. Is this possible?"

The Mysterious Woman thereupon bestowed upon the Thearch the Talismans of the Military Tokens of the Six *Jia* Cyclicals and the Six *Ren* Cyclicals, the Five Numinous Treasure Talismans, the Document on Forcing Ghosts and Spirits into Service, the Seal of the Five Bright-Shiners for Regulating the Uncanny and Communicating with the Numina, the Formula of the Five Yin and Five Yang for Concealing the *Jia* Cyclicals, Charts for Grabbing the Mechanism of Victory and Defeat of the Grand Unity from the Ten Essences and Four Spirits, Charts of the Five Marchmounts and the Four Holy Rivers, and Instructions in the Essentials of Divining Slips. [She also gave him] jade tallies of the nine radiances, pennants of the ten cutoffs, swords which commanded demons, auroral cloud caps and fire belt pendants, dragon halberds and rainbow banners, kingfisher carriages and green palanquins with sinuous dragons as the inner pairs of the draft teams and tigers riding astride, a thousand flowered canopies, eight simurgh carts, feathered flutes and mysterious staffs, rainbow standards and jade battle axes, creations of the divine transcendents, seals of the five dragons, pearls of the nine bright-shiners, and tallies of the nine heavens.[95] All [of these] were used for

---

94 Feng Hou invented the south-pointing chariot, traditionally considered China's first compass. The use of the compass in China is attested since the Han dynasty at the latest. On magnetics in China Needham 1954-2005, 4.1: 229-334.

95 The list of texts, tokens, and objects goes back to the "recipe masters" or magicians of the Han dynasty, as well as to the Celestial Masters and Great Peace movements of the

military communications. [18a] Five-colored banners distinguished [the armies of] the five directions.

Then the Thearch once again led all. The feudal lords fought] again to attack. The Wormy Rebel drove his demons and assorted ill-omened creatures, setting them against [the Thearch's armies] in battle array. He used Rain Master and Wind Lord as guards, while responsive dragons stored up water to attack the Thearch. But the Thearch controlled them all. Thereupon he destroyed the Wormy Rebel in the wilds of Jueben. The Thearch buried [the Wormy Rebel] at a grave mound in the township of Zhongji, having divided his four limbs. Subsequently Yu Gang resisted the mandate and the Thearch punished him as well, in the wilds of Banquan. Then the Thearch pursued Xun Yu to the north, and greatly settled the four quadrants. He exhaustively paced to the four extremities, traveling altogether over twenty-eight thousand *li*. Then he cast tripods to set up the nine provinces, and established vassals of the nine circuits and nine virtues to observe Heaven and Earth, sacrifice to the ten thousand numina, hand down models, and establish teachings.

---

late Han, filtered through the beliefs of the Shangqing school. On transmission of texts and numinous objects from early Daoist religious movements to the Shangqing school, see Robinet 1979b; 1984,1:137. None of the texts Du Guangting cites in his account here appears under exactly the same name in the *Daozang*, but there are numerous close relatives.

Part 2
Matriarchs

3. Mother Liang

Mother Liang 梁母 is Du's first human subject in the "Records." She was a good-hearted innkeeper who ascended to transcendence in 476. We do not know her given name. She lived during the tumultuous and brief southern Liu-Song dynasty (420-479). Born to a southern family, she later ran an inn for travelers in what is now Shandong province in the northeast. We know nothing of her youth or marriage. When Du introduces her, Mother Liang is a childless widow with no family to obstruct her religious activities. Her specific practice, belonging to the highly valued category of hidden virtue or hidden good works, consists of living frugally and taking care of travelers and the poor.

Du emphasizes good works as the Daoist equivalent of the popular Buddhist notion of merit. Merit leads to good karma, leading to a good rebirth and finally to the opportunity for enlightenment and nirvana. Daoist good works pave the way for the austerities and meditations that result in transcendence. The special quality of hidden virtue or good works is that they are acts of compassion that are neither witnessed nor publicized, and the performer expects no earthly recognition or reward. This is the first mention in Du's account of a very important virtue and vehicle to immortality.

The gods must have heard of Mother Liang's accomplishments, as they sent the Small Lad of the Eastern Sea (Donghai xiaotong 東海小童) in disguise to investigate her. The Small Lad, also known as the Azure Lad (Qingtong 青童), was an important deity in both the Celestial Masters and Lingbao traditions. Serving here as heavenly detective, the Azure Lad must have verified her progress. Du Guangting next reports that the Daoist Master Xu Daosheng 徐道盛 encountered her in 476, traveling in splendor with three divine lads in attendance. If Master Xu is the same person as Xu Lingqi 徐靈期, he provides another connection to the Lingbao school of Daoism. That Daoist Master Xu was the recipient of Lingbao scriptures transmitted by Ge Chaofu 葛巢甫, a descendant of Ge Hong and founder of the Lingbao school. Master's Xu's testimony further testifies to Mother Liang's transcendence.

As it happens, Mother Liang was on her way to heaven. As she passed Mount Tai, she luckily encountered master Xu and asked him to carry a message back to the community of Daoist nuns in eastern China. That she uses him as a messenger suggests her superior status. The mention of nuns suggests that she had disciples and perhaps was abbess of a convent. Her message is one of encouragement in times of difficulty, telling her followers to look forward to the era of Great Peace, a time of universal bliss and cosmic harmony that will certainly come in the future. Her mention of Great Peace provides a link to the utopian and apocalyptic Great Peace movement of the Later Han, also known as the Yellow Turbans, leaders of the first historically attested peasant uprising in Chinese history. Great Peace scriptures and hopes survived the slaughter of the Yellow Turbans rebels by the Han army in 184 C.E. They must have seemed as timely during the Southern Song era of Mother Liang as they were in Du Guangting's own period era at the end of the Tang and beginning of the Former Shu dynasties.

The Grand Supreme who summons her is the Grand Supreme Lord of the Way (Taishang daojun 太上道君), one of the highest gods of both the Shangqing and Lingbao schools. This deity's presence advances Du Guangting's project of uniting schools in his record of female religious figures. Through Mother Liang's story and the characters she meets, Du joins the traditions of Great Peace and Celestial Masters Daoism from the Han dynasty with the two great medieval schools Shangqing and Lingbao. Her summons further testifies to her transcendence and sainthood. With the life of Mother Liang, Du continues his lineage from the goddesses of his first two entries to human women. With Mother Liang's parting words to the nuns, we see her lineage continuing to the next generation of disciples.

Translation

[115.1a] Mother Liang was a person from Xuyi [in Jiangsu]. A childless widow, she ran an inn for travelers at the Pingyuan [Flat Plains] Pavilion.[96] Whenever

---

[96] Another account of Mother Liang may be found in *Taiping guangji* 261. Xuyi municipality is on the Huai River. The Pavilion may be located in the Pingyuan municipality of the Liu-Song dynasty (420-479), in modern Shandong. The reading *pingyuan* appears later in the text. I use it to replace *shiyuan* ("ten plains") here.

strangers came for a rest, she treated them no differently from [family members] returning home. No matter how much or how little a guest paid her, she never said a word about it. And if a guest stayed for months, she was not annoyed. After [buying her own] rough garments and coarse food, she would distribute whatever she had left to the poor and sick.

Once a youth stayed there several months. His activities were different from those of ordinary people. When he was about to depart, he told her that he was the Small Lad of the Eastern Sea.[97] But Mother [Liang] did not know what sort of person this Small Lad might be.

In the fourth year of the Primal Tenuity reign period of the Song dynasty [476], on a C-dragon (*bingchen*) day, Daoist Master Xu Daosheng of Mount Ma'er [Horse-Ear] arrived in Mengyin [in Shandong], to the west of Feng City.[98] [1b] He encountered a carriage drawn by a blue goat. The carriage stopped of its own accord, and he saw a small lad who summoned him, saying: "Daoist Master Xu, come forward." [When Xu] Daosheng approached and stopped about three steps from the carriage, he saw two more lads, about twelve or thirteen years old, wearing yellow garments lined in scarlet, with horned chignons on their heads. In appearance and clothing they were proper and correct, peerless in this world. The person in the carriage sent one lad to transmit a message [to Daoist Master Xu]:

> I am the Pingyuan innkeeper, Mother Liang. Just now I have been summoned by the Grand Supreme to return home. Responding, I passed Mount Penglai and sought out Wang Ziqiao.[99] As I

---

[97] The Small Lad of the Eastern Sea is another name of the Azure Lad. He was the teacher of Celestial Masters founder Zhang Daoling and is also associated with revelations of the Lingbao school. See Kroll 1985; Bokenkamp 1997, 275-373. Confusingly, the same term Azure Lad may also refer to the minor deities who serve as messengers of the great gods. Context usually makes the choice clear.

[98] Xu may be Xu Lingqi, a transcendent elixir master of the Liu-Song period from the southern marchmount, Mount Heng. He has a biography in th *Lishi zhenxian tidao tongjian* (Comprehensive Mirror through the Ages of Perfected Immortals and Those Who Embody the Tao, DZ 296) by Zhao Daoyi, dated to about 1300. According to this, in 401, he received transmission of the Lingbao scriptures from Ge Chaofu, a second generation descendent of Ge Hong and heir to that master's library. Xu achieved realization on the date mentioned in this text, and appeared to several great Tang Daoist masters. Mother Liang is passing Mount Tai, the sacred mountain of the east, also in Shandong, where mortals are judged at the end of their lives. For her it is a step on the way to the heavens.

[99] Penglai is a legendary island of the immortals in the Eastern Sea. Wang Ziqiao, a Zhou dynasty prince of the sixth century B.C.E., was one of the earliest transcendents. He could call phoenixes with his music. He ascended to heaven in broad daylight from Mount

crossed Mount Tai, I examined my summons, [discovering that] its intent was that you and I were to meet one another. And so it is that you have indeed come here. My numinous rig has wheeled and soared, while dark cliffs loomed steep and precipitous. Fords and post stations were few, so that every day we had to travel three thousand *li*. As the time when I will meet [the Grand Supreme] face to face approaches, my heart grows depressed and weary.

Moreover, I still must mount smoke and ride up to the Three Clear Realms.[100] These three boys will see me off to the Dark Capital [above]. Could you take leave of the Female Masters of the Clear Faith [Daoist nuns] from the eastern quadrant for me?[101] [Tell them that] the era of Great Peace approaches. The greater and lesser good omens [of the end of time] have almost certainly begun. [2a] [Heaven and this world will open to each other] so that people can cross over to salvation. This situation is neither depressing nor dangerous.

Then she lifted her hands, bade farewell [to Daoist master Xu] and departed, saying "See you in the era of Great Peace!" She urged on her carriage and soared, traveling to the limits of Xu's vision before she disappeared.

[Master Xu] Daosheng returned from his travels and asked about these events. It turned out that the day upon which Mother Liang passed from this world was exactly when they met one another.

Goushi near Luoyang, riding a crane. There were many shrines to him during the Tang dynasty, including a famous one at Mount Song. See Kaltenmark 1953.

[100] The Three Realms of Clarity (*sanqing*) are the highest heavens of Shangqing Daoism: the Jade- (*Yuqing*), Supreme- (*Shangqing*), and Grand Realms of Clarity (*Taiqing*).

[101] These Female Masters are female disciples or ordained Daoist nuns of the Lingbao tradition, formally known as Clear-hearted Women Masters (*qingxin shinu*).

4. Bao Gu

In contrast to Mother Liang, about whose origins we know nothing, Maiden Bao 鮑姑 had impeccable Daoist and literati credentials. She was the daughter of one famous Daoist patriarch, Bao Jing 鮑靚, and the wife of another, Ge Hong. In time-honored Chinese fashion, she gains attention through her family connections. Maiden Bao's biography suggests that the Daoist religion supports family values. Daoism can run in families. In fact, filial piety demands that the children follow their parents' religious practices. As Chinese Buddhists express filial piety by dedicating the merit obtained through good acts to their ancestors, Daoists express their filial devotion by crediting their religious achievements to virtue they have inherited along the patriline. Bao Gu's experience teaches that the rewards of secret or hidden virtue, highest in Du's hierarchy of good works, may be also be inherited.

Du Guangting emphasizes Maiden Bao's importance and sanctity by associating her through her father with patriarchs of several Daoist traditions. Bao Jing was the teacher of Xu Mai 許邁, a member of the family of Eastern Jin officials to whom Yang Xi 楊羲 revealed the Shangqing scriptures. Bao Jing's teachers, Zuo Ci 左慈 and Yin Changsheng 尹長生 (Long-Life Yin), were famous masters of the late Han dynasty. Zuo Ci was an ascetic, shape-shifter, and magician supposedly executed by General Cao Cao in 220. Long-Life Yin was an elixir alchemist reported to have ascended to heaven in broad daylight.[102] Both the Shangqing and Lingbao schools claim Maiden Bao's husband, Ge Hong, the great alchemist and author, as an ancestor.

When Du reports that Bao Jing moved south to take up a military position, he actually refers to Bao's participation in the mass flight of elite Chinese to the south that took place after the Jin capitals of Luoyang and Chang'an were sacked in 311 and 317. This movement of literati officials helped spread the Daoist religion southwards and exposed Daoist think-

---

[102] On this personage, see Campany 2002, 274-75, 279-86.

ers to southern influences such as shamanism and drug cults.[103] Southern influences in turn had a huge impact on the emergence and development of Shangqing and Lingbao Daoism. After Maiden Bao's father moved south, he married her to Ge Hong, a southern official who also wrote and conducted alchemical experiments.

A little later, Maiden Bao's paternal aunt, her father's younger sister, died young and unmarried. She was buried at Mount Luofu in Guangdong province, a site holy to Daoists and Buddhists alike. After death, her flesh did not decay, demonstrating that she had achieved transcendence through liberation by means of the corpse. The transformation of a deceased unwed female to a perfected person would have seemed remarkable in the fourth century. In medieval times, a girl who died before marriage was likely to return to her family as an angry and dangerous ghost. Having died childless, she had nobody to carry out ancestral rites for her and would be forced to wander for all eternity. If Du convinced his readers that Daoism provided a good afterlife for women who died unwed, thus preventing haunting by vengeful maidens, he might reassure worried relatives and win converts.

The companionate relationship of Maiden Bao and Ge Hong provides a rare illustration of marriage as a Daoist religious vocation, what Du Guangting in his introduction calls "the Way of one yin and one yang." This unusual case argues that Daoism is a couple-friendly religion: husband and wife can share the faith. They may have had a sex-free marriage. Her unusual nickname *gu* 姑, "Maiden," suggests either that she was celibate within marriage or that marriage and childbirth did not deplete her original purity. Several later subjects in Du's collection who are called Maidens (# 17, 18, 19, 25) are clearly solitary wandering ascetics.

The maiden's father Bao Jing obtained liberation by means of the sword at the end of his earthly life, following earlier instructions from his teacher Master Yin. Liberation by sword is a form of liberation by means of the corpse, a way of transformation from this world to the next. In liberation by means of the sword, the adept appears to die and leave a corpse for proper ritual burial, but he has actually escaped while a magical sword simulates his remains.[104] Bao Jing thus departed in the same manner as his sister. And at the end of their lives, in 343, Maiden Bao

---

[103] For a detailed account of early Shangqing history, see Strickmann 1978.
[104] On this form of transformation, see Robinet 1979a; Cedzich 2001.

and her husband Ge Hong ascended together into transcendence. Not only did they practice together, they also achieved perfection together.

Translation

[2a] Bao Gu [Maiden Bao] was the daughter of Grand Protector of the Southern Seas, Bao Jing.[105] She was the wife of Ge Hong, Constant Attendant of the Scattered Cavalry of the Jin dynasty.[106]

[Bao] Jing, whose cognomen was Taixuan [Grand Mystery], was a person of Chenliu Commandery [near Kaifeng in Henan]. As a youth, he already had comprehensive understanding and deeply grasped the Dark Prime. But he sank his heart and obscured any display, so no one knew about this. Both Jing and his younger sister received the accumulated secret virtue of previous generations, so that blessings and health accrued to Jing [and his sister]. Therefore the whole family all attained the Way. [His daughter] Bao Gu, together with his younger sister, ascended to the category of transcendents.

After Jing had studied and penetrated the scriptures and apocrypha, he took as his teacher Master Zuo Yuanfang.[107] [Zuo] bestowed upon him both the Methods of the Middle Bureau and the Essentials of Commands and Summonses for the Three Illustrious Ones and the Five Marchmounts. He practiced these and proved divinely effective. He could employ ghosts and deities as messengers, seal up mountains, and regulate demons.

---

[105] On Bao Jing in the *Shenxian zhuan*, see Campany 2002, 295-97. Bao is important to the Shangqing school as a teacher of Xu Mai, one of a family of Eastern Jin officials to whom the medium Yang Xi revealed the Shangqing scriptures. The *Zhen'gao* mentions him several times. He also has a biography in *Jinshu* 95.2482. The Southern Seas refers to present-day Guangdong (Canton) province.

[106] On Ge Hong, see *Jinshu*. 72 and his autobiography in *Baopuzi waipian* 50. He is a descendant of the Daoist patriarch Ge Xuan and an ancestor of the Lingbao founder Ge Chaofu.

[107] Zuo Ci (d. 220) was a renowned Daoist "recipe master" who also taught Ge Xuan, an ancestor of Ge Hong and a Daoist patriarch. Zuo has several biographies in the *Daozang*, in the *Shenxian zhuan* (Campany 2002, 279-86) as well as in the *Sanguo zhi* and *Hou Hanshu* (see DeWoskin 1983). He is also mentioned in the *Shanhai jing* and *Bowu zhi*. An ascetic, shape-shifter, and magician, he was imprisoned and executed by Cao Cao. The texts bestowed by Master Zuo are Daoist talismanic and ritual works that enable the adept to control spiritual forces, protect himself and others, and effectively perform his practices in pursuit of immortality. See Kohn 1993.

[2b] During the primal year of the Grand Uplift reign period of the Primal Thearch of the Eastern Jin dynasty [318], on a D-tiger [*wuyin*] day, Jing encountered the realized person Long-Life Yin at Mount Jiang [near Nanjing]. From him, Jing received the art of liberation by means of the sword. When his accumulated official honors had reached the level of Attendant Esquire of the Yellow Gate, Jing sought to go out and become Grand Protector of the Southern Seas. He married his daughter [Bao Gu] to Ge Zhichuan [Ge Hong]. Zhichuan then sought [a transfer] from his position as Constant Attendant of the Scattered Cavalry to the office of Commandant of Zhulou county [in Guangdong] so that he would be in the right place to refine cinnabar granules [to make elixir drugs].[108]

While Jing was in the Southern Seas [south China], his younger sister reached the age of pinning up her hair [marriageable age]. Without presenting any symptoms, she suddenly died. At that time, he received his guests without expressing sadness or grief [over her early death], then buried her at Mount Luofu [in Guangdong]. Her countenance and flesh were like those of a living person, so everyone said she had achieved liberation by means of the corpse.

Jing returned to Danyang [near Mount Mao] where he died. He was buried at Little Stone Cliff. Afterwards, during the chaos [rebellion] of Su Jun [327-8],[109] when his coffin was extruded from the ground, it contained no corpse but only a big sword. When thieves [rebels] went to seize the sword, they heard sounds of soldiers and horses to the left and right of the tomb mound. Turning to look back at the tomb, they felt startled and alarmed. Right in their midst, the sword made a crashing sound, like thunder booming. The pack of thieves rushed off in flight. After the thieves were pacified, someone took the sword and reburied it. [3a] So Jing as well as his younger sister had achieved liberation by means of the corpse.

---

[108] Zhulou (Great Leak), in the northeastern part of modern-day Beiliu county in Guangxi province, is named for its limestone mountains full of high caves eroded by streams. Here Ge Hong conducted his alchemical experiments.

[109] Su Jun, an official originally from Shandong, led a rebellion in 327-328 that reached present day Jiangsu province, killing tens of thousands of people. He died in battle with the Eastern Jin imperial armies near the town of Danyang in the vicinity of Mount Mao in 328. In this paragraph, the term translated "thieves" refer to the rebel armies.

Part 3

Inhabitants of the Grotto Heavens

Inhabitants of the Grotto Heavens

The next ten entries (# 5-14) cover the lives of eleven women and will be discussed as a group. All brief and sketchy, the accounts share several characteristics. Not every biography has every feature outlined here, but all have most of them. The subjects are all young women who lived at the end of the Han dynasty or just afterward. Their fathers, when we know anything about them, were literati officials. They were mostly southerners, connected by residence and cult to southern holy mountains. Du Guangting does not comment on their marital status, suggesting that they remained single.

Several inherited merit from ancestors who had practiced hidden virtue, underlining the central value of that form of good works for Du Guangting. Others inherited Daoist technologies through their patrilines. These women had the opportunity to study and practice the Dao and they did so with enthusiasm. Some of them apprenticed to famous Daoist masters. Several of them ingested elixirs or learned to absorb divine vapors; these represent the traditions of both elixir and meditative alchemy.

They were rewarded for their practice by gaining special powers such as being able to fly or communicate with animals. After their lives in this world ended, they became earth transcendents of the most elevated class; they took up responsible positions in the divine bureaucracy and resided in palaces in grotto heavens under holy mountains. A grotto heaven is an underground microcosm where Daoist initiates and deities dwell in protection from earthly cycles of destruction.[110] At least six of them ultimately lived in the Palace of Transformation and Transcendence (Huaxian gong 化仙宮) in the Floriate Yang Grotto Heaven (Huayang dongtian 華陽洞天) under Mount Mao, a place especially holy to Shangqing Daoism. The grotto heaven under Mount Heng, the Southern Marchmount, known as the Vermilion Palace (Zhugong 朱宮), is mentioned twice, while Mount Song, the Central Marchmount, appears once.

---

[110] On grotto heavens, see Verellen 1995; Hahn 1988, 2000.

The ten biographies present a cumulative picture of study, practice, and accomplishment. In one case (# 8), Du explicitly mentions her practice as "female transcendence" (*nüxian* 女仙). This suggests a separation of male and female practice, a trend that becomes prominent in the following Song dynasty. In the double biography of Liu Chunlong and Guo Shuxiang (# 9), Du editorializes, praising several female transcendents. Their appearance and performance of rituals were impressive, he observes, and their talents and knowledge outstanding. Then he makes the powerful statement that they were "raised to the responsibility of Attendant Esquire because of their excellence and talents, unrestricted by distinctions between male and female." This suggests a certain egalitarianism in posthumous celestial titles and by extension equality between male and female adepts. It seems to contradict Du's earlier mention of a separate Way to transcendence for women. I would argue that this apparent contradiction shows ambivalence towards women's practice and achievements in Du Guangting in particular and in the male Daoist institutional hierarchy in general. All of Du's biographies of women, I believe, reveal a tension between women's possible spiritual equality and their clear social inferiority that characterizes medieval Chinese Daoism and society at large.

This series of brief biographies also reflects Du's continuing debate with Chinese Buddhists. One of his subjects, Fu Lihe (# 11), converted from Buddhism. And Du competes in the realm of ideas as well. Hidden virtue rivals the Mahayana Buddhist supreme virtue of *dāna*, compassionate giving. And the Daoist notion of inherited merit that appears in several entries rivals the popular Buddhist idea of transfer of merit. Chinese Buddhists taught that a devotee could transfer to others the merit accumulated by performing good deeds. They had constructed this idea in response to criticism of their faith, with its goal of individual enlightenment, as selfish, unfilial, and anti-family. Daoists, such as Du, who also promoted individual liberation, found the idea of inherited virtue especially useful and compatible with traditional Chinese patrilineal values. And according to this scheme, women could accumulate hidden merit as well as men. Merit was not based on gender, and keeping one's good deeds secret complied with traditional ideas of female virtue that stressed modesty.

These eleven women with their various practices embody Du's statement in his introduction that there is only one Way but there are many methods to reach it. The biographies carry out his effort to unite the various schools and practices of Daoism in one great tradition. Practitioners of astral and physical disciplines, inner and outer alchemy, heiresses of family merit and knowledge, linked with the ancient cults of the holy mountains of the five directions, the women create a mini-lineage within the larger lineage register that is Du's whole work. They are foremothers of Daoism who link the schools and technologies of the Han dynasty with the medieval Shangqing and Lingbao schools that Du brings together. Their stories show that earth transcendents, while not as elevated in the hierarchy as celestial transcendents, were nonetheless important beings who participated in the divine bureaucracy that controlled human destiny.

Their lives also encourage the readers by holding out the promise that there is a safe place where faithful Daoists, even women, can find peace at the end of the world age. The grotto heavens must have been as timely a utopian vision at the end of the Tang as they were to the Celestial Masters at the end of the Han dynasty.

5. Sun Hanhua

[115.3a] Sun Hanhua 孫寒華 [Bitter-Cold Flower] was the daughter of Sun Xi, a person of Wu.[111] She took Du Qi as her master, receiving from him the Essentials of the Dark and White.[112] Her face and countenance daily grew younger. After wandering various mountains of the Wu and Yue region [southern China] for over ten years, she obtained the Way of the transcendents and departed.

---

[111] Wu was one of the states of the Three Kingdoms period (222-280, located in southeast China. I have not been able to identify Sun Xi.

[112] Du Qi or Du Guangping was a Daoist master of the third century. He excelled in elixir arts, especially compounds of the "dark and white" (combinations of gold, mercury and lead). He lived on the eastern side of Mount Mao, and could disappear at will. He is mentioned in the *Zhen'gao* and thus associated with Shangqing Daoism. He has a longer biography in *Lishi zhenxian tidao tongjian* (DZ 296).

6. Li Xizi

Li Xizi 李奚子[Personal Servant] was the grandmother of Li Zhong, the Jin dynasty Grand Protector of Dongping commandary [in Shandong].[113] We do not know her native surname or clan. [Li] Zhong's grandfather practiced virtue and restraint [as a hermit] in the hills and gardens. Being naturally merciful and sympathetic, he made hidden virtue his business. Xizi and her husband shared one ambition: to devote themselves to saving people. When great snows fell and bitter cold weather froze the roads, they stored grain in their garden and courtyard, afraid that wild animals and birds might otherwise starve to death. This is how she applied her heart.[114] Now she has obtained the Way and dwells in a palace inside the Floriate Yang Grotto [beneath Mount Mao].

7. Han Xihua

[3b] We do not know where Han Xihua 韓西華 [Western Flower] came from. She showed compassion and love for all creatures, constantly practicing hidden good works. Even when it came to short-lived creatures such as spiders and feathered ones, she loved and protected them in all cases. She studied the Way and obtained transcendence. Now she resides within the Grotto Heaven at [the Central Marchmount of] Mount Song.

8. Dou Qiongying

Dou Qiongying 竇瓊英 [Rose-gem Blossom] was Dou Wu's younger sister.[115] Their seventh generation ancestor, whose given name was Zhi,

---

113 Dongping commandery was in eastern Dongping county in present-day Shandong province, a region noted for its many *fangshi*, "recipe masters or technicians" during the Han dynasty. I have not been able to identify Li Zhong

114 "To apply one's heart" (*yongxin*) means to form intentions.

115 Dou Wu was an Eastern Han classicist whose daughter became empress during the Extended Felicity period (158-167) of the Powerful Thearch (Huandi). Dou Wu gained

had regularly made it his business to bury dry bones with the proper rites, and had set his heart on caring for invalids [lit., "living dead']. For this reason, blessings reached Qiongying, causing her to practice female transcendence. She resides in the Palace of Transformation and Transcendence [in the Floriate Yang Grotto under Mount Mao].

9. Liu Chunlong

[4a] We do not know where either Liu Chunlong 劉春龍 [Spring Dragon] or Guo Shuxiang 郭叔香 [Gathered Fragrances] came from. Because their ancestors had practiced hidden virtue, they both managed to escape worldly change, refine their phosphors, and enter the Palace of Transformation and Transcendence in the Floriate Yang Grotto.

Liu Chunlong, Dou Qiongying, Han Xihua, and Li Xizi [# 6-9] all possess a heavenly appearance and the strictest beauty. Their proper ritual comportment and ceremonial headdresses [are so impressive as to] startle the masses. Their talents and knowledge shine forth heroically. All have attained the celestial office of Attendant Esquire of the Bright Chronograms and dwell in [various] grotto [heavens]. One is raised to the responsibility of Attendant Esquire because of excellence and talents, unrestricted by distinctions between male and female.[116]

10. Zhao Sutai

Zhao Sutai 趙素臺 [Plain White Platform] was the daughter of Zhao Xi, the Goading Notary [military governor] of the Han dynasty province of

---

higher and higher positions after his young grandson became Numinous Thearch (Lingdi) upon the Powerful Thearch's death in 168. Dou served as regent for most of that year. He was executed later in 168 after losing a struggle with the eunuchs for power at the Han court. His execution ushered in a period of oppression for scholars. See Twitchett 1986, 287-89, 317-22.

116 Or "They were raised…"

Youzhou [in the far northeast of China].[117] Ever since Xi was young, he had engaged in good works. He helped the poor and suffering, and he saved Wang Hui's and other clans. He went to extremes in practicing hidden virtue. After several decades Xi was able to pay a ceremonial visit in person to the Vermilion Tumulus [inside Mount Heng], and his children obtained the ability to travel to the grotto heavens. [4b] Sutai has resided within the Palace of Transformation and Transcendence [under Mount Mao] for four hundred years already and she is unwilling to move away. She herself says the subcelestial realm has no greater delight than this place. She has traveled several times in disguise to peek at famous mountains and waterways, and that is enough for her. Her rank is that of a Lady of the Palace of Transformation and Transcendence.

11. Fu Lihe

Fu Lihe 傅禮和 [Ritual Harmony] was the daughter of Fu Jian of this place [Mount Qingcheng in Sichuan where Du was writing]. Her whole family served the Buddha. But every day, as she sprinkled and swept before the [altar of the] Buddha, Lihe vowed: "I will revere only the Way of the transcendents." She constantly ingested the essence of the five asterisms [planets], until her body emitted a radiant florescence.[118] Attaining the Way, she departed as a transcendent. She was skilled at composing Songs about the Empty Grotto [-Heavens].[119] When she sang them, wild birds soared and danced, flying together in flocks to gather before her and listen. She is indeed a case of responding with perfect sincerity and thus capturing the Way.

---

117 I have not been able to identify Zhao Yi or Wang Hui. Could Wang Hui be an ancestor of the Wang family that founded the Former Shu dynasty? If so, Du ingratiates himself with his ruler and patrons by praising their ancestors.

118 Ingesting essences of astral bodies is a technique for attaining immortality that combines meditation, visualization and breathing exercises. This system is favored by Shangqing Daoists. What ascetic adepts actually ate is disputed and varies from school to school and text to text.

119 I am interpreting the phrase "Song(s) of the Empty Grotto Heavens" as a type of Daoist tune, perhaps used in ritual practice, rather than the name of a single song.

12. Huang Jinghua

[5a] Huang Jinghua 黄景華 [Phosphor Florescence] was the daughter of Minister of Works Huang Qiong of the Han Dynasty.[120] When Jinghua was young, she already loved the Way of the transcendents, regularly practicing its perfected essentials in secret. Later she took Lord Han as her master, and he bestowed upon her a recipe for Min Mountains' cinnabar [elixir of immortality].[121] Ingesting it, she obtained entry to the Palace of Transformation and Transcendence, where she took up her position as Lady Who Coerces the Chronograms.[122] She leads the ladies of the nine palaces as well as generally instructing and bestowing [texts and ordinations] upon them.

13. Zhang Weizi

Zhang Weizi 張微子 [Master Tenuity] was the daughter of the Great Artisan Zhang Qing,[123] who held office during the reign of the Illuminating Thearch [Zhaodi] of the Han dynasty [r. 86-73 B.C.E.]. We do not know her commandary of residence. Because Weizi loved the Way since youth, she obtained liberation by means of the corpse and departed. She now resides in the Office of the Director of Destiny of the Grand Prime of the Floriate Yang Grotto [beneath Mount Mao], where she lives on Terrace of the Realized Ones. [In life] she took as her master the Eastern Floriate

---

[120] Huang Qiong was a Later Han paragon of virtue with an official biography in *Hou Hanshu* 91.

[121] I have not been able to identify Lord Han. Several Han dynasty masters surnamed Han are included in biographical accounts in the *Daozang*. The Min Mountains are a range in modern Sichuan province that includes Wushan (Shamanka Mountain), and Qingcheng shan (Blue Walled-City Mountain). Both were holy mountains for Daoists.

[122] This title implies that she set in motion and regulated the constellations the Chinese used to mark seasons and years. The title continues the link of the ladies in this text with astronomical phenomena, and the link of astral bodies with Shangqing practices. Like other subjects of this section, Huang Jinghua lived beneath Mount Mao.

[123] Grand Artisan is the title of the chief minister in charge of palace buildings in the capital during the Han dynasty. I have not been able to identify Zhang Qing or the specific Shangqing deity known as Donghua yufei, the Eastern Floriate Jade Consort.

Jade Consort. [The Jade Consort] bestowed the Way of Ingesting Misty Vapors upon Weizi, telling her: "Mist is the florescence of water and fire from the mountains and waterways, the overflowing breath of metal and stone. After ingesting it for a long time, you can disperse your form, enter the void, and mingle your body with clouds and mist."[124] Weizi practiced this, and that is how she obtained her transcendent Way.

14. Ding Shuying

[5b] We do not know where Ding Shuying 丁淑英 [Pure/Chaste Blossom] came from. Possessing the hidden virtue of saving the destitute, she delivered Zhao Fu from extreme difficulties.[125] She moved the illustrious ones from on high to bestow upon her the essentials of their Way. Now she is a Consort of the Vermilion Tumulus and has wandered many times to the Three Clarities.[126] In addition, the Director of Destiny has told her to consult in his decision-making.

---

[124] Many Shangqing meditative practices involve inhaling vapors of celestial bodies, but this technique has her ingesting misty vapors of the earth. She obtains the ability to dissolve herself at will into clouds and mist, then travel anywhere or join with the great void. The idea of a goddess appearing in misty vapors is as old as the Han dynasty prose poems, such as the "Rhapsody on the High Altar" by Song Yu, the "Rhapsody on the Goddess of the Luo River" by Cao Zhi, all found in *Wenxuan* (Literary Selections) 19.393 -97 and 401-05. See Watson 1971.

[125] I have not been able to identify Zhao Fu. The theme of rescuing others recalls the story of Zhao Xi saving Wang Hui's family (# 10) and then visiting the Vermilion Tumulus.

[126] The Vermilion Tumulus is a palace located in the third of Du Guangting's thirty-six grotto heavens, deep inside Mount Heng, the holy mountain of the south.

Part 4
Tang Saints and Transcendents

15. Wang Fajin

Starting with this biography, Du Guangting's entries become longer and more detailed. His Tang dynasty subjects lived closer to him in time, and he had more and better sources of information.

Wang Fajin 王法進 (Dharma Progress, d. 752) is one of the most remarkable figures in Du's collection. Her biography centers on the transmission of a fundamental ritual of the Lingbao school of Daoism. By honoring a Lingbao saint and ceremony, Du pays homage to that school and demonstrated the seriousness of his intent to weave together the Lingbao and Shangqing traditions. In addition, Du appropriates Buddhist ideas and terms in telling the story of Wang's life. He also shows the subject overtly playing a male role, indicating that at least in this case he regards gender as a performance rather than as essential identity. All the action in this narrative takes place in Sichuan province, where Du moved with the Tang court in exile in 882, and where he later lived as an honored courtier and Daoist master under the rule of the Wang family during the Former Shu dynasty. Du emphasizes the sanctity and Daoist credentials of the region. Striking scenes of famine and human suffering attributed to Wang Fajin's era parallel the situation in Du's own times, without insulting the ruler by referring directly to bad times under his reign.

Wang Fajin was born in Jian province in modern Sichuan. We know nothing of her family except that they lived near an abandoned Daoist temple. Fajin already loved the Way as a child, as she demonstrates with spontaneous reverence to the images in the deserted belvedere. When she was around ten, a Daoist nun passed through town and Wang Fajin's parents gave her to the nun. Her parents may have been Daoists or they may have been too poor to raise her. In any case, they made no objections to Fajin's childhood devotions. Ordained as a novice, she learned ritual protocols and assisted at public ceremonies. Her religious name Fajin, "Dharma Progress," sounds more Buddhist than Daoist and exemplifies the high degree of sharing that went on between the two religions. The Dharma, or the teachings of the Buddha, is one of the Three Treasures of Buddhism. Chinese Buddhists had used the term *fa* 法, meaning method or law, to translate the Sanskrit word. Daoist nuns and

Daoist authors like Du Guangting borrowed it back. In the same manner, the Chinese Buddhists borrowed the term *dao* or Way to refer to their faith. Such words of great potency were passed back and forth between the two religions.

Wang Fajin's briefly sketched youthful religious practice included fasting and ingesting elixir foods. "Cutting off the five grains" refers to severe fasting in which the adept eats no carbohydrates. She also cannot share food with people who are not fasting, even her own family. This extreme form of asceticism restricts her social and family life. The practitioner may become extremely emaciated, and her survival may seem miraculous to her admirers. According to Du, Wang's efforts proved effective, attracting visits from Daoist celestials. One such visit set in motion the events leading up to her most important contribution to Daoism.

According to Du Guangting, the central event of Wang Fajin's life was her transmission of a Lingbao rite of confession from the heavens to the Daoist community in Sichuan. This very public contribution contrasts to the hidden good works of most of his other subjects. Her experience, which seemed to pass in a flash, actually lasted three months of human time. It all began during a horrible famine. Two blue lads, messengers from the deities to humans, visited her, bringing orders from the Supreme Thearch. The Supreme Thearch (Shangdi 上帝), a mighty deity of Shangqing Daoism and important source of revealed texts, was ruler of the Supreme Clarity Heaven. The Supreme Thearch praised Fajin's diligence and resolution, saying her transcendence had been predetermined at her birth by "transcendent bones" (*xiangu* 仙骨). Following her destiny, her virtuous practice resulted in this summons to visit the Supreme Thearch in his heavenly capital. There he presented her an elixir in the form of broth made of dawn vapors. He also gave her a lecture.

The Supreme Thearch reveals to Wang Fajin that he caused the current famine in order to punish the people for their wrongdoing. They have fallen away from their proper reverence and work. But now he wishes to save them by giving them a ritual means of confession and repentance. This ritual is intended to compete with the great public rituals of Buddhism, and its rationale, voiced by a high Daoist god, borrows from Buddhist beliefs. The Supreme Thearch asserts that people are lucky to be born in human form, a belief imported to China along with Buddhism from India, where people believed that there were six possible paths of rebirth (Skt.: *gati*): the realms of gods, giants, humans, animals, hungry ghosts, and hell dwellers. Human birth is a blessing, despite the suffering it entails, as it is the only path of life from which one can attain enlightenment and escape from the wheel of life and death. The thearch continues, here drawing upon traditional Chinese cosmology, that humans are naturally endowed with the breaths of Heaven and Earth and the five phases. The same forces produce food to nourish us. The Supreme Thearch criticizes the people for not appreciating their good fortune.

Lately, the Supreme Thearch contends, people have wearied of their work in agriculture and sericulture. Du Guangting's description clearly assumes that women and men inhabit separate spheres in the economy. As the Chinese folk saying puts it: "Men till and women weave." As a result of neglect, agricultural and textile production has ceased, with disastrous results. People are starving. Heaven and earth and all the spirits oppress rather than support them.

Despite the Supreme Thearch's severe penalties, the people still have not realized their errors. Here Du uses the term "awaken" (*wu* 悟), most frequently chosen by Buddhists to translate the Sanskrit term *bodhi* or "enlightenment." Accordingly, another strategy is necessary. In a rare submission of Shangqing to Lingbao, Du declares that the command of the Grand Supreme, a Lingbao deity, supersedes the previous orders of the Shangqing deity called the Supreme Thearch. The people need the communal rituals that the Lingbao school can provide. In particular, they need a way to confess and repent their wrongdoing. Such communal repentance rituals were a feature of the Celestial Masters school during the late Han dynasty and afterwards. At the time of its origins in the fifth century, the Lingbao founders stressed individual self-cultivation, as did the Shangqing leaders. But by the Tang, the Lingbao school was associated with public and state rituals.

The deity transmits a saving ritual using Wang Fajin as his messenger. He orders her to serve as one of his "unsurpassable attendant lads." Her performance of a male role suggests that Du Guangting views gender as a way of acting in society. She becomes the part she plays, at least while she performs it.

The Supreme Thearch sends Wang Fajin back home as celestial messenger to lead people to resume their proper attitude and work. The people must revere the Rectified Way (Zhengdao 正道), that is: Daoist traditions such as Shangqing and Lingbao that claimed the Celestial Masters school of the Han dynasty as their ancestor. If the masses lived properly and practiced the liturgy Wang Fajin bestows upon them, harmony and prosperity would be restored for families and for the whole nation. When he says farewell to Wang Fajin, the Supreme Thearch predicts her future return to heaven. Predictions of enlightenment and even buddhahood figure in Mahayana Buddhist scriptures like the *Lotus Sutra*. Similarly, the prediction is a conventional Daoist sign of future immortality.

The ritual of repentance and gratitude, titled "Method of the Pure Fast of the Numinous Treasure for Reporting to and Thanking Heaven and Earth," is also known by other names. It corresponds with several ritual texts in the current Daoist canon, belonging to the great community ceremonies of the Lingbao school. Du's elevation of a Lingbao saint and Lingbao ritual shows the depth of his determination to unite Lingbao and Shangqing Daoism. In addition, the descriptions of the ritual itself show how similar relations between deities and humans were to transactions between emperors and bureaucratic officials.

At the end of her earthly life, Wang Fajin ascends to heaven as the Supreme Thearch predicted, welcomed by cloud cranes. The crane was a symbol of longevity and a favorite means of transportation among Daoist immortals. Wang's ascension verifies her sainthood and the worthiness of her cult. Fulfilling the Supreme Thearch's prediction by returning to heaven in a dragon-tiger year, the saint controls her own death. Wang Fajin is one of only two Tang women in Du Guangting's records who achieve the highest form of departure for the next world. They ascend directly to heaven in broad daylight. The other is Bian Dongxuan, Du's foremost exemplar for the Shangqing school (# 22).

Translation

[115.5b] Wang Fajin [Dharma Progress] was a person of Linjin County in Jian Province [Sichuan].[127] As a young child, she naturally loved the Way. Her household was near an old belvedere [Daoist monastery]. Although no Daoist master lived there any longer, she never belittled or insulted the revered images, even in play. Whenever she saw them, she felt compelled to join her hands in prayer and do obeisance; she trembled before them as if afraid.

When [Wang] was just over ten years old, a Daoist nun from Jian Province who was traveling through other townships passed her household.[128] [Wang's] father and mother, because of her longing for the Way, asked the Daoist nun to safeguard and protect her. The nun, [ordaining her as a novice,] bestowed upon Ms. Wang the "Register of Rectified Unity for Extending Life,"[129] and gave her the religious name Dharma Progress. [6a] She then became especially diligent at the incense fire [rituals]. She protected and assisted at fast and abstinence ceremonies. She also ate fungus and cedar seeds while cutting off [the five] grains.[130] Sometimes descents of deities took place in response [to her religious practice].

That year a famine took place in the Three Rivers region [Sichuan], with attendant shortages of food. Grain prices soared. The dead numbered five or

---

[127] A biography of Wang Fajin is found in *Taiping guangji* 241, from a source identified as *Xianzhuan shiyi* (Picking up What Was Dropped from the Transmissions Concerning the Transcendents), a text now lost. The version is very similar to Du's but is condensed and contains a mistake in dating her death (as year twelve of the Heavenly Treasure reign period, 753, a date that does not agree with the cyclicals recorded.) The *Taiping guangji* version is translated in Idema and Grant 2004, 161-63.

[128] The term for nun is *nuguan*, "female official," often replaced by its homophone "female cap," using a part of her ritual costume to refer to the whole nun.

[129] No text with this exact title is listed in the *Daozang*; it may be a general term for Rectified Unity registers. Having originated in the Celestial Masters school, these were bestowed at ordination. See, for example, the *Zhengyi wailu yi* (The Rectified Unity Liturgy for the Conferral of the Outer Registers, DZ 1243) of the fifth or sixth century, which contains rules and writs for transmitting the "Register of the Seventy-Five Generals of the Celestial Masters" to women and foreigners.

[130] "Cutting off grains" or "cutting off the five grains" refers to a specifically Daoist type of fasting in which the adept abstains from eating grains, the major food staple of medieval China, thus disciplining the body severely as well as separating the Daoist ascetic from normal, grain-eating society. On cutting off the five grains, see Lévi 1983; Eskildsen 1989. See also # 22 below.

six out of every ten. People often pulled up mountain taro and wild creepers to satisfy their hunger. Suddenly two blue lads descended into [Wang's] courtyard, proclaiming the Supreme Thearch's decree:[131]

> Because you were endowed from birth with transcendent bones, your submissive heart is essential and sincere, and you have not been negligent regarding the Way, I now summon you by means of these blue lads to receive a position in the Jade Capital [heaven].

Thereupon Fajin followed the blue lads as they soared up bodily and skimmed the void, passing through to the place where the Supreme Thearch was located.[132] He ordered that she be given auroral broth in a jade cup. After she finished drinking, the Thearch told her:

> People's natural endowments are the great embodiment of the five phases and of the harmonious breaths of Heaven and Earth. It is extremely difficult to obtain human form and in addition to dwell in the central land [China]. Moreover, heaven causes the breaths of the four seasons to revolve, while the earth receives what is necessary for the five phases to flourish, producing the five grains and five hundred fruits to provide nourishment for the people. [6b]

> But the people have not been acknowledging the nurturing mercy of Heaven and Earth: they belittle and reject the five grains, and irritably forsake fabrics of hemp and silk. As a result, husbands who do the tilling and farming, along with their wives who do the spinning and weaving, exhaust their bodies in labor without obtaining their fill, and exert their strength with utmost effort without avoiding the cold. They provide their labor in vain; no one spares or pities them. Thus when they are oppressed by divinely brilliant [spirits], Heaven and Earth do not protect them.

---

[131] Blue lads are minor Daoist deities and messengers of the higher gods. The Supreme Thearch, Shangdi, is one of the highest Daoist divinities, lord of the heaven known as the Supreme Clarity, one of the three highest heavens. Here he dwells in his Jade Capital), located by Lingbao Daoists in the Great Veil Heaven (Daluo tian) beyond the world that is not destroyed even in revolutions of the great kalpas or world ages. This is where the holy texts wait out the destruction at the end of each great kalpa. Daluo tian is another term shared with the Buddhists.

[132] I am treating the reference to the Grand Thearch (*Taidi*) here as a mistake for Supreme Thearch (*Shangdi*). The Grand Thearch is another high deity who rules the Grand Pure Realm, one of the three heavens of Shangqing Daoism

Most recently, [the deities of the] marchmounts and water-ways that are my earthly offices have daily produced memorials saying: "The people detest and despise rice and barley; they do not treasure the basis of their clothing and food [sericulture and agriculture]."

In response, I ordered the Bureaus of the Grand Florescence to restrain the spirits of the five grains and commanded the grain that has already been planted not to mature. I sent down famine and starvation to the people to show my criticism and punishment, in order to correct their hearts. [And yet] this generation's foolishness is so far-reaching that they still have not experienced awakening or enlightenment. Now we have received the Grand Supreme's [new] command to cherish life by means of the Great Way.[133] We must not harm the masses of good folk on account of some evil people. Although Heaven and Earth and the divinely brilliant [spirits] find them guilty [and punish them], the ignorant people still do not understand the arising of their transgressions. Thus they do not take the road of repentant prayer or confession of original [sins]. So they receive bitter suffering in vain.

You must, acting as one of my unsurpassable attendant lads, enter and wait upon the Heavenly Storehouse Chronogram [to obtain the rituals].[134] [7a] After that, I order you to descend to the mundane world to report and teach the inferior people how to send away their regrets and sins. Have them treasure mulberry and silkworm, value and revere agricultural matters, and love the five grains and hundred fruits. They must recognize that the Great Way nurtures the people while the abundant earth nourishes all creation. They should elevate and honor the Rectified Way, venerating and serving the divinely brilliant [spirits].[135] When it comes to the use of water and fire [in rit-

---

[133] The Grand Supreme or Grand Supreme Lord of the Dao is a revealer of sacred scriptures from the Heavenly Honored Ones to humanity. He is a high god originating in the Lingbao school of Daoism.

[134] She is commanded to function as a male rather than a female deity. The Heavenly Storehouse Chronogram (Tianfu chen) is the fourth star of the second constellation among the twenty-eight lunar lodgings in by medieval Chinese astronomy. Since stars are lodgings of high deities, the ritual must have been stored there prior to its revelation to humans.

[135] The "Rectified Way" refers first of all to the Celestial Masters School of the Han dynasty, ancestor of the later schools of the Tang. Followers of these later schools who

ual and daily life], they may not reject them in annoyance. When it comes to the nurturing of clothing and food, they must be frugal with themselves and restrain their bodies. If they can practice these bright prohibitions, then Heaven and Earth will love them and the divinely brilliant [spirits] will protect them. Wind and rain will prove favorable and harmonious, while family and nation will become peaceful and prosperous. [These practices] will also increase your own hidden accomplishments.

Then [the Supreme Thearch] ordered his attendant girls to unroll white gemstone book bags and pearl-beaded containers, bringing out the "Method of the Pure Fast of the Numinous Treasure for Reporting to and Thanking Heaven and Earth" in one scroll.[136] He gave it [to Wang Fajin] for transmission and practice in the world, telling her:

The people of the world can lead one another to a high, clear place on a dark mountain. There they can establish a fast to repent and give thanks. Within one year, they can do this twice, in the spring and autumn. In the spring, let them pray for abundance in the earth's harvests; in the autumn; let them thank the strength of the Way. In this manner, their indwelling faults will be exterminated and the deities known as Grain Father and Silk Mother [ancient folk deities] will arrange overflowing riches on their behalf. In a dragon-tiger year, I will summon you again.

[The Supreme Thearch] ordered the blue lads to accompany her as she departed. When she returned home, it had already been three months. The text she received was precisely the same as today's "Method of the Pure Fast of the Numinous Treasure for Reporting to and Thanking Heaven and Earth." This method is simple and easy, belonging to the same category [of ritual] as the "Spontaneous Fast of the Great Universal from the Numinous Treas-

---

traced their origins to the Celestial Masters might also consider themselves part of the Rectified Way.

136 Ritual is the center of Lingbao practice. This text describes the liturgy of one of the nine main types of *zhai* (fast or purification ceremonies, sometimes including meals so bountiful that we might translate the term "vegetarian feast"), called "Fast for Spontaneity" (*ziran zhai*), used to dispel disasters. No text with this exact title survives, but the Lingbao texts concerning purification rituals found in DZ 524 and DZ 532 are possible candidates. Citing variant names may be Du's strategy for including ritual texts with different titles or from variant traditions. On Lingbao *zhai*, see Yamada 2000. For details, see Kohn 2003.

ure."[137] Whenever it is practiced among people, it produces immediate results. But if there should ever be the least display of levity, tardiness, turbidity, or dirtiness among the sets of ritual utensils, or if anyone with the least sign of an inequitable heart should be present among the people offering up the rite, then whirling wind and violent rain will destroy the altars and prayer mats, while swift thunder will roar, and lightning will destroy the utensils.

Thereafter, people of the Three Rivers, Liang, and Han River regions [Sichuan] all reverently performed this affair each year. Even officials who were fools or dolts, even crazy or violent men, all trembled equally in dread of such warnings. Grave and reverent, kneeling in awe, they learned how to carry out this method. Whenever caterpillars and locusts or droughts and floods hurt crops and harmed agriculture, the masses would sincerely and obediently exert themselves to practice [this rite] and make offerings. Then after they burned incense and sent their reports to the mysterious ones, dawn and evening they received echoes and responses, increasing their blessings to the utmost. [Even] for impious and unbelieving persons, this established proof and witness [of the efficacy of the rite]. South of Ba [eastern Sichuan], they call this rite the Pure Fast. In Shu territory [western Sichuan], they call it the Fast of Heaven's Accomplishments. It is probably the same holiday.

In the eleventh year of the Heavenly Treasure reign period [752], an I-dragon [*renchen* = dragon and tiger] year, cloud cranes welcomed Fajin and she returned to heaven. This tallies precisely with the [calendrical] revolutions of the dragon and tiger as [foretold in] the words of the deity.

---

[137] This might be related to *Lingbao ziran zhaiyi* [Obserservances of the Lingbao Fast for Spontaneity, DZ 523].

16. Ms. Wang

This biography presents a life that was fascinating and informative for several reasons. Until her death, Ms. Wang's 王氏 practices were identical to those carried out by men of the Shangqing tradition. Her life provides evidence that at least some men and some women during the Tang dynasty pursued Daoist perfection using the same religious practices, even if they were not necessarily practicing together. During the following Song dynasty, as we have seen, separate Daoist regimes were set for men and for women. In addition, Ms. Wang's story and her own words criticize the householder's life as a possible ground for religious transformation. This contradicts Du Guangting's statement in his introduction that marriage (the Way of one yin and one yang) can be a religious vocation for women. Ms. Wang's dramatic deathbed speech vigorously condemns the daily life of a married woman as an impossible situation in which to practice religious self-cultivation, because of its unavoidable attachments and aversions. And, perhaps the most extraordinary event in this biography, Ms. Wang persevered in her practice beyond the grave, to achieve posthumous liberation by means of the corpse twenty years after her death. This is the first case I have encountered of such a method of transformation. As Du Guangting says in his introduction, there are many paths that lead to the Way.

In this account, Du associates Ms. Wang, and by extension himself and the royal court where he served, with the great Shangqing Daoist Master Wu Yun 吳筠 (d. 778). Master Wu Yun, a poet and friend of another famous Daoist poet, Li Bo 李白 (701-762), served thirteen years at the court of the emperor known posthumously as the Mysterious Ancestor, Xuanzong (r. 712-756), a ruler to whom Du seems particularly drawn. In this account Du implicitly compares himself to Master Wu Yun, and likens his royal patrons to emperor Xuanzong. The comparison suggests that Du's patrons, the Wang family rulers of the Former Shu state, are as legitimate and as fully Daoist as that famous monarch. Du also takes the occasion of Ms. Wang's tale to deliver one of his mini-lectures, explaining that the highest classes of celestial transcendents do not reside here on earth.

Du Guangting reports nothing of Ms. Wang's family or childhood. We first meet her when she marries the official and advanced degree holder, Xie Liangbi 謝良弼. Xie was a southerner and descendent of a military leader of the Eastern Jin. After her marriage, Ms. Wang becomes a chronic invalid, unable to follow her husband to his post. Nevertheless, she apparently bears him several daughters. (Alternatively, the "daughters," mentioned only near the end of the biography, when she addresses them from her deathbed, may actually be her disciples.) Relatives appeal to Daoist Master Wu Yun, fortuitously wandering in the area, to save her. Master Wu cures her overnight, using the ashes of a written Daoist talisman dissolved in water. According to Daoist beliefs, this talisman or charm, written in special, spiritually effective characters by a holy man, channels divine powers to restore her health. Daoist believers attribute her return to health to the efficacy of Master Wu's treatment. Doubters might suspect a placebo affect.

After this miraculous event, Ms. Wang converts to Daoism and becomes Wu Yun's disciple. As part of her worship, she burns "Brahman incense" (*fanxiang* 梵香), an expensive and prestigious aromatic, perhaps sandalwood, imported from India along with Buddhism. The use of the term *fan*, a transliteration of the Sanskrit "Brahman," shows Daoists borrowing terminology from Buddhism for a shared practice. (Ultimately the term comes from Indian Vedic traditions; Brahma is a Hindu deity and Brahman is the universal energy Hindus believe underlies all phenomena.) She receives registers giving her access to deities, meditates in a quiet room, performs astral visualizations, and fasts: all religious practices dating back to the Celestial Masters school of Daoism continued and developed in the following centuries. She also ingests celestial vapors, a well-documented Shangqing Daoist practice. Her diligence begins to pay off, and her body becomes light and fragrant, proving she had reversed the aging process. Divine clouds light up her dwelling; realized ones and spirits secretly visit her. All is going well, when she suddenly realizes she is going to die.

In her vividly rendered last speech to her daughters or disciples, Ms. Wang credits Master Wu Yun with saving her life after ten years of illness. In a close parallel to the language of Buddhism, she calls her conversion to Daoism "taking refuge with Heavenly Master (Wu Yun)." When Buddhists affirm their faith, they chant the Triple Refuge: "I take refuge in the (founder and teacher known as) Buddha, I take refuge in the Dharma (teachings of the Buddha), I take refuge in the Sangha (the Buddhist community or order)." The Triple Refuge, also known as the Three Treasures, is a universal and early part of Buddhist doctrine. In using this word, she compares her teacher to the Buddha. In addition, when she describes her conversion, she says she entered the Way of "enlightenment," using the same term for enlightenment as the Buddhists. Ms. Wang next acknowledges that she began her religious practice late and still has a long way to go. She blames her physical and emotional infirmities on the "sickness inherent in ordinary behaviors of everyday life," a powerful condemnation of the householder's life as a ground for religious formation. This concern about daily life in a family erecting a powerful obstacle to religious attainment is also shared by Buddhists.

After this, Ms. Wang's deathbed words enter a familiar world of Shangqing Daoist practices and ideas. She describes her inner organs and their functioning in terms drawn from the realm of microphysiology, joining medical and religious ideas. She realizes that she needs about twenty more years of self-cultivation before she can transform herself into a transcendent, leaving her body behind as a husk, the way a cicada sheds its shell. She predicts her own ascent, showing the foreknowledge and control over death that mark a Daoist saint. She requests that, counter to the dictates of filial piety and normative funerary practice, her daughters (or disciples) carry her body into the woods and leave it there, with only a cedar screen for burial goods and grave marker.

She dies the same night and is buried as she instructed: with a simple ceremony, laid in a grove of trees as if she were sleeping in her bed. This shocking transgression of traditional Chinese funerary custom by exposing the body of the deceased may reflect the practices of a southern ethnic minority. In any case, the unorthodox burial is effective in supporting her posthumous practice. Twenty years later, thieves disturb her place of rest, leaving her body on a pile of dirt. Lightning and thunder later signals her family that something unusual has taken place. When they go to her gravesite and lift her abandoned corpse, they find it almost weightless. Her skin, nails, and hair are all intact; that is, her external shell is perfectly preserved. But Ms Wang is no longer there. A scar on her chest shows where she has escaped. As she predicted earlier, she has achieved liberation by means of the corpse. Her family then buries her with appropriate rituals.

The case of Ms. Wang must have been tremendously encouraging to parents or children of Daoist believers who went to their graves unperfected, as well as to adepts who believed their own transformation to be incomplete as the time of death approached. Du even suggests here that abandoned or improperly buried corpses may have a good outcome in the next world. Toward the end of the Tang dynasty and in the years that followed its fall, a time of sporadic warfare and great economic hardship, many people migrated, leaving behind dead and even unburied relatives. They could take comfort from such a tale. Such consolation must have played a big role in gaining converts for Daoism.

After describing Ms. Wang's secret ascent and public funeral, Du cites Lady Wei Huacun 魏華存 as an authority on transcendence. Lady Wei is a great Shangqing goddess and revealer of texts who appears in several of Du Guangting's entries, but inexplicably does not have her own entry in the version of the text translated here. Lady Wei comments upon the highest and the second highest classes of transcendents. Both are celestial and not of this earth. She pronounces liberation by means of the corpse as a valid means of transcendence. Finally, addressing a controversy among Daoists over what precisely climbed to heaven, she clearly asserts that the entire physical body of the adept ascends. This contradicts Du Guangting's own statement in his introduction (p. 36). This discrepancy may result from a disagreement between Du's sources, and reveals conflict on this doctrine among the Daoist community.

Lady Wei also explains in no uncertain terms that the two highest types of transformation—ascending to heaven in broad daylight and liberation by means of the corpse—lead to a heavenly rather than earthly home. Even the famous mountains and Marchmounts of earth are not adequate for their final resting place. Thus the transcendents of the grotto heavens (# 5-14 above) have achieved a lower form of transcendence than the subjects who ascended to heaven in broad daylight or achieved transformation by means of the corpse.

At the end of his account of Ms. Wang, Du adds the information that her husband, Xie Liangbi, also became a disciple of Wu Yun. This suggests that some Tang dynasty women might have influenced their husbands' religious choices. Xie's conversion also tempers Ms. Wang's denunciation of marriage as a possible Daoist vocation, suggesting that some extremely devout practitioners might succeed in their religious goals despite being married.

Du Guangting reports that Xie Liangbi wrote a biography of Wu Yun. I believe that this is the short text preserved in the current Daoist canon between two works attributed to Wu Yun, the *Wu zunshi zhuan* 吳尊師傳 (Transmissions Concerning Venerable Master Wu, DZ 1053) and the *Nantong dajun neidan jiuzhang jing* 南統大君內丹九章經 (Scripture in Nine Chapters on Inner Alchemy According to the Great Lord Who Rules the Southern Empire [Wu Yun], DZ 1054). Schafer noted the anachronisms in the latter text and interpreted them as evidence that the text was a forgery. I argue that this text was written by Wu Yun's disciple and Ms. Wang's husband, Xie Liangbi, to explain and spread Master Wu Yun's teachings and that he added Wu's biography, also found in the other *Daozang* text, as a preface. The biography reports on Wu Yun, and also expresses some of Du Guangting's favorite teachings: that practicing hidden virtue is a powerful way to accumulate merit, that the Dao is not outside our own bodies, and that we can attain transcendence through our own efforts.

Translation

[115.8a] Ms. Wang was the wife of the Resident of the Central Secretariat, Xie Liangbi. [138] A descendent of [Xie] Yishao of the Right Army of the Eastern Jin Dynasty [317-419], he was a person from Kuaiji [Zhejiang]. When Liangbi passed his Advanced Scholar exam, he became Secretary of the Region East of the Zhe River, and [Ms. Wang] married him. Thereupon she embraced sickness, sinking into chronic invalidism. Several years passed without improvement. Liangbi attended the watchtowers [took up his office], but she was unable to accompany him. Instead, her sickness just continued, increasing in extent and gravity. [8b]

At that time Heavenly Master Wu Yun was wandering through the Four Bright [Mountains] [in Zhejiang]. [139] He passed Mount Tiantai, the Orchid

---

[138] I have not identified Xie Yishao beyond what Du Guangting states here. Ms. Wang's husband, Xie Liangbi, was also a disciple of Wu Yun (d. 778) and his writings probably served as a source of Du Guangting's information.

[139] On Wu Yun (d. 778), the famous Daoist master and poet, see Schafer 1981, 1982; DeMeyer 1998, 1999. Wu Yun was a friend of Li Bo, another Daoist poet, drinker, and wanderer in southern regions. Like Du Guangting, Wu Yun took the Advanced Scholar (*jinshi*) exam, but did not pass it. Wu spent some time at the court of Xuanzong, and has an official biography by Quan Deyu (759-818) that exists in several versions, including *Jiu Tangshu*, 192

Pavilion, and Yu's Caverns, and then stopped on the shady side of Whip Mountain.[140] A relative of Ms. Wang made a formal visit to him, seeking his saving powers. He prepared holy water for her and had her swallow a talismanic text [dissolved in that water as medicine]. She recovered overnight.

Moved by the power of the Way to save and protect, Ms. Wang made formal visits to the Heavenly Master [Wu Yun]. She received registers [of deities signifying initiation], purified her practice, and burned Brahman incense. She contemplated in stillness, dwelling alone in a quiet room. She intended and hoped to fly to the chronograms. Accordingly, she [fasted by] cutting off the five grains. She swallowed vapors, so that her spirits became harmonious and her body light. Sometimes there was a rare fragrance [about her], or strange clouds drew near and illuminated her residence. It seemed that realized ones descended to her and she secretly communicated with numina, but nobody knew about it.

Suddenly she said to her daughters [or disciples]:

> My former illnesses had lasted nearly ten years when I took refuge with Heavenly Master [Wu Yun], who cured me and extended my already exhausted lifespan. My entering the Way of enlightenment was already late, and I have not yet become essential in practicing what I received. When I seriously examine my past excesses, I regret them no end. For my whole life, because of the sickness inherent in ordinary behaviors of everyday life, I have inclined towards cherishing jealousy and envy. Now my heart is still obstructed, my storehouses [organ systems] black, and not circulating [vital breath] along the proper pathways. I must [visualize] my secluded interior, refine my form, wash my heart, and transform my storehouses.

(16.5129-5130). Wu Yun, one of whose religious names was Zongxuan (Ancestral Mystery), is the attributive author of several texts in the current Daoist canon. These include *Zongxuan xiansheng wenji* (Collected Works of the Prior-Born Ancestral Mystery, DZ 1051) and *Zhongxuan xiansheng xuangang lun*, A Discussion of the Mysterious Mainstays of the Prior-Born, Ancestral Mystery, DZ 1052). Like Du Guangting a Shangqing master, he stresses the importance of hidden good works and asserts that that the Dao is not outside one's own body. We can and must attain the Way through our own efforts..

[140] Mount Tiantai in Zhejiang is holy to both Buddhists and Daoists. Du Guangting lived there for a while. The Orchid Pavilion (*Lanting*) in the Kuaiji mountains in modern Shaoxing county was made famous by a preface commemorating a poetic gathering there in 353 by Wang Xizhi (321-379), the Eastern Jin calligrapher and Celestial Masters follower. (see Owen 1996, 282-84). Yu's Caverns (Yuxue), named after Yu the Great, the legendary hero who saved the world from the flood in prehistoric times, are also located in the Kuaiji Mountains. All these locations are in modern Zhejiang.

> After twenty years [of practice], I will certainly be able [to transform] like a cicada [breaks through its shell]. [9a]

> When I die, do not use a coffin. You may make me a screen of cedar wood. Convey my corpse into the wilds. At the right time, you may depute someone to examine it.

That very night she died. People from her household prepared her for burial as she had instructed; everything was simple and frugal. They set her up in a grove in the hunting park, reclining as if in bed. There were no changes or alterations [in her appearance]. Some twenty years later, thieves discovered her interment and abandoned her form [body] on a mound of dirt. During the cold winter months that followed, reverberations of thunder and lightening were suddenly heard beside her screen. Her whole household, finding this startling and strange, rushed to look at her. When they arrived and lifted out her corpse, her body was as light as an empty husk. Her flesh, nails, and hair were all complete, but on the right side of her rib cage a scar more than a foot long had split open. Later she was reburied with proper rites.

As the Lady of the Southern Marchmount [Wei Huacun] once said:

> Members of the highest class of those who attain the Way ascend to heaven in broad daylight. Their forms and bones fly up together to fill vacancies as realized officials. Members of the next class shed their skin like cicadas. They also soar and rise up with forms and bones, their flesh and material substance climbing to heaven. In both of these cases, they become heavenly transcendents; they do not dwell in [earthly] mountains and marchmounts.[141]

[Her husband Xie] Liangbi also grasped the rites of discipleship and in person attended the Heavenly Master [Wu Yun]. He established a transmission about [biography of] the Heavenly Master, to record in detail the traces of his affairs.

---

141 Wei Huacun (252-334), a libationer of the Celestial Masters, later became a matriarch of Shangqing Daoism. Although born in Shandong, she attained the Dao on the southern marchmount and became especially associated with that site (see Schafer 1977b). The southern Marchmount, identified with Mount Heng during the Tang dynasty, may have been located at Mount Huo in Lady Wei's own time. (A private communication from James Robson is my source for information on the transfer of Lady Wei's cult site from one mountain to the other).

17. Hua Gu

Hua Gu 花姑, the Flower Maiden (640-721) was another south-easterner. Most of the events recorded in her biography took place in the forests and mountains of the modern state of Jiangxi. Hua Gu is the first of four Tang women in Du Guangting's collection called "maiden." The term suggests celibacy if not necessarily virginity, and three of the four Tang maidens were solitary, wandering ascetics who lived in wilderness areas, far from the comforts of family or convent. Another became a wanderer upon her retirement. Their life stories show that during the Tang dynasty, women as well as men could live as hermits.

Hua Gu's story exemplifies several of Du Guangting's themes. Her life's work consisted of acts of hidden virtue, a step to transcendence Du favored. Du associated the Flower Maiden with the Shangqing goddess, Lady Wei Huacun, and especially with two shrines commemorating sites of that deity's religious practice and ascent to heaven. Hua Gu's tale also modeled Du's ideal of the mutually supportive relationship between the Daoist church and the Tang imperial bureaucracy. And in telling her story, Du Guangting promotes Daoism and diminishes its rival, Buddhism, by co-opting two major Buddhist images: the elephant and the lotus. Like the previous subject, Ms. Wang, Hua Gu requested and received an unusual burial. In her case, the unconventional funerary arrangements enabled Hua Gu to demonstrate her immediate ascent to transcendence.

We do not know where the Flower Maiden was born, nor do we have any information about her childhood, family, or social class. Du identifies her family and given names: Huang Lingwei 黃靈微. She first appears to the reader as an old woman of eighty with skin as fresh and soft as a baby's. This testifies to her successful Daoist practice that has allowed her to reverse the aging process and become younger with each passing year. The image of a baby in Daoist writings also suggests the undifferentiated, pure, and free state of the human being before life experience and cultural teachings corrupt and limit us. Hua Gu moved like a goddess. She traveled all over to auspicious and holy places, protected by divinities. She was a well-known and revered figure, treated as a deity by the people.

The Flower Maiden is best known for her work in restoring the shrine at Linquan associated with Lady Wei Huacun. Lady Wei, a leader of the Celestial Masters school of Daoism during her lifetime, later became a great goddess and transmitter of texts of Shangqing Daoism. In the Tang dynasty, she was believed to dwell on Mount Heng, the holy mountain of the south. Although the Lady herself does not have her own entry in Du Guangting's collection, she plays crucial roles in several accounts such as this one.

The Flower Maiden heard of an abandoned altar to Lady Wei at Linquan 臨泉 in modern Jiangxi, and sought it out. When locals proved unable to help her find the overgrown site, she visited Daoist Master Hu Chao in 693 to ask him about the altar. Drawing on his ability to communicate with deities, Master Hu directed her to a stone statue of a headless tortoise in the fields not too far away. She located the tortoise and found the remains of the altar on either side of it. The discovery of images and ritual utensils confirmed the identity of the shrine. She uncovered and repaired the shrine complex. Next she dreamed that Lady Wei herself showed her a nearby pool with steps, which the Maiden also found. These stories attest to the religious origins of archaeology: one of the primary reasons for digging up old things was to locate or restore a holy place.

The Flower Maiden's restoration work came to the attention of the court in 711, when Emperor Ruizong (r. 710-712) dispatched the famous Daoist official and magician, Master Ye Fashan 葉法善 (616-720), from the capital city of Chang'an. Master Ye brought images, sacramental cloth, and other gifts to the altar and re-consecrated it by performing Daoist rituals there. He established a convent and ordained seven nuns. The site remained continuously active under Xuanzong (r. 712-756). It was known as a sacred site where purification was taken seriously and uncanny or auspicious omens might be sighted.

But by the time the Linquan shrine became a religious establishment officially recognized by the Tang court and Daoist church, the Flower Maiden was long gone. One of the many spirits with whom she communicated told her that there was another ruined holy site at nearby Mount Shijing (Stone Well). After confirming this message through divination, she set out to locate and repair the establishment. Smelling delightful fragrances and hearing divine music, she wandered through the wilderness feeling as if she were being led along. She slept outdoors without fear or injury. Fearlessness in the wild is often the mark of a saint. Perhaps saints were so in tune with the Way that all of nature protected them. Hua Gu discovered remains of an earlier Daoist establishment, apparently the place where Lady Wei had ascended to transcendence, and built a small hut there where she lived and devoted herself to practice.

When the Flower Maiden was living at the shrine on Stone Well Mountain, she fearlessly removed an arrow from a wild elephant that approached her seeking help. A special rapport with wild animals is also frequently a sign of sainthood. Later the elephant showed his gratitude by bringing her a lotus whenever she performed rituals. The elephant and the lotus are classical Indian images given new meanings by the Buddhists; these motifs were exported together with Buddhism to China. The elephant is a symbol of the power, royalty, and virility of the Buddha, while the lotus that grows out of the mud and remains clean is a sign of the pure Buddha nature within each human being. But the elephant and lotus were motifs in native Chinese art long before Buddhism arrived. For example, a late Shang or early Zhou bronze ritual vessel is cast in the shape of an elephant, and lotus ponds appear in relief on the walls of Han dynasty tombs in Sichuan province. Du Guangting reclaims these powerful symbols for Daoism and for his saint.

The death narrative of the Flower Maiden is particularly rich. The Maiden predicted her own departure, in 721, when she suddenly told her disciples that her "transcendent journey has become urgent." Knowledge of one's own time of death, indicating control, signifies sanctity. Like Ms. Wang, Hua Gu made a shocking request about her own funeral arrangements, contradicting customary burial practice. She asked her disciples not to nail her coffin shut, but just to cover her body with a fine piece of red silk. Perhaps she worried that nailing her inside the coffin might impede her escape. Then she died overnight without ever suffering illness. Her corpse remained uncorrupted and emitted a beautiful fragrance, another sign of sainthood. Her disciples, complying with her wishes, covered her only with light silk cloth. Suddenly lightning struck, the Maiden's disciples saw a hole the size of an egg in her red silk cover, and her coffin was empty but for some wooden writing strips and her shroud. A hole in the ceiling appeared, big enough for a person to pass through. Two gourds laid in offering beside her coffin miraculously sprouted and bore fruits like peaches (the fruits of immortality). All these supernatural events provided evidence of her ascent to transcendence. Her incorruptible and later disappearing body proved that she obtained transcendence through liberation by means of the corpse.

The Flower Maiden's biography is unusual among Du's entries in providing information about subsequent history of the site. Du Guangting, who himself took a deep interest in Daoist holy places, traces the shrines that were the Maiden's life work up to his own time. The compound, including the old ruins, her grave, and her former dwelling remained numinous even after her departure. On each anniversary of her death, nature put on a light and sound show. Emperor Xuanzong heard about this phenomenon and had an official investigate it. Convinced of her sanctity, the emperor ordered Daoist Master Cai Wei 蔡偉 to write an account of the Maiden for the "Transmissions Concerning Later Transcendents," a now-lost text that probably served as a source for Du.

Later, in 740, the emperor had Daoist Masters perform a major ritual there. A white deer, vehicle of Daoist transcendents, appeared in response and then vanished, while a flock of multi-colored moths gathered. The auspicious omens of the white deer and transcendent moths show nature responding with approval to her cult. Moved by this event, the military governor Zhang Jingyi set up a stele (no longer extant) at the site, narrating her life. This text probably provided information for Du Guangting. Nuns performed ceremonies there regularly in 750. But by 768, when the great calligrapher and official Yan Zhenqing 顏真慶 (709-785) served as military governor of the region, all traces of the Flower Maiden at the site of Lady Wei Huacun's former shrine were lost. Yan Zhenqing took it upon himself to summon Daoist masters from the capital to establish a monastery and convent there, and wrote an inscription about the Flower Maiden's that does survive and was clearly a resource for Du. Incorporating Yan and his activities adds luster to the tale and also gives his entire work an implied Confucian imprimatur.

Translation

[115.9b] Hua Gu [Flower Maiden] was the female Daoist Master Huang Lingwei.[142] At the age of eighty, she had a youthful face and the appearance of a baby. Her Daoist practices were lofty and pure. Contemporary people called her Hua Gu. When she was stepping along at a stately pace, galloping horses could not catch her. We do not know where she came from. From the beginning of the Tang dynasty, she came and went by the Yangtze and Zhe rivers and among the lakes and mountain passes. There was not a single famous mountain or numinous grotto to which she did not go. When she visited a place, if she dwelt in the wilds of the forests, then local divinities and numina would protect her. If anyone had incorrect thoughts about her, intending to mistreat or assault her, he would immediately topple down into difficulties. Far and near, people revered and respected her. They made offerings to her and served her as a divine brilliant [spirit].

She heard that in the place where Lady Wei of the Southern Marchmount always used to cross the Yangtze to practice the Way, an altar had once been established. [She had heard that] there was an altar to the transcendents in Linquan Commandary, west of the Linru River near Stone Well Mountain [in Jiangxi].[143] [10a] Accordingly, she visited that place to seek [Lady Wei's altar]. As years and months had stretched out over a long time, the altar had become overgrown, with thorny trees and weeds engulfing and screening it. So none of the people at the time knew about it.

In winter, during the tenth month of the second year, an I-dragon (*renchen*) year, of the Prolonged Longevity reign period of Empress Wu Zetian [693], Hua Gu paid a ceremonial visit to Daoist Master Hu Chao in the Western

---

[142] Du Guangting does not label Hua Gu the regular term *nüguan* (female cap or female official) commonly used for a nun or female religious. Instead, he calls her a *nü daoshi* or "female Daoist master," using the unisex term for "Daoist master," preceded by the modifier "female." Kirkland (1991) translates and analyzes several biographies of Hua Gu, including Yan's *Fuzhou Linquanxian Jingshan Huagu xiantan beiming* (Stele Inscription on the Transcendent Altar of the Flower Maiden from Well Mountain in Fuzhou City in Linquan County) in *Quan Tangwen* 240.4359-60, and *Wei furen beiming* (Stele Inscription at [the Shrine of] Lady Wei) in *Quan Tangwen* 340.4366-69. Kirkland also discusses Du's account.

[143] On the restoration of the shrine of Lady Wei Huacun in Tang times, see Schafter 1977b. Yan Zhenqing's accounts do not mention Stone Well Mountain, and situate this story in Crow-Black Tortoise Plateau. They may well refer to the same place, with Crow-Black Plateau being a part or peak of the mountain. The textual variations make it likely that the author refers to two peaks in the same range, with two separate shrine sites to the goddess. On Yan, see Kirkland 1986; McNair 1998.

Mountains of Hongdu [Jiangxi] to ask him about [the altar].[144] Chao, whose cognomen was Basu [Rooting out the Vulgar], could communicate with divine brilliant [spirits]. He pointed to Crow-Black Tortoise Plateau some six miles away in the southern suburbs. Long ago there had been a stone tortoise around there who was always damaging sprouts in the fields until the people struck him and cut off his head: *that* was the place. When the Maiden visited there, she saw traces of an altar to the left and right of the tortoise. It seemed that the very place she stood must have been the middle of the altar. From beneath she retrieved such things as images of the venerable ones, oil vessels, awls, knives, and oil cups from lamps. Accordingly she repaired the altar and made it usable. Later she dreamed that Lady [Wei herself] pointed out a pool with nine turns on the south side of the altar. She visited [the place] and discovered [the sacred pool]. Its stepping stones were all still there.

In the middle of the reign period Spectacular Cloud [711], the Astute Ancestor [Emperor Ruizong] sent Daoist Master Ye Shanxin [Ye Fashan, 616-720], bringing an embroidered image together with streamers and flowers, to come and practice Daoist teachings there.[145] Accordingly [Master Ye] established the Belvedere of Grotto Numina west of the altar, and ordained seven female Daoist Masters as presiding servers. [10b]

During the reign of the Brilliant Illustrious [Emperor, 712-756] [Master Ye and the nuns] performed of cosmodramas, sacrifices, and prayers there without ceasing.[146] When there was wind or rain, sometimes people heard the sounds of syrinx and pitch pipes. Everyone who visited this place for rites had to undergo the strictest purification. If they did not, uncanny manifestations, such as snakes or tigers that startled them by roaring, would occur. Sometimes cloud phenomena resembling crows flying in a flock would descend in a belt straight down to the top of the altar. Then suddenly they

---

[144] Wu Zitian was the de facto ruler of China after the death of her husband Gaozong in 684. In 690, she declared herself emperor of China and founded the Zhou Dynasty [690-705] (see Guisso 1978). Although a Buddhist herself, she supported Daoist enterprises. Yan Zhenqing's account of Hua Gu mentions that Empress Wu confiscated the relics from Lady Wei's shrine. Master Hu is Hu Huichao (d. 703), a Tang theurgist. Here he is portrayed as a shaman. He is involved in the cult of the dragon-slayer Xu Xun who in turn is mentioned in Du Guangting's introduction to the current work. Hu Huichao has several biographies, the fullest in *Lishi zhenxian tidao tongjian* (DZ 296)

[145] Ye Fashan has biographies in *Jiu Tangshu*. 192.5107-8 and *Xin Tangshu* 204.5805. For studies, see Kirkland 1992; Benn 1991.

[146] The cosmodrama (*jiao*) is one of the two main types of Daoist ceremony in Tang times. (The other is the *zhai* or fast). The cosmodrama is a ritual meant to confirm the special relations of a group or place with its deities. On the cosmodrama, see Saso 1972; Lagerwey 1987.

would exit westward towards Well Mountain. There has never been anything like this, before or afterwards.

Hua Gu communicated with a host of numina, and one of them secretly announced to her: "At Well Mountain there are old remains that you must reverently restore." Suddenly she sensed a strange fragrance coming from the west. The Maiden repeatedly obtained auspicious prognostications, so she herself went to repair and renovate [the holy site]. She went and spent a night in the mouth of a grotto, where she heard the resonance of sounding stones. Although the place had been an abandoned wilderness for a long time, it seemed as though someone were leading her along. She spent a night amidst forest undergrowth, feeling delighted and extremely peaceful. The next day she entered the mountain and indeed encountered the altar, basilica, and other remains. Accordingly she set up a room [and stayed] there. She heard transcendents pacing the void, and the fragrance of Brahman incense surrounded the altar to a distance of several *li*. If anyone who was not essential and pure came along to collect firewood in the forest, he would have been alarmed at such an odd, bizarre situation. [11a] Once a wild elephant who had been hit by an arrow came to seek help from Hua Gu. She removed it for him. After that, whenever there was to be a fast [ceremony], he would bring a lotus in his mouth to offer the Maiden.

In the ninth year of the Opened Prime reign period [721], an H-rooster [*xinyou*] year, when the Maiden was about to ascend and transform, she told her disciples: "Because my transcendent journey has become urgent, I cannot stay here any longer. After my body is transformed, do not nail my coffin shut. Just cover the coffin with crimson silk gauze." The next day she came to her end without even being sick. Her flesh and skin were fragrant and pure, her physical form and breath warm and genial. A strange fragrance filled the courtyards and halls. Her disciples followed her orders and did not nail her coffin shut, simply covering it with crimson silk gauze. Suddenly they all heard lightning and thunder strike. On the top of the silk gauze was a hole about as big as a hen's egg, and in the coffin were only her shroud and some wooden [text] slips. In the ceiling of the room a spot had been penetrated [leaving a gap] big enough for a person to pass through. At the base of the coffin, where offerings had been placed, a gourd sprouted creepers several days later and then set two fruits like peaches.

Each time the anniversary of her death came around, the wind and clouds grew thick and suddenly entered right inside the room. The Brilliant Illustrious [Emperor] heard about it and was amazed. He ordered an official to examine the case. [11b] The next day he ordered Daoist Master Cai Wei to edit an entry on her in the [now lost] "Transmissions Concerning Later Transcendents."[147]

In the twenty-eighth year of the Opened Prime reign period [740], a G-dragon [*gengchen*] year, in the third month, on a B-rooster [*yiyou*] day, the emperor induced Daoist masters carrying dragon [imperial] insignia in the form of a jade disc to come and perform a cosmodrama. Suddenly a white deer emerged from east of the altar, reached the middle of the Maiden's grave mound, and then utterly disappeared. It was exactly the same place where Hua Gu had been buried, the place of her empty coffin and wooden slips. Five-colored transcendent moths [alternatively: girls] also gathered at the altar. Moved by her incomparable virtue, Goading Notary Zhang Jingyi set up a stele to eulogize her and narrate this tale.[148] In the eighth year of the Heavenly Treasure reign period [750], an E-ox (*jichou*) year, two female Daoist Masters were ordained to tend the incense fire regularly at the place where Lady Wei had ascended on high.

Later, in the third year of the Great Calendar reign period [of Emperor Daizong, 768], an E-monkey [*wushen*] year, the State-Opening Common-lord from Lu Commandary, Yan Zhenqing was made Goading Notary [military commandant] of Fuzhou [Shandong]. By then [Hua Gu's] former traces were overgrown and destroyed, and nobody [that is: no clergy] was there to preside over services. [So Yan Zhenqing] summoned Daoist Masters Tan Xianyan and Huang Daojin from the Transcendent Platform Belvedere [along with others], altogether twenty-seven men, to come and reside in the Belvedere of the Grotto Numina.[149] In addition, there were seven female Daoist Masters of lofty practice residing in the Transcendent Altar Close. Common-lord Yan narrated the "Transcendent Alter Stele Inscription" and wrote it out himself in order to record the traces of [Hua Gu's] affairs.

---

[147] According to Yan Zhenqing, Master Cai Wei came from the Hongdao Belvedere in the capital city of Chang'an.

[148] "Transcendent moths" may become the homophone for "transcendent girls," as Kirkland has noted (1991, 61n5). Zhang Jingyi is mentioned in *Jiu Tangshu* 185B.4810 and *Xin Tangshu* 100.3948. He became a great official under Xuanzong. He was a native of Fanyang, near modern Beijing, the region from which An Lushan led the rebellion of 756. Li Bo also came from that region, as did Bian Dongxuan (# 22). Zhang was Goading Notary (Military Commander) of Fuzhou before Yan Zhenqing. His now-lost account of Hua Gu may well have been available to Yan and Du.

[149] I have not located Tan Xianyan or Huang Daojin. Xiantai, The Transcendent Platform Belvedere was probably a Daoist monastery-temple compound near the capital of Chang'an. The Belvedere of the Grotto Numina (Dongling guan) must have been the Daoist monastery established at a site near Lady Wei's restored shrine and Hua Gu's tomb. The Transcendent Altar Close (Xiantan yuan) would have been the associated convent.

18 . Xu Xiangu

Transcendent Maiden Xu 徐仙姑 is another southerner. She is also another "maiden." Hua Gu in the previous biography, Gou Xiangu in the following, and Shen Gu (# 25) are the other Tang maidens. Judging from their lives, *gu* was a title for solitary female ascetics, not necessarily ordained nuns, who wandered to holy places and might be popularly regarded as deities in their own lifetimes. They were celibate if not virgins. A period of celibacy was often required as purification in preparation for Daoist rituals. Some Daoist adepts, male and female, made permanent celibacy part of their practice. By not wasting time or energy on sexual intercourse or human attachment, they conserve their essence so that they can achieve perfection more quickly. Xu's biography expresses Du's ambivalence about family life as a field for practice. In addition, Du Guangting takes this opportunity to mount a strong, even crude, attack upon Buddhism. He presents Xu Xiangu as a remarkable magician and defender of her faith. Du does not inform us of her time or manner of departure, but provides evidence of her popular cult and transcendence.

Du opens his account with her family background. Xu Xiangu is the daughter of Xu Zhicai, a learned official and famous wonder-worker of the Northern Qi dynasty (550-577) who also held office under the succeeding Sui dynasty (589-618). Du himself held office under two dynasties and may seek here to justify his own choices by the comparison. Du expresses ignorance concerning Xu's Daoist masters and training. But near the end of the account, he contradicts himself and supports her claims that her father was her teacher. Through her father, Xu Xiangu is linked to the Han dynasty tradition of the "recipe masters," technicians or experts of magic and the supernatural. Her gifts verify her assertions. Like Hua Gu, Xu Xiangu had unusual qualities Du interprets as signs of sainthood. She too looked young in old age, traveled great distances with ease, and slept in the wilderness without fear.

Xu Xiangu even lodged in hermitages intended for Buddhist clergy. This habit led to her most dramatic adventure. Once a group of monks insulted her. She fired back curses at them, which only increased their rage. When they took out knives to stab her, she laughed and dismissed them with one of the most amazing statements in Du Guangting's work. She said: "I am a woman, and yet I have been able to reject the household life and travel amidst clouds and rivers. I shun neither serpents and dragons nor tigers and wolves, so why should I be afraid of you rats?!"

Xu's retort packs several layers of meaning. The first is pure Daoist propaganda. Du borrows her voice to denounce Buddhist clergy as violent and libidinous in an *ad hominem* attack that would certainly anger Buddhist readers. The monks prepare to break their vows of celibacy and inoffensiveness without a second thought. Xu dismisses them contemptuously as rats, not even worthy fearing. In fact, she feels comfortable with fierce predators such as serpents and wolves, and with the symbolic animals of the four directions, including the dragon and tiger—a sure sign of holiness. Secondly, Xu's statement acknowledges that it is difficult for a woman to renounce the household life and to travel freely on her own. Furthermore, she implies that domesticity is harder than living with wild animals, at least if you want to be a female Daoist adept. This contrasts with Du Guangting's praise of family lineages, such her own, that passed Daoist practices along from one generation to the next. Du demonstrates an understanding that the patrilineal system could be good for Daoist men, but was full of conflicts for women.

The plot thickens as the Maiden, ignoring the furious Buddhist monks, lies down and falls asleep. The monks happily plan a gang rape. But Xu foils them, rendering them mute and stiff like corpses. Through her magical techniques, she achieves poetic justice: they are speechless after insulting her with words, and as stiff as erect penises after intending sexual battery against her. Only after she leaves are the monks released from her spell. The modern reader is left wondering what actually happened: was it magic, hypnotism, Freudian hysteria?

Like the Flower Maiden, Transcendent Maiden Xu stayed young in old age. The people regarded her as a divinity. Du Guangting's account claims that she lived at least two hundred and fifty years. In 859, she told Daoist Master Kui Yuntao her story, claiming to be her father's heir in Daoist arts. She further asserts that she inherited his "secret accomplishments," a type of Daoist accumulated virtue that, Du implies here, is superior to the merit that brings good karma in Buddhism. Kui recorded her tale; his now-lost text probably served as a primary source for Du Guangting.

Du closes his account with an exclamation validating Xu Xiangu's claim to have attained her father's Way: "She actually was [Xu] Zhicai's daughter!" Du usually ends with his subject's departure and posthumous celestial office. These twin accomplishments serve to legitimate her as a Daoist saint. But here they are omitted. His case for Xu Xiangu's sainthood rests upon her family connections, miraculous talents, and meritorious work in battling Buddhists, as well as the cult that grew up around her in her own lifetime.

Translation

[115.12a] Transcendent Maiden Xu was the daughter of Assistant Minister Xu [Zhicai] of the Sui dynasty.[150] We do not know who her master was. After several hundred years, her appearance was still that of a twenty-four or – five year old. She was skilled in the arts of interdictions and spells.

She wandered alone within the seas to the Three Rivers, Five Marchmounts, Four Brights, Mounts Luofu and Guacang;[151] there was none of the famous mountains and surpassing scenic spots to which she did not travel. She often spent the night inside forest caves in cliff sides or foothills. She would also stay over in Buddhist monks' closes [hermitages].

Once she was suddenly set upon by several ranks of Buddhist monks who used insulting expressions and insinuating words. The Maiden abruptly and unceremoniously cursed them. Roused to anger, the flock of monks was about to stab her with knives. The tone of their words became increasingly urgent. The Maiden just laughed as she said: "I am a woman and yet I have been able to reject the household life and travel amidst clouds and rivers. I shun neither serpents and dragons nor tigers and wolves, so why should I be afraid of you rats?!" Then she undressed and lay down, quickly snuffing out her candle. [12b] The crowd of monks was happy, thinking they would have their way with her. But the Maiden had devised a plan to emerge safely from

---

150 A short account of Xu Xiangu is found in *Taiping guangji* 295. Her father, Xu Zhicai, was a literatus, shaman, and wonder worker of the Northern Qi dynasty (550-577, absorbed by the Northern Zhou in 577, and taken over by the Sui dynasty in 581). Xu Zhicai also held office under the Sui (589-618). He has biographies in *Bei Qishu* 33 and *Beishi* 90.

151 The Three Rivers region is part of Sichuan province. The Five Marchmounts are the holy mountains of the five directions.. The Four Brights are holy mountains in Zhejiang province. Mount Luofu is a mountain sacred to both Daoists and Buddhists, located in Guangdong province. Guazang is a Daoist holy mountain located in modern Zhejiang.

the mountains the next day. For that whole night, all the monks were stiff-ened, standing like corpses or sitting as if bound in restraints. Their mouths were stopped so that they could not speak. After the Maiden had departed several *li* [the next morning], the monks returned to their former selves.

[The Maiden] came and went south of the Yangzi River. The people of Wu saw her for over forty years.[152] Her color and countenance stayed just as they had been in former times, and she moved as if flying. Wherever she went, people feared and revered her as if she were a divine brilliant [deity]. No one dared treat her incorrectly, belittle her, or insult her.

At the beginning of the Total Comprehension reign period [859-73], she said to Daoist Master Kui Yuntao of the White Crane Belvedere in Zhan county: "My late father held office successively under the Zhou and Sui dynasties. He made his reputation through his prescriptions and arts. His secret accom-plishments reached even to creation. Now I also have obtained his Way. Therefore I have been able to reach beneficent places and extend my years into long life."

Based on this, [Kui Yuntao] made a detailed report on her. She actually was Zhicai's daughter!

---

[152] Wu refers to a Warring States (480-221 B.C.E.) kingdom in the south, and a Three Kingdoms (220-280 C.E.) dynasty, located mostly in Zhejiang. From those early states, Wu comes to refer to southeast China in general.

19. Gou Xiangu

Transcendent Maiden Gou 緱仙姑 (ca. 790-870) is third in a series of Maidens and the second given the title "Transcendent Maiden" in place of a given name. She was another celibate ascetic, and another southerner, from Changsha in Hunan province. She lived at Marchmount Heng, the holy mountain of the south, where she entered the Way. Like the other maidens, she remained youthful looking in old age. Like Hua Gu, she was associated with a shrine of the Shangqing goddess and revealer of texts, Lady Wei Huacun. Like Xu Xiangu, she fought evil Buddhist monks and prevailed. Her biography illustrates several of Du Guangting's favorite themes. He links female subjects like Gou Xiangu with Shangqing deities, creating a divine lineage register that starts with the oldest and highest female deity and ends with the most recent human saint. Du stresses individual self-cultivation as a means of salvation. He attacks the religious competition, Buddhism. He ingratiates himself and his religion with the imperial court and with the official bureaucracy. He shows that women Daoists may teach male disciples, even famous officials. He commends Daoism to the rulers and the people as a source of comfort in apocalyptic times ahead.

Transcendent Maiden Gou practices extreme austerities at a shrine of Lady Wei Huacun located at Mount Heng, perhaps one restored by Hua Gu. She lives alone in the wild, at peace with animals that terrified most travelers. After over ten years of the strictest practice, the Transcendent Maiden receives a visit from a blue bird, a divine messenger of Daoist high divinities and an old symbol of transcendence. This particular bird has red markings on its neck and a long tail, perhaps one of the beautiful pheasants native to southern China. The bird speaks to the Transcendent Maiden, the only person who can understand its language. This cross-species communication is another sign of her sanctity.

The bird explains that she represents Lady Wei Huacun, who admires the maiden's severe asceticism and solitary existence. The Lady has sent the bird to accompany and serve her in her solitude. Later the bird reveals to Gou Xiangu that the maiden is a descendent of the Queen Mother of the West, the subject of Du Guangting's first biography and the divine head of this yin lineage. The Queen Mother herself sends bird messengers, and also had the surname Gou. And the bird hails from Goushi Mountain, where the Queen Mother cultivated the Way and famous immortals such as Wang Ziqiao ascended into heaven. The bird encourages Gou Xiangu, assuring her that the Queen Mother, impressed with her diligence, will send her a realized master to bestow the Way.

In the meantime, the blue bird serves as a psychic butler to the Transcendent Maiden, announcing visitors in advance and describing them in detail. Its predictions always prove accurate. When the bird warns her that violent Buddhist monks are approaching with mayhem in mind, the maiden does not worry. In due course, ten monks arrive, intending to burn her hut and destroy the altar to Lady Wei. But they can neither see the saint nor budge the altar. The ability to disappear at will is a superpower specific to Daoist saints. The altar, a huge stone slab resting on another block of stone, turns out to have an ingenious and perhaps magical mechanism that protects it. This contrivance allows the top slab to move in response to the gentle touch of a single well-intentioned hand, but to lock fast if wicked people attack it, even if they are numerous. When the Buddhist monks try to wreck Lady Wei's altar, the earth trembles and quakes. The monks, unable to budge the stone slab, flee in terror. Tigers eat nine of the monks; only the single monk who abstained from vandalism is spared. The altar and Transcendent Maiden remain unharmed as the blue bird foretold, while enemies of the faith who threatened Daoist holy ground and the saint are punished drastically. Here Du Guangting again resorts to slanderous accusations to besmirch the reputation of Buddhist clergy. At the same time, he highlights the power of the Way to annihilate its enemies and save the faithful from danger in a time of crises.

On the advice of the blue bird, the Transcendent Maiden later moves south. In the meantime, the high court official Zheng Gongtian 鄭公畋 (Zheng Tian), demoted around 870 from his position in the Grand Secretariat in the capital city of Chang'an, is appointed as military governor in Wu county in modern Guangxi. There Zheng encounters the maiden and becomes her disciple. In a poignant farewell to her student, Transcendent Maiden Gou tells Zheng that hard times are coming soon, during which the whole world will suffer. As Du Guangting knew when he compiled this account, the Huang Chao rebellion (878-880) and the final collapse of the Tang dynasty were not far off. The maiden tells Zheng that she can no longer live among humans. After a final divination, she departs for the Nine Uncertainties Mountains (Jiuyi shan). This suggests that Daoist believers during the Tang dynasty regularly turned to divination when faced with important decisions. Her departure is the last we know of her.

Later, in 882, after demonstrating his heroism and loyalty during the Huang Chao rebellion, Zheng Tian was recalled to the imperial court where he probably met Du Guangting. Perhaps disciple Zheng told Du Guangting the story of his teacher.

Translation

[115.13a] Transcendent Maiden Gou was a person from Changsha [Hunan] who entered the Way and dwelt at Mount Heng.[153] At over eighty years of age, her countenance and color seemed extremely youthful.

At the altar of Lady Wei beneath Marchmount [Heng], [Gou] made her practice essential and [performed rituals using] incense and fire for over ten years. She was alone without a companion. Right near the altar were many tigers and wolves. Usually when people traveled there they had to join companions and carry weapons before they dared to enter. But the Transcendent Maiden, deeply concealed within [the altar], was never afraid of anything.

After several years, there was a blue bird, similar in shape to a dove or pigeon, with a red neck and long tail, that came flying to her dwelling.[154] The bird said, quite naturally: "I am an emissary of the Lady of the Southern Marchmount Wei Huacun]. Because the Maiden practices the Way essentially and harshly, perching alone at the extreme end of the forest, [the Lady] has ordered me to become your comrade."

Another day [the bird] spoke again: "The Queen Mother of the West has the surname Gou. She is in fact the Maiden's incomparable ancestor. She heard that the Maiden has been practicing the Way so that your diligence is perfected. She will send down a realized official to bestow the Way upon you. But that time has not yet arrived. You should exert yourself in practice and be sharp."

---

[153] Another account of Gou Xiangu is found in *Taiping guangji* 296. An earlier translation of Du Guangting's biography appears in Schafer 1979. Changsha is today the provincial capital of Hunan. It was an important Daoist center in the Han dynasty, with artifacts and manuscripts unearthed at nearby Mawangdui.

[154] The blue bird is an emissary of the great goddesses; she is employed by Lady Wei and also by the Queen Mother of the West. See # 1 above.

Whenever anyone was traveling in the mountains in the area, the blue bird always announced his or her name to the Maiden in advance. When the day arrived [that the traveler came, the bird] she proved correct in every detail. [13b] [The bird] also said, "The place south of the Yellow River on Mount Goushi [in Yanshi, Henan], where the Queen Mother cultivated the Way, is my old mountain home."

Another day the blue bird came flying to say: "This evening there will be violent strangers but [they can do you] no harm, so do not fear them." That evening indeed ten or more Buddhist monks came. Now the Lady Wei's transcendent altar was a huge stone slab some ten feet in circumference. Underneath, it seemed to float upon another projecting stone. If a single person were to push it with his hand, [the altar] would tremble and move. But if many people did so, it would just stand there like a mountain peak.

That night, the group of monks entered her apartment carrying fire and grasping swords with the intention of harming the Transcendent Maiden. The Maiden was on her bed, but the monks did not see her. After going out the gate, they shoved the transcendent altar in order to harm it. Suddenly there was a rumbling noise; mountains quaked and valleys split open. One would have thought that the altar had already toppled off, but in the end [the monks] could not budge it. Those monks all scattered and fled. At dawn one of them reached a distant village. The other nine monks, having separated and scattered, were gnawed to death by tigers. [14a] Only the monk who had not joined in the evil deed when they were shoving the altar escaped being harmed by tigers. The Lady's transcendent altar remained upright and undamaged. The Maiden was also uninjured. Over a year later the blue bird told the Maiden to move her dwelling to a transcendent place. Accordingly she moved to dwell south of the lakes [Hunan]. The bird also followed her. Other people never understood its speech.

After our National Minister, the Civil and Luminous Zheng Gongtian, was demoted from the office of Scholarly Gentleman who Receives Decrees to become the Shepherd of Wu, he served the Maiden as his teacher.[155] The Maiden told the Civil and Luminous Worthy: "After the present time, all within the four seas will encounter many difficulties. I cannot dwell much longer among humans. I will perform divinations, and then retreat into Jiuyi shan [Nine Uncertainties Mountains in southern Hunan]." And so one morning she departed.

---

[155] Zheng Gongtian is the Tang court official Zheng Tian. During the period 869-874, he was demoted from a position in the Grand Secretariat in the central government in the capital city of Chang'an to a provincial post as military governor of Wu county in modern Guangxi. Zheng has biographies in *Jiu Tangshu* 178.4630-38 and *Xin Tangshu*. 185..5401-05.

20. The Tea Granny of Guangling

This odd story seems out of time and place in Du Guangting's collection. Some of the biographies fit well in the genealogical scheme I discern in Du's work. Others like this one remind me of how incomplete and even tautological such constructions after the fact can be. The Tea Granny of Guangling (Guangling chalao 廣陵茶姥) resembles a character from folk legend more than a historical individual. She may simply have been a favorite of Du and his patrons, or the center of a now-vanished local cult. Nevertheless, her story brings several ideas to light. Her teapot reminds us of the beginning of widespread use of tea in China during the Tang dynasty and of tea's connection with medicine, wakefulness, and both Daoist and Buddhist meditation.[156]

Like the maidens, the Tea Granny is a southerner who travels alone without fear. She looks old, but nowhere near her real age, which must be at least two hundred and fifty years. Her youthfully keen senses and thick black hair testify to her transcendence. As a crone of unknown name, clan, or origin, she is also the stereotype of a Chinese granny: ancient, wise, and slightly frightening. In the Tang, old women functioned as midwives, go-betweens, and healers: liminal people who could cross the boundaries between women and men, family and outsiders. They play important roles in Buddhist as well as Daoist tales. Tea Granny crosses the lines between old lady and witch, human and spirit, humor and hagiography.

Tea Granny has literary precursors such as the Incomparable Mother of the Eastern Tumulus (Dongling shengmu 東陵聖母), a fourth-century saint whose husband had her jailed for neglecting her wifely duties to pursue religious practices. The Incomparable Mother also escaped by flying out of the prison window. Ge Hong tells her story in his *Shenxian zhuan*. Du was familiar with the Incomparable Mother, for he mentioned her in the biography of Xue Xuantong (# 27), whose husband also criticized her when she chose religious over domestic practice. Many such tales appear in collections that combine legend, ghost story, and biography. Some were privately produced, like Ge Hong's work and Duan Chengshi's 段成式 (800-863) *Youyang zebu* 酉陽雜俎 (Tray of Meats from

---

[156] On tea in Buddhism and Chinese culture, see Kieschnick 2003, ch. 4.

Youyang). Others were published with imperial sponsorship, such as the Song encyclopedia *Taiping guangji*.

Like Du's other subjects, Tea Granny possesses magical powers. Du usually stresses the rigorous religious practice required to attain supernatural abilities. Hers are simply taken for granted. Tea Granny's calling card is a bottomless teapot. No matter how much tea she sells in the marketplace, her pot is always full. And no matter how long she serves the tea, it is always fresh. This resembles the bottomless wine pot and wish-fulfilling tree of Yangping Shi (# 24). It also recalls the wish-granting carp in Duan's story of Yexian, the world's first Cinderella tale.

Tea Granny's story warns the reader that regular ignorant folk often cannot recognize immortals. We may become suspicious of them and even abuse or imprison them. We may mistake them for madmen or dishonest merchants. This presumably is not good for the merit of the abusers. We should be on the lookout for transcendents in disguise who may appear at any time to test our faith. This will become an important theme in the cult of the Daoist Immortal Lü Dongbin 呂洞賓 in the centuries to come. In the present case, all ends well as Tea Granny calls on another of her magical powers to escape her captors and leave them baffled. She simply flies out of the jailhouse window and departs. That is the last we see of her. Du implies but does not specifically record her ascension.

Translation

[115.14a] As for the Tea Granny of Guangling [Jiangsu], we do not know her surname, clan, or home village.[157] She usually looked like a person seventy years old, yet she was light and sturdy and possessed strength. Her ears were keen and her eyes bright. Her hair was thick and black. Descendents of the immigrants who had crossed to the south at the beginning of the [Eastern] Jin Dynasty [317] passed it down that they had seen her from days of old and that her face and appearance had not changed in over a hundred years.[158] [14b] Whenever she went to town carrying her pot of tea to sell, townspeo-

---

[157] A later biography of the Tea Granny is found in *Taiping guangji* 66.297.

[158] Immigrants to the south refers to the flood of northern refugees after the Western Jin dynasty (265-317) capitals of Luoyang and Chang'an were sacked in 311 and 317. At this time numerous people moved from the central plains of the Yellow River valley to the Yangtze River regions. The Eastern Jin dynasty, formed after the southern crossing, lasted from 317 to 420.

ple competed to purchase [tea from her]. From dawn to dusk she sold a great deal of tea, yet the tea inside her pot always seemed newly steeped and never disappeared or diminished. Most people found this very strange. The officials of the province, using laws regarding fraud, bound her up in jail. The granny then grasped the pot she had been using to sell tea and departed by flying out the [jailhouse] window.[159]

---

[159] For a study of the granny figure in later Chinese literature and culture, see Cass 1999. On the immortal Lu Dongbin, see Katz 1999. For a translation of the first Cinderella tale, see Ko 2001, 26-27. A beautifully illustrated children's book that retells the same story and includes a facsimile of Duan's text is found in Young and Louie 1982.

21. The Lady of the Southern Stygian Realm

This puzzling entry seems, at first glance, imperfectly related to other accounts in Du Guangting's "Records." The name Lady of the Southern Stygian Realm (Nanming furen 南溟夫人) suggests that she is another southerner, but it also links her to underworlds. Also, the account does not really seem to be about her. The opening reads like the official account of a great goddess, then quickly turns into a meandering and extremely entertaining yarn about two hapless male adepts and their farcical struggles with the celestial bureaucracy.

But under its odd characters and twisted plot, the tale reiterates several central themes of Du's collection. The language rivals Buddhist sutras in doctrine, setting, and drama. The plot line is a comic version of the pilgrim's progress to the Way that Du renders so earnestly in other entries. And a story within the story narrates the love of a minor goddess in the entourage of the Lady for a beautiful youth from Canton. Their union produces a semi-divine child who descends to the Southern Marchmount. Du flatters the Tang and Former Shu emperors by providing them with a divine lineage, suggesting dynastic legitimacy and uncontested possession of the mandate of heaven.

Du Guangting refers sarcastically throughout his account to Yuan Zheng 元徵 and Liu Shi 柳實, our unheroic and otherwise unknown Daoist buffoons, as "our two masters." They retire together to cultivate the Way at Mount Heng, ancient holy mountain of the south (in Hunan province). Perhaps unnerved by the rigors of ascetic life, they next travel by boat even further south, to Hanoi. There they remain alone on board while the sailors enjoy a local festival. When a hurricane springs up, they are swept out to sea, and come ashore at a mysterious island. After entering a deserted temple containing Daoist images along with signs of recent worship, they look back over the ocean where they watch a huge sea god surface, look around, and sink back under the waves.

Still gazing out over the water, they are astounded to see a purple cloud emerge, followed by a hundred-foot lotus that surges up and then opens, petal by petal. Inside is a white silk tent: the Lady's dwelling. A rainbow-colored bridge stretches from the lotus platform to the island, and a divine female attendant comes down to burn incense before the image in the temple. Surprised, the attendant asks them what they are doing there. Our two clueless adepts blurt out their whole story, begging her to save them and show them the road home. She, being just a functionary, tries to pass them up the bureaucracy. A Daoist gentleman riding a white deer fortuitously joins them. When they make their pitiful pleas to him, he tells them to follow the female attendant and pay respects to the Lady of the Southern Stygian Realm.

Soon they kowtow before the Lady's silk tent and tell her their tale of woe. It happens that her master, the Honored Teacher of the Jade Barrens (Yuxu zunshi 玉虛尊師), is about to visit her. He arrives and they have a celestial feast reminiscent of the celebrations the Queen Mother of the West shares with King Mu of the Zhou and the Martial Thearch of the Han. The ceremonial banquet is part of a Daoist transmission ritual. Amid music and delicacies, the Honored Teacher gives sacred scrolls to the Lady. But here Du pushes to the margins of his story the scriptural transmission that often occupies the center of a hagiography. The Honored Teacher tells the two visitors that they will find their way home as long as they keep the breath of the Way, that he has just the right drug to help them, and that he is not their master but they are destined to meet one. Encouragement and predictions from deities often feature in Du Guangting's accounts. The Honored Teacher departs on deer-back, suggesting that he is the same gentleman who told our seekers to request an audience with the Lady in the first place.

Suddenly a martial giant one hundred feet tall appears, clad in gold armor and brandishing a huge sword. Deferentially, he reports to the Lady that, according to her instructions, he has executed the ancient sea deity known as Tianwu 天吳 for dereliction of duty. Apparently Tianwu was a secret service dragon, commissioned to secure the roads for divinities.

After the giant warrior departs, the Lady of the Southern Stygian Realm gives our silly masters leave to depart and sends her female attendant to direct them home. The Lady gives them a magical jade pot to strike if they need help *en route*, then produces an uncanny bridge woven from snakes and dragons that leads back to the island. Crossing it, they see Tianwu's decapitated corpse and discover that he was executed for failing to recognize and divert the two of them.

Now things become even more complicated. The accompanying female attendant tells her charges that there must be a divine purpose in their meeting. Giving them an amber box, she confesses that she is a water-transcendent who had a passionate affair with a mortal human man and bore him a child. The theme of love affairs between female immortals and mortal men is endlessly replayed in the Daoist tales and literati ghost stories of the Tang. The attendant's confession calls to mind shamans, fox fairies, and the Shangqing goddesses who use the language of seduction to teach human adepts.

The Lady forced her attendant to give up her son for adoption to the Esquire Ruler of the Southern Marchmount (Nanyue langwang 南岳郎王) when the child was only three years old. This reminds the reader of the instability of unions between divinities and mortals, and of the separation between Heaven and Earth that both gods and humans long to cross. It also calls our attention to the power of the superior goddess, similar to that of the first wife in a polygamous Tang household, that allows her to dispose of the children of lower-ranking females as she sees fit. After the adoption, the attendant asked a minor deity from Mount Heng who happened to be passing through to take her boy a beloved plaything, his jade ring. But the envoy betrayed her and pocketed the precious object. Seeing a chance for redress, she asks the two adepts to take an amber box to the peak on Mount Heng from which the treacherous deity had come, throw it into his ancestral temple, recover the stolen jade ring, and deliver it to her son.

Our hapless duo journeys home, obtaining food when needed by knocking on the jade pot, which turns out to be a wish-fulfilling vessel like the Teapot Granny's. But when they arrive, they find that twelve years have passed, their families believe them lost at sea, and their wives have died.

Even more convinced that they should renounce the world, Yuan Che and Liu Shi set out to honor their transcendent guide's request and toss the amber box into her betrayer's ancestral hall. When they do so, an enormous black dragon rushes out, knocking down trees and houses, and destroying the offender's ancestral temple at Mount Huiyan (Returning Wild Goose Peak). As our two masters shake with fright, a celestial appears in space and hands them the stolen jade ring. As promised, they take it to the temple of the Esquire Ruler of the Southern Marchmount.

Returning home again, they find a lad clad in yellow garments who respectfully presents each of them with a golden box as a gift from the grateful Esquire Ruler of the Southern Marchmount. It holds a potent ointment for resurrecting the dead, even those departed for a full cycle of sixty years. The two masters use the ointment to anoint the heads of their deceased wives, restoring them to life.

Then the real reward comes. During a freezing snowstorm, the two masters take pity on an old wood-cutter and offer him wine. Suddenly the characters "Grand Ultimate" appear on his hat. They realize that have at last met their teacher and pay him reverence. The deity in disguise in turn reveals his identity as the Prior-Born of the Grand Ultimate (Taiji xiansheng 太極先生), sent by the Grand Supreme to ordain them. He recognizes their jade wish-fulfilling pot as the old wine jug in which he had long ago stored his jade liqueur. They return the pot, then happily follow their teacher into a grotto heaven palace called the Vermilion Tumulus at Zhu Rong's Peak in Mount Heng. This place has already figured in several of Du's biographies of transcendents of the grotto heavens. After passing through the appropriate bureaus of the celestial bureaucracy, they ascend to heaven together with their wives.

While some earlier entries directly attack Buddhism by denigrating Buddhist monks, the story of the two Daoist stooges employs the subtler rhetorical strategy of co-opting Buddhist language, scenes, and teachings for Daoist uses. Here Du appropriates terms, stories, and visual descriptions found in sacred texts such as the *Lotus Sutra* and *Pure Land Sutra*. These Buddhist scriptures, the most illustrated in medieval Chinese art, figure prominently in paintings at the cave temples of Dunhuang on the Silk Road. Such art helped spread Buddhism among the Chinese masses.

Du Guangting phrases his descriptions of Daoist heavens, even the minor heaven of the lady of the Southern Stygian Realm, to rival paradise scenes from the Pure Land of Amitabha Buddha. His portrayals of Daoist feasts and ceremonies compete with the most elaborate and theatrical stagings of the sermons of Shakyamuni Buddha in the *Lotus Sutra*. As in other biographies, Du appropriates Buddhist terminology, calling the Daoist high gods "Heavenly Honored," a term Buddhist translators associated with the cosmic and eternal Buddha. And he repossesses the powerful symbol of the lotus from Buddhists, along with the meanings that the Buddhists had added to that symbol, such as purity and human potential. In illustrations of the Pure Land Sutras, the new-born souls of the devout sit on lotus flower seats, listening to the wisdom of the cosmic Buddha Amitabha. Here the lotus provides a stage for a small above-water dwelling of the goddess, and suggests her ability to move between the underwater and earthly realms.

Du's Daoist rhetoric competes with Buddhism in describing spectacles. In creating suspense and entertainment, several stories in Du's collection, including this one, rival the Buddhist tales designed for public performance, and intended to instruct and convert the audience. Examples would include some of the Tang and earlier "transformation texts" found hidden in a cave at Dunhuang in Gansu province. One of the most famous is the story of Maudgalyayana saving his mother from hell, a story addressed to a Chinese audience that combines violence, horror, filial piety, and Buddhist teachings. This account reads like the script for a just such a lively public performance. It has everything: comedy, sex, murder, mischief, magic, danger, and suspense. The Daoists must also have proselytized by giving sermons in the marketplace that included an entertaining mix of moralizing and fabulous tales. Perhaps one such tale is the origin of this account. It is also easy to imagine the adventures of the Lady and the two masters as a puppet show or temple drama.

Through the vehicle of his two comic actors, Du Guangting proclaims the efficacy of the Way. Daoism is so infallible that even these fools can be saved. Here Du responds to the popular story from the twelfth chapter of the *Lotus Sutra* about the dragon's daughter, a learned young lady the text recognizes as a future Buddha. The Mahayana Buddhist message is that everyone has buddha nature and the Middle Way is so effective that even a woman, even a child, even a nonhuman can follow it and achieve full and complete enlightenment. Taking on the *Lotus Sutra*, Du implicitly claims that Daoist practices are so potent that they too can save even these idiots, and by implication, even women.

The literary image of the Daoist master as innocent fool is a character that goes back at least to pre-Qin times, to the Zhuangzi and the *Yufu* 魚

父 (Fishing Father) poem of the *Chuci* 楚辭 (Odes of Chu). The guileless bumblers, saved almost despite themselves, remind us of Zhuangzi's misfits and cripples who challenge conventional virtue and aesthetics. There is nothing heroic about these two weeping cowards. They try to practice the Way on a mountain like good hermits, but wander off in a boat, only to encounter a hurricane and be blown to paradise. For the Chinese reader, this entry would recall the famous story called *Taohua yuan* 桃花源 (Peach Blossom Spring) by Tao Yuanming 陶淵明 (365-427), in which a lucky fisherman loses his way and enters a utopian lost world. The comic adventures of our two masters read more like a Daoist soap opera. Just trying to go home, they experience one extreme event after another, continually helped by celestial bureaucrats and even major gods, until they fumble their way into immortality.

The account of Yuan Che and Liu Shi is reminiscent of another famous story by Du Guangting: "The Curly-Bearded Hero." That tale presents a fictional account of figures involved in the founding of the Tang dynasty and the rise of Li Shimin 李世民 (599-649) to become emperor Taizong in 618. From Du's standpoint, at the end of the Tang and beginning of the Former Shu, he interprets the earlier dynastic succession from Sui to Tang in terms of establishing order and legitimacy.

Running through Du's collection of lives of female transcendents is a thread linking his own era to that of Xuanzong, recognized as a high point and also a turning point for the Tang dynasty. Du implies that the Former Shu inherited the mandate of Heaven from the Tang. (And if this is true, Du commits no disloyalty by serving first the Tang and then the Former Shu.) Du Guangting hints that the baby boy of mixed divine and human parentage might even be the emperor Xuanzong. In the following biography of Bian Dongxuan, a transcendent disguised as an old man identifies Xuanzong as a divinity, specifically the Realized Person of the Southern Palace of the Grand Unity from the Vermilion Yang. This Realized Person may be the adopted son of the Esquire Ruler of the Southern Marchmount. The assertion of such an eminent lineage would flatter both the Li and the Wang families, providing them with a divine ancestry that the Wang clan rulers of Former Shu inherit from the Li clan rulers of the Tang dynasty. Such a claim about the imperial lineage would help explain the presence of this entertaining and theatrical account of two Daoist Masters in a book about female transcendents.

Within the Daoist world, Du Guangting asserts the supremacy of Shangqing revelations over Daoist cults and schools of the past. The Lady of the Southern Stygian Realm rules the old god of the sea, Tianwu, and the ancient water goddesses.

In summary, Du Guangting could have justified his inclusion of this apparently incongruous tale in his records on several counts. The story shows humans interacting with and learning from deities, women receiving and transmitting holy scriptures, and husbands and wives ascending together to heaven to join the celestial bureaucracy. It takes place at a location (Mount Heng) sacred to Daoists. The narrative competes with Buddhist offerings of visual spectacle and dramatic entertainment, and it supports Tang and Former Shu claims to divine descent and legitimate rule.

Translation

[116.1a] The Lady of the Southern Stygian Realms lived in the middle of the South Seas [Canton].[160] We do not know the degree of her class or rank. She probably descended as a divine transcendent who had obtained the Way.

Once there were two men, Yuan Cheng and Liu Shi, who formed the same intention to search for the Way They wove together a thatched hut on Mount Heng within which to roost and retire. After over a year, they went south together, reaching Hepu district in Guangzhou province.[161] They climbed into a boat, intending to cross the Viet Sea to its southern shore. They got off at Jiaozhi [Hanoi] and tied their boat beside the bank. It so happened that the villagers were just then making offerings to their deities, with syrinxes and drums giving a loud performance. The boatmen and longshoremen, along with the servants and messengers, all went over to watch it. Only our two masters remained inside the boat. [1b]

---

160 This biography was previously translated in Schafer 1979. On Buddhist influence on Daoism, see Zürcher 1980. For a translation of the story of Maudgalyayana, see Mair 1994b. For a translation of the "Fishing Father" poem, see Hawkes 1959, 90-91. For a translation of Tao Yuanming's "Peach Blossom Spring," see Hightower 2000; Bokenkamp 1986. For a translation of "The Curly-Bearded Hero," see Birch 1974. For other traditional tales, see Ma and Lau 1978. The Southern Stygia and Northern Stygia appear in the *Zhuangzi*. One referent of Stygian Sea is the eastern sea around the magical Mount Penglai, the island abode of the immortals.

161 On the south of China during the Tang dynasty, see Schafer 1967.

Suddenly a hurricane blew in, severed the ropes, and spun the boat off into the sea. Nobody knew where they went. They came close to sinking two or three times. All of the sudden they came to shore at a single lonely island. The wind and waves also settled down. When our two masters climbed onto the bank, they looked as far as they could on the island and saw a white jade image of the Heavenly Honored [One], residing resplendently inside a stone room.[162] In front of it was a golden brazier, its incense all burned to ashes, but nobody was there. Our two masters looked all around. Gazing off dejectedly into the far distance, they saw a huge beast emerge from inside the waves. It looked as if it detected something. After a good long time, it sank back down.

Suddenly a purple cloud burst from the surface of the sea, flowing abundantly for three or four *li*. In its midst was a great lotus flower, over a hundred feet high. Petal by petal, it revolved and opened. Inside was a curtained tent of white tabby-weave silk with embroidery of a complexly interwoven [design]. A rainbow bridge several tens of feet wide reached directly down to the top of the island, where a female attendant offered up incense in front of an image of the Heavenly Honored One. Before the incense had finished burning, our two masters mournfully beseeched her, seeking rescue and requesting to be shown the road home. The female attendant exclaimed in surprise, "How did you get here so quickly?" After they explained the whole business to her, the female attendant said, "In a little while the Lady of the Southern Stygian Realm has an appointment with the Honored Teacher of the Jade Barrens. [2a] You masters may try to make your request to her."

Before the female attendant had even departed, there was a Daoist Gentleman who arrived riding over the multi-colored clouds on a white deer. Our two masters wept mournfully as they made their report to him. The Daoist Gentleman said: "You may follow this woman [the female attendant] to pay respects to the Lady of the Southern Stygian Realm."

After our two masters received his instructions, they followed the female attendant and climbed the bridge to arrive in front of the curtains [of the Lady's] tent. They repeatedly bowed and kowtowed. The told her how they

---

162 Heavenly Honored One (Tianzun) is a title reserved for the three highest deities of Daoism, including the Queen Mother of the West's teacher, the Heavenly Honored One of the Primordial Commencement. The term is used by Buddhists to honor the Buddha. It is thought to translate Sanskrit Tathāgata, which is also translated into Chinese as *rulai* or *ruchu*, meaning the "Thus-Come or Thus-Departed One." It is likely that Daoists borrowed the term or took it back from Buddhist sutras translated from the Sanskrit.

came to be drifters and wanderers, narrating their surnames and chosen names. The Lady ordered them to sit down. Then the Honored Teacher also arrived. They sat in a ring while music was performed, and in a short time were presented with delicacies. The Honored Teacher said: "Our two guests need delicacies suitable for humans." So these were presented to them.

When the delicacies were finished, the Honored Teacher gave the Lady a scroll written in cinnabar seal script. The Lady bowed and accepted it. When this was completed, the Honored Teacher announced his departure and told our two masters: "You have the breath of the Way, so don't worry about the road home. It just happens that I have numinous drugs to give you. It is your lot not yet to have joined with a suitable master for yourselves. I am not your proper master. But you'll see him another day." Our two masters bowed in farewell. The Honored Teacher departed, riding his deer. [2b]

Shortly afterwards, a martial hero over one hundred feet tall, wearing gold armor and holding a sword, advanced and said: "According to the commission I received, [the water spirit] Tianwu did not clear the roads according to the standard, and so he had to be executed as an example. Now I have carried out that punishment." Thereupon he hurried away and sank out of sight.

The Lady then ordered the female attendant to show our two masters the road home. She told them: "Depart following the Hundred Flower Bridge." She gave them a jade pot and said: "If you have any problems on the road ahead, just knock on this pot." At that, they took leave of the Lady, climbed onto the bridge, and departed.

The bridge was long as well as wide, and all along the railing were strange flowers. Our two masters, peering among the flowers, saw a thousand snakes and a myriad dragons, knotted and woven together so as to make the bridge. They saw the huge beast they had seen earlier, its body and head floating in different places among the waves. Our two masters asked the envoy accompanying them [the Lady's female attendant] the reason for the beast's dismemberment. She replied: "The reason is that he did not recognize you two guests."

Then their envoy told the two strangers: "I was not [originally] supposed to serve as an envoy and accompany you. So there must have been some deep meaning to my wanting to accept the assignment." From within the belt of her robe, she untied a box of amber and gave it to them. [3a] Inside it was something that vaguely resembled a spider in shape.

She told our two masters "I am a water transcendent. Once I experienced the ultimate of passionate delight with a youth from Panyu [Canton]. We had one son who was three years old when I was fated to abandon him. The Lady ordered me to give [my son] to the Esquire Ruler of the Southern Marchmount to become his [adopted] son. In the middle of all this, an envoy from Returning Wild Goose Peak had business with the Bureau of Waterways, so I commissioned [this envoy] to take the jade ring that my son used to play with and give it to him. But the envoy hid the ring, and in the end my hopes were disappointed by him. You two guests may take this box to Returning Wild Goose Peak and throw it into the ancestral temple there. Then if you obtain the jade ring and accompany it to the ancestral temple at the Southern Marchmount, my son will certainly reward you. Take care that you neither open nor reveal it." So our two masters accepted the box and hid it inside their robes.

Then they inquired [of the envoy] about what the Honored Teacher of the Jade Barrens had meant when he said they would have a teacher of their own. Who had he meant? She told them: "[Your teacher] is in fact the Prior-Born of the Grand Ultimate from the Southern Marchmount. You will be meeting him yourselves." In an instant the bridge came to an end and the envoy departed from them. They had already reached the shores of Hepu. When they asked about what era it was, twelve years had already passed. [3b]

Thereupon they planned to return to Mount Heng, but in the middle of their journey they became extremely hungry. When they tried knocking on the jade pot, rare treats arrived. Once our two masters had finished eating, they did not feel hunger or thirst again. When they finally returned, their wives had already departed from the world, and their family members said: "It has been over ten years since my lord esquires drowned at sea!" From this time on, our two masters increasingly wanted to abandon the mundane world and no longer had the heart to become famous statesmen.

They did indeed climb Marchmount Heng and throw the box into the ancestral temple at Returning Wild Goose Peak. Between a blink and a breath, along came a black dragon several tens of feet long, blasting wind and snorting thunder, splitting trees and scattering houses. With a single sound of thunder, the building and grounds of the ancestral temple were smashed. As they trembled in fear, a person appeared in the midst of empty space. He gave them a jade ring. Our two masters took the ring and accompanied it to the ancestral temple on the marchmount.

Upon their returning home, there was a yellow-clothed youth holding two golden boxes who toasted our two masters, saying: "The Esquire Ruler of the Southern Marchmount has been keeping this ointment for restoring the soul in order to repay milords. Now if someone in your household has died a violent death, even after a whole *jiazi* [sixty-year] cycle, if you anoint the top of [the victim's] head with this ointment, then she will come [back] to life. As soon as they took it, they lost sight of that messenger. Our two masters accordingly, by means of anointing them with this ointment, brought their wives back to life. [4a]

Afterwards, on the occasion of a great snow they saw an old firewood carrier, bearing his burden in the freezing bitter cold. Taking pity on his old age, our two masters gave him wine to drink. Suddenly they saw on his hat brim the characters: "Grand Ultimate." Accordingly they paid him ritual respects and treated him as their teacher. He told them: "I have obtained the Way of the divine transcendents. I have listed my name at the Grand Ultimate. Now the Grand Supreme has ordered me to come and ordain you masters." Then when he saw the jade pot, he said: "This is the pot in which I stored my jade liqueur. I lost it many tens of *jiazi* [sixty-year cycles] ago. I am so happy to see it again!" So they offered him the jade pot. Then our two masters followed the Prior-Born of the Grand Ultimate and entered the Palace of the Vermilion Tumulus at Zhu Rong's Peak.[163] They wandered through the various transcendent bureaus, and together with their wives they obtained the Way of ascending to heaven.

---

[163] The Palace of the Vermilion Tumulus at Zhu Rong's Peak is located inside Mount Heng. Du Guangting lists it as third of thirty-six lesser grotto heavens. This location is associated with several others subjects of Du Guangting's collection, especially the transcendents of the grotto heavens. Zhu Rong is an ancient god of fire and metallurgy.

22. Bian Dongxuan

One of the most powerful accounts in the entire collection, Du Guang-ting's life of Bian Dongxuan 邊洞玄 (Grotto Mystery, 628-711) is replete with Du's signature themes. He clarifies doctrinal issues, carries on his running argument with Buddhism, portrays the ideal female adept ac-cording to the Shangqing school of Daoism, and links Daoism to the Tang royal family. His comments add to our information about the con-tested subjects of family and gender roles in medieval China. He even provides clues about the economic foundations of Tang Daoist convents.

Du's account of Bian Dongxuan resonates with modern as well as me-dieval issues. An extreme example of asceticism, Bian takes control of her life by fasting and entering a convent. She embodies the current de-bate about predominantly female disorders such as anorexia and self-mutilation, behaviors that some psychologists have interpreted as at-tempts on the part of their practitioners to heal themselves and exercise some self-determination in their own lives. We might understand both medieval religious practices and modern women better if we compare them. To an outsider, and even to her fellow nuns, Bian Dongxuan's fast-ing and ingesting drugs that led directly to her death looks like deranged self-destruction. When we know her own interpretation of her behavior, it makes more sense. She believed that she was approaching perfection and transcendence through her rigorous physical practices.[164]

Du Guangting would agree, drawing upon the entire Shangqing Daoist tradition of individual self-cultivation that lay behind him. With her hidden good works, fasting, and ingesting elixir drugs, Bian Dongxuan is Du's ideal female Shangqing adept. She and Wang Fajin (# 15), Du's personification of the ideal Lingbao Daoist woman, are the only Tang subjects in his book who unambiguously attain the highest form of tran-scendence available to human beings: ascending to heaven in broad day-

---

[164] On anorexia and fasting in the medieval Christian west, see Bell 1985. On women and fasting in the medieval Christian west, see Bynum 1987. On the practice of women cut-ting themselves, see Strong 1998. On asceticism, including fasting, for Chinese Daoist women, see Cahill 2003.

light. Since they receive the greatest reward, we may conclude that Wang Fajin and Bian Dongxuan represent female perfection for the two schools he attempts to join in so many of his writings.

Perhaps Bian Dongxuan's biography provides a clue about distinctions between Daoist religious practice for women and for men in medieval China. Women are associated in the medieval Christian West with fasting and eating only special sacred foods while feeding others. What is more, medieval Western women might also abstain from sexual intercourse and childbearing as part of their austerities. Bian Dongxuan exhibits the same complex of behaviors. These women were giving up what they could give up, controlling what they could control: their bodies and the corporeal functions of eating and childbearing. Both Western and Chinese male ascetics tended to give up wealth, public position, and family ties, their arena of action and so their biggest sacrifices. But we must not make too much of this distinction, as Daoist male practitioners also fasted and remained celibate. Apparently the normative family activities of eating and reproducing were harmful to the religious aspirations of both male and female Daoists.

In the life of Bian Dongxuan, one of the most detailed in his records, Du Guangting touches upon several of his favorite themes. He engages in a debate with Buddhism by appropriating titles such as "Heavenly Honored" and virtues such as compassion. He presents Bian's hidden virtue as the Daoist answer to compassion, a quality that Mahayana Buddhists had long claimed exclusively. Hidden virtue also figures as the most powerful form of good works, leading to immortality as merit leads to enlightenment in Buddhism. Du describes his subject as a model saint, compelling enough to rival any cult figure in Buddhist literature.

Du Guangting continues his program of associating Daoism with the Tang royal family and its heavenly mandate. The Emperor Xuanzong (r. 712-756) figures in this tale, as does his younger sister, the Tang princess and Daoist nun, Yuzhen or Jade Realization. Du implies that the emperor's deep interest in Daoism and the princess's ordination were both due to Bian Dongxuan's influence.

In his life of Bian Dongxuan, Du Guangting also affirms the Confucian family values held by royalty and literati officials. He praises his subject for her filial piety in caring for her aging parents and mourning them so fiercely. And he commends her womanly virtue and discipline as a skilled weaver. In these ways, she fulfills the ideals of Confucian female virtue. In other ways, as we will see, her behavior flies in the face of everything the traditional patrilineal family holds dear.

Bian Dongxuan represents the rare northerner in Du Guangting's collection. She came from the region around modern Beijing, an unimportant town at the time. The rebel An Lushan (d. 756) and the Daoist poet Li Bo (701-762) hailed from the same place. A precocious child in both intelligence and compassion, she fed starving creatures. They in turn recognized and flocked to her. As in other biographies, here animal friends bespeak virtue.

At the age of fifteen, Bian told her parents that she wanted to become a Daoist nun and devote her life to practicing austerities. This instigated a family crisis, with filial piety and religious vocation in conflict. From her parents' point of view, to remain unmarried and childless would be both unfilial and disloyal. But nothing was stronger than her desire to practice Daoist self-cultivation, so she refused to marry.

Instead, she performed daughterly duties by nurturing her parents in their old age. Perhaps already elderly when she was born, they soon conveniently died. She mourned them with unusual intensity, to the point of endangering her own life. This is part of a pattern of extreme behavior typical of Bian. After completing her period of mourning, Bian requested admission to a Daoist convent. As she had no surviving close relatives to support her financially or to object, the nuns accepted her.

Once settled in the convent, Bian Dongxuan turned out to be a skilled and industrious weaver. She worked tirelessly to support her new household, earning the other nuns' respect. Du remarks that this establishment supported itself entirely by textile work, giving us a glimpse at the economic foundations of female religious institutions during the Tang dynasty. This particular convent may have been completely self-supporting through textile production. He also depicts weaving nuns as the epitome of female industry, discipline, and chastity, an image harmonious with social expectations of women and womanly work in Tang China.

Whenever she earned extra money, Bian used it to buy food that she hid away. This detail tells us that, in her order at least, individual nuns might keep a portion of their earnings. The other nuns, perhaps suspicious of a poor orphan's motives for entering a convent in the first place, teased her about eating secretly during the long cold nights. She did not bother to reply, but in fact she was feeding rats and birds. As a result, no animals ever bothered the nuns' food stores. Du interprets this as the creatures' natural response to her hidden virtue. This reflects the Daoist notion of reciprocity between adepts and the natural world, as well as Daoist beliefs in a holistic and interconnected universe.

Bian Dongxuan loved elixir drugs and was eager to experiment with almost anything that came her way, even if it made her deathly ill. She followed the path of external alchemy, actually ingesting physical substances. Others among Du's subjects practiced inter alchemy, in which

A divine lady busy at her loom

the elixir of immortality is compounded within the adept's body through a process of energetic circulation and visualization. Du himself elsewhere favors internal alchemy, and he takes pains here to assert that it was only after decades of austere practice that Bian achieved immortality through taking elixirs. Du graphically describes Bian's agonizing digestive symptoms, remarking that she never complained but just started again as soon as she recovered. Her sisters worried about her excessive drug use and pleaded with her to stop this risky behavior, but they had no better luck in the face of her determination than her parents. Bian continued to fast, ingest elixirs, and distribute food to the needy.

After many years, a Daoist immortal turned up at the convent, disguised as an aged seller of herbal medicines. His appearance introduces an interlude in which Du employs comedy to make his arguments. The comic element and the dialogue make this a great piece for public performance, like the preceding account of the two silly heroes and the Lady of the Southern Stygian Realm (# 21). When the old man told the nuns that he had an incredibly effective elixir of immortality, they laughed in his face. They took him for a quack. They figured that if he had such a great remedy for prolonging life, he would have taken some himself and rejuvenated his decrepit body. He patiently explained that he could not just randomly ingest the miraculous medicine but had to take it together with another person who sought transcendence.

The nuns again doubted his sanity, for they knew that everybody wanted long life. In a religious community like theirs, it was insulting for him to insist that he could not find anybody serious about pursuing immortality. Again taking their questions seriously, he pointed out that everybody loves the Way, but not everyone wants to engage in the difficult and time-consuming religious practices necessary to attain it. Still mocking him, the sisters asked why he did not give this fabulous elixir to the current Tang emperor, Xuanzong. The old gentleman answered that since the emperor was already immortal, he had no need of an elixir. Unconvinced, the sisters inquired as to just which transcendent the present emperor really was. He unabashedly replied that Xuanzong was the Realized Person of the Supreme Primordial of the Grand Ultimate of the Vermilion Yang. By this time the nuns were becoming uneasy about this peculiar and uncanny fellow. They shrank back, dumbfounded. Nature responded with a dramatic and stormy display.

The strange old man, revealing the true reason for his visit, then asked where he might find the female Daoist master whose reputation for fasting and secret virtue had already reached him. After the sisters directed him to Bian Dongxuan, he walked right into her room without ceremony and informed her that he had the elixir drug she needed. She inquired about the price, and he cited an outlandish sum. When she protested her poverty, he told her that her forty years of practice counted as full payment. First he gave her three pellets of middle-grade medicine that would allow her to transform her body and ascend to heaven after fifteen days. Then, impressed with her diligence, he reconsidered and presented her with a medicine he blended for her on the spot out of water and a peach gum-like substance. (The peach was a long-standing symbol of longevity, associated with the Queen Mother of the West.)

After she took both drugs, Bian could ascend to heaven without experiencing the pain of transformation in just seven days. Du's description does not give away the ingredients of the elixir of immortality, but it does indicate that those who ingested elixirs did not expect the process of transformation to be painfree. After handing over the goods, the old guy disappeared. Bian reported to her sisters the events that had transpired in her room. The convent community remained divided about the authenticity of the elixir.

Next Bian Dongxuan told her sisters that she wanted to rest atop a locked building in the corner of their courtyard and flew up there. Dense clouds and fragrance, harbingers of an otherworldly event, filled the courtyard. People gathered from far and near; officials and the masses all revered her. Here Du records the beginning of her cult. The community prepared a grand parting ritual. As music and clouds drifted in, Bian Dongxuan ascended to heaven in broad daylight, witnessed by a huge audience. Her vividly rendered departure verifies her transcendence. The government officials present immediately sent word of this miracle to the capital.

Meanwhile back in Chang'an, Xuanzong sat in his audience hall, conducting his imperial affairs. Suddenly he saw purple vapors and smelled an enticing fragrance. Four blue lads, minor Daoist deities, appeared, leading a female Daoist master who looked about sixteen. Her youthful appearance showed the effectiveness of Daoist practice in reversing the aging process. Bian Dongxuan introduced herself to the emperor and bade him a ceremonious farewell. The emperor immediately questioned his officials about this event. At the same time, the messengers arrived to report on her ascent. Realizing that it was the same girl, Xuanzong bestowed honors on her convent. Thus he recognized a local cult honored both by bureaucrats and the masses. Du also credits Bian Dongxuan for the emperor's well-known devotion to Daoism, asserting that his interest in the affairs of transcendents started with his encounter with Bian. And Du implies that Bian inspired the emperor's younger sister, Princess Jade Verity, to enter a convent in 711.

Translation

[116.4b] Bian Dongxuan [Grotto Mystery] was the daughter of a person of Fanyang county [near Beijing].[165] When young she was lofty and pure, clever and perceptive, humane and compassionate, and she loved virtue. When she saw the life of the most minute creature in danger or extremity, she would always bend over to save it. Until she had succeeded in saving it, she forgot her own hunger and thirst. Whenever frost and snow congealed and froze so that birds and sparrows roosted hungrily, she sought foodstuffs like rice and grains to scatter and feed them. As years and months deepened, birds and sparrows came to look for her and to recognize her from afar. Some led in front, calling out as they flew, while others followed behind, dancing as they soared.

When she was fifteen, she revealed to her father and mother that she wanted to enter the Way and to refine her body by cutting off grains and nourishing her vital essence. Her father and mother were moved by her benevolence and compassion as well as her filial piety, but would not permit it.

When she reached marriageable age, [Bian] vowed not to marry, but to serve and nourish her parents with sweet delicacies. Several years later, she mourned her mother and father. Broken down and emaciated, she would not eat. Her fasting almost reached the point of extinguishing her life force. When she laid aside her mourning clothes she went to the Daoist nuns in the region and requested permission to become a Daoist master. In the end, since her older and younger brothers had all died young and she had no close relatives, [she was admitted to the convent]. Her nature was clever and perceptive. She was skilled with a loom shuttle. The flock of nuns sympathized with and respected her. Her spinning and weaving were so industrious! She worked from daybreak until night without ever idling.

---

[165] Different accounts of Bian Dongxuan are found in *Taiping guangji* 63.274 (based on the *Guangyi ji* [Record of General Oddities]), and the *Lishi zhenxian tidao tongjian* (DZ 296). All versions are translated in Cahill 2000.

Whenever she had some income, aside from [buying] sesame, China root fungus, ginseng, incense, or paper money, she would frequently purchase and store things like the five grains. People questioned her about it, asking: "Since you have not eaten these past several years, why do you store up rice and wheat? [5a] Can it possibly be that during those eternal nights and freezing dawns you think about hunger and thirst?" She smiled, but did not respond. And so it was that each morning she scattered rice and grain in the courtyard to feed the wild birds, and under the eaves to feed the rats. Years accumulated this way. She never once had the appearance of idleness. The whole household of nuns in this belvedere [convent] wove silk as a service [to make a living]. From the time Dongxuan began living with them, there were never any cases of rats harming things. People all passed on this story, interpreting it as an example of hidden virtue achieving a response among creatures.

It was also [Dongxuan's] nature to love to ingest special morsels. Whenever someone handed cinnabar [elixir] drugs to her or bestowed pills or powders upon her, she always made sure to burn incense, make offerings, and pray in the Audience Hall of the Heavenly Honored Ones [highest gods].[166] Only afterwards would she ingest [the drugs]. Often, when she suffered on account of the drugs, she would vomit them up, and her retching and diarrhea would bring her to the point of exhaustion and distress. But she was never resentful nor did she sigh in complaint. After her symptoms ended, she would swallow the drugs as usual. Those sharing the same Way worried about her. With indirect insinuations, they repeatedly urged her to shake [this practice] loose. But her heart with its perfected belief was as solid as a rock and could not be moved. Numerous times, when farmers encountered famine at harvest time, she would divide up the rice and wheat she had stored and distribute it to the people. [5b]

One day an old gent carrying a cloth sack on his back entered the belvedere to sell herbal medicines. The group [of nuns] accordingly asked him what drugs he was selling. The old gent said: "Morsels of Great Recycled Cinnabar– whoever ingests it will gain prolonged life and become a realized transcendent who ascends to heaven in broad daylight!"

---

[166] The Audience Hall, consciously styled like those of Chinese emperors, was the main public hall for the Daoist community and was usually located front and center in the convent compound. It would have contained statues of the deities. On Daoist temples, their architecture and organization, see Kohn 2003; for more on Daoist statues and art work, see Little and Eichman 2000.

All those who heard this took it for a joke. For the old gent's gaze was hazy and dark, his countenance wizened and shriveled, and his walking posture stooped and hunched. When his voice had only just left his mouth, the group laughed and said to him: "If this recycled cinnabar can bring deathlessness, extended life, and ascent to the heavens, then why are you so dried up and burned out? Why not take pity on yourself [and eat some of your own medicine]?"

The old gent replied: "When I first boil up and concoct this cinnabar, I must establish merit by delivering someone else. In this case, my requirement of saving someone is not yet satisfied. Those who seek transcendence are not easy to come by. I cannot just ingest this at my own convenience and then fly and soar up to the heavens."

The group asked him: "All people in the world wish for prolonged life without death, extended years, and increased longevity. Since all people have such hearts, how can you say that people who seek transcendence are hard to come by?" [6a]

The old gent answered: "People all have hearts that love the Way, but they are unable to refine their practice. To be able to love the Way and in addition to refine your practice so as to keep the essential spirits from retreating, to be diligent for a long time in these matters, to avoid being enticed by sounds and colors, moved by fame and profit, or led around by right and wrong, but to keep your heart as it was in the beginning, unchanging as metal or stone: that is difficult! In a hundred thousand myriads of people, there might not be even one single such person. So how can you talk about 'loving the Way'?"

Next they asked him: "Now since we have someone as noble as our Son of Heaven [Xuanzong], whose wealth includes all within the four seas, if you have such gold and cinnabar drugs, why don't you submit them to the throne and allow his majesty to obtain prolonged life and eternal longevity?"

The old gent replied: "Supra-Celestial Great Incomparable Realized Persons, Lofty Supreme Realized Transcendents, and the Seven Primal Lords of the Northern Dipper descend in cyclical order among the people, each in turn to become the Son of Heaven.[167] On the day his term is fulfilled, each returns

---

[167] The old man names ideal beings of Shangqing Daoism. The Seven Primal Lords are powerful gods of the seven major stars of the Big [Northern] Dipper (Beidou), an important constellation in Shangqing meditations and older protection rituals. See Schafer 1977.

and ascends to the Supreme Heaven; why should they pretend to ingest elixirs to obtain the Way?"

Then the audience also asked: "Since you know everything, which transcendent is the present Son of Heaven?"

He answered: "[He is] the Realized Person of the Southern Palace of the Grand Unity of the Vermilion Yang [near Mount Mao]."

In the astuteness of his replies to questions and in the matters he discussed, he was different from other people. His words came out fluently. The people could not fathom him and shrank back uncertainly. [6b] Suddenly violent wind, thunder, and rain arose. They kept looking back and forth at each other, startled and alarmed at his being so different from the ordinary. The flock of people gradually diminished, scattering as they departed. The old gent inquired of the group: "There is a female Daoist master around here who loves practicing secret virtue and who has cut off eating grains for many years. Where is she?"

Accordingly they showed him by pointing to her cloister. The old gent entered the cloister without knocking or asking permission. Going straight across to stand before Dongxuan, he said: "I have here the great drug known as recycled cinnabar. I have come from afar to save you. Can you take it?"

Dongxuan, startled and pleased, extended an invitation to him to sit down and asked him how much money she would need to spend for the drug. The old gent said: "It doesn't cost much – only 500,000 in gold."

Dongxuan then said: "This impoverished and distressed one has been in extreme want for many years now. I really don't have that kind of money. How could I ever obtain such a drug?"

The old gent replied: "Don't worry. It has been forty years from your childhood until today. For thirty of those years you accumulated and stored the five grains to provide food for birds and bugs. When we calculate it this way, [what you have already paid] is no less than the price of the drug."

With that, he opened his bag and showed her some two or three dippers of drug pellets that were blue-black in color and about the size of paulownia seeds. He ordered her to feel around among them for herself inside his bag. [7a] Following her whim, Dongxuan grasped three pellets from his drug bag. The old gent said: "If you ingest this cinnabar, it will change your intestines and transform your blood. It will take exactly fifteen days, and then you can ascend to heaven. This is a drug of the middle grade."

Then again he took a box the size of a coin from inside the overlap of his robe and brought out a little bit of a drug that had the appearance of peach gum. Its fragrance was also like peaches. The old gent himself drew water from the well to blend with this peach gum, then ordered her to swallow the pill. The old gent became happy, saying: "Your perfected sincerity has moved me to great gratitude. The Grand Supreme One has given me a command ordering me to summon you. After you take these two drugs, you will no longer need to change your intestines and transform your blood. Then, dwelling suitably in a pavilion on top of a platform, you will join with realized ones and meet with transcendents, never again to live in stinking and turbid rooms. After only seven days, you will be able to ascend to heaven. Of course, heavenly clothes and heavenly music will come of their own accord to welcome you."

In an instant the rain cleared and the old gent disappeared. The flock of nuns rushed to visit Dongxuan's room to ask her whether or not she had obtained the drug. She reported to them in full. [7b] Some scoffed at her strange exaggerations; others sighed over her encounter. Startled and alarmed, they stared at each other.

After this, some among the flock of residents of that province who knew about the incident raced to be first to see her. Thereupon Dongxuan notified the people: "I don't want to live here. I would like to climb to the top of the storied building over the gate [of our compound]." When she turned back to look at it, the storied building in the corner [of the convent] was still barred and locked [so she could not enter it and climb to the top]. Then Dongxuan notified the people: "I won't stay here." Before she had even finished her words, she soared up bodily to the top of that storied building. A strange fragrance overflowed, while extraordinary clouds scattered, filling the whole prefecture.

Within the whole region, those who viewed her were so numerous as form a solid wall [blocking the roads]. The Grand Protector, staff officers, and people from far and near all performed ritual obeisance and formal visiting ceremonies to her. Dongxuan notified the masses: "On the morning of the

Central Prime Day,[168] I will ascend to heaven. You may come to take leave of me [then]."

The masses then brought about a great communal fast.[169] On the fifteenth day of the seventh month, from the hours of 7 to 9 a.m., heavenly music filled the void. Dense and impenetrable purple clouds would around the upper stories of the [buildings in the] belvedere. Masses of people saw Dongxuan ascend, with heavenly music preceding and following her, with standards and pennants spread out and arrayed. She departed straight to the south. By noontime, the clouds had just scattered. [8a] The Grand Protector and the flock of officials all memorialized the throne.

That day between the hours of 7 and 11 a.m., the Brilliant Illustrious One [Xuanzong] of the Tang Dynasty, dwelling at ease in his basilica, suddenly sensed a strange fragrance as variegated purple vapors filled the courtyard. There were four blue lads leading a woman Daoist Master whose age might have been around sixteen or seventeen. She approached [the emperor] and said: "Your handmaiden is the Woman Daoist Master Bian Dongxuan from Youzhou [near Beijing]. Today I have attained the Way and am ascending to heaven. I have come to say farewell to your majesty [literally: you below the stairs]." Her words finished, she slowly departed.

Thereupon the emperor summoned and questioned his officials [who were responsible for religious affairs]. At the same time the memorials and letters [written by local officials concerning Bian Dongxuan's ascent] had just arrived. The two [versions of the] event matched each other precisely. He ordered that her belvedere be called the Belvedere of Climbing to Transcendence and that the storied building [from which she ascended] be called the Purple Cloud Storied Building, in order to publicize this matter. That year [711] the Illustrious One's younger sister, Princess Jade Verity,[170] requested permission to enter the Way, and donated her enfeoffed land and towns as

---

168 The Central Prime Day (*zhongyuan*), held each year on 7/15 of the lunar calendar was one of three major Daoist holidays observed with public liturgy. Based on the early ritual cycle of the Celestial Masters, much of its celebration was developed under the influence of the Buddhist Ullambana (see Teiser 1988).

169 The great communal fast was actually a vegetarian feast of celebration, with the occasion and the food considered sacred. Because of the holiness of the ceremony, it was named for religiously prescribed eating, i.e., fasting. Many of the rich banquets held by deities that Du describes elsewhere in his text are similarly called "fasts." For details of the ceremonies, see Kohn 2003.

170 On Jade Verity (Yuzhen), see Schafer 1985; Benn 1991 She was ordained together with her sister, Golden Transcendent (Jinxian).

well as the tax income from the enfeoffed territories [to the Daoist church]. From this time on, his highness loved affairs of the divinities and transcendents, becoming even more diligent and faithful towards the Way. Thus he ordered the Esquire of the Office of Comparative Texts [editor], Wang Duan, respectfully to make a stele to record this splendid affair of the divine transcendents.[171]

23. Huang Guanfu

Huang Guanfu 黃觀福 (Fortune of the Belvedere, d. ca. 665) was another southerner, who spent her short life in what is now Sichuan province. She lived near the city of Chengdu, where Du lived a couple of centuries later. Huang, worshipped at a roadside spirit shrine, was the center of a popular local cult. Du recommends her to the court as an auspicious omen and protector.

Du's biography of Huang Guanfu reads like a ghost story: a maiden commits suicide to escape marriage, then returns from the dead. However, instead of haunting her parents, Huang helped them. Du shows through this case that Daoism can save even a female suicide from the dire fate of being abandoned in the next world. Although Huang committed the supreme unfilial and disloyal act of killing herself, and although she died before entering a patriline and bearing sons to revere her as an ancestress, she still obtained a place in the Daoist heavens. Rather than turning into the most dangerous sort of vengeful ghost who harms her family and others, the usual destiny of a virgin suicide, Huang Guanfu became a benevolent guardian spirit. In his account of her biography, Du joins his ghost story with another type of supernatural tale: that of the banished immortal, sent temporarily to earth to answer for some minor crime. Along with presenting this individual as a saint, Du's composite account would also comfort the parents of suicides and release them from guilt.

The story embodies several of Du Guangting's central themes. Huang Guanfu practiced diligently, gaining superpowers and earning her tran-

---

171 Wang Duan was a literatus who held office under Xuanzong. He has a biography in *Xin Tangshu* 149.4808. Wang Duan's "Record" was probably a major primary source for Du.

scendence. She refused to marry, enacting Du's ambivalence about marriage as an institution favorable to Daoist salvation. She saved people from calamity, competing with the Buddhist deity Guanyin 觀音 and even earning a Buddhist following and a Buddhist name. Du claims her as an exclusively Daoist saint. Her inclusion here shows also Du's co-optation of the ancient folk practice of worshipping the unappeased souls of people who died a violent death at spirit shrines. What the Daoists could not reform among popular religious customs, they transformed and absorbed. And the cult of Huang Guanfu links Daoism with the Tang and Former Shu royal families.

She is said to have lived in the mid-seventh century and died around 665. Her family was very poor. As a child she already fasted, purified herself, performed rituals, and meditated. She embodied the Daoist meditation practice of "sitting in forgetfulness" (*zuowang* 坐忘). As a result, she gained the ability to foretell the future. Her parents worried, but allowed her to continue her religious activities until she reached marriageable age. Then they urged her to marry, precipitating a crisis. Huang tricked her parents into following her to the riverbank, where she committed suicide by throwing herself into the uncharacteristically raging river. When her parents dredged the river, they pulled out a gilded and painted wooden statue of their daughter in the form of a high Daoist deity. Only then did the water calm down. Weeping, they set the statue beside the road. Placing her statue signifies the beginning of her cult.

Later, as the mother worshipped at Huang Guanfu's roadside shrine, her daughter descended with three female companions, accompanied by a heavenly host. She reassured her mother and told her not to worry. She was not a suicide at all, but rather an immortal who had come down to earth in punishment for a misdemeanor. Her term of banishment over, she has returned to heaven. Her companions were goddesses from each of the Three Realms of Clarity. Predicting that this would be her last visit, she warned her mother about a terrible epidemic coming to the region next year. She gave her parents gold to help them leave the plague area, then departed and ascended with her entourage. Her parents moved away. As Huang had foretold, a dire epidemic occurred. Her ability to predict the future indicates her sainthood.

After these events, the people of the region honored Huang Guanfu with a cult. An alternate form of her name, Guanfo 冠佛 or "Capped Buddha," reveals that Buddhists as well as Daoists worshipped her. Du Guangting argues that Guanfo was a mistake in transmission, due to common folks confusing her image with that of a Buddhist deity, and to similarity in sound between the two versions of her name. Du claims her as a heavenly honored one, a high Daoist deity.

Huang Guanfu's ascent is not recorded. Du would have classified it as a return to heaven. Her original transformation occurred before this account begins. Her sojourn on earth, disguised as the familiar story of a banished immortal, is really prompted by compassion. She shows a skill in saving people that rivals that of Guanyin in the *Lotus Sutra*.

Translation

[116.9a] Huang Guanfu [Fortune of the Belvedere] was the daughter of commoners from Baizhang county in Ya province [Sichuan].[172] From youth she did not eat meat or spicy foods, loving what was clear and clean. Since her household was so poor that they had no incense, she took cedar leaves and cedar seeds and burned them. She often sat in quietude, looking as if she were frozen. She would sit through a whole day without doing anything, yet she never wearied of it. Sometimes she ate cedar leaves and drank water, but she was not fond of the five grains. Her father and mother worried about her, but they allowed her to follow her nature and carry out her intentions.

When she reached marriageable age, [her parents] wanted her to marry. Suddenly she said to her father and mother: "There is something extremely strange in the river at the head of the gate." Now she had often discussed odd matters with her father and mother, and her previous prognostications had frequently proved to be true. So when they heard this, [her parents] believed it and followed her to go to look at the river. In fact, it was tumultuous and restless. Then [Huang Guanfu] threw herself into the water.[173] After a good long time passed without her emerging, her father and mother dredged the river and obtained a wooden statue, like those of the heavenly honored ones [high deities] made in the old days. Its gilding and painted colors were already mottled. Its form and appearance were no different from their daughter. The river thereupon became settled and clear as before, and there were no more [strange] phenomena. Then [her parents] took that wooden image and set it up beside the road, calling out and weeping [as if

---

172 Another account of Huang Guanfu is found in *Taiping guangji*. 63.276..

173 On suicide, see Jamison 1999. For its role in Chinese culture, see Lin 1990.

mourning her]. Frightened by the strangeness of the whole affair, they returned home.

[Huang Guanfu's] mother would often go and peek at the statue, remembering and recalling her ceaselessly. Suddenly [on one of these occasions,] there were multi-colored clouds and transcendent music, along with extremely numerous forerunners and guards. [Huang Guanfu] descended together with three female companions into the courtyard and said to her father and mother:

> Your daughter was originally a person of the Realm of Supreme Clarity. Because of a small transgression I was banished to live among humans. When the years of my sentence reached their limit and it was finished, I returned again to the Supreme Heavens. Please do not be too sad or worried. Of the three serving girls who came with me, one is Serving Girl to the Jade Illustrious One, one is Serving Girl Who Attends the Chronograms for the Grand Thearch, and one is Serving Girl of Supreme Clarity.[174] My surname is Huang. My given name is Guanfu. When I leave here [this time], I won't come back again. This year there will be an epidemic in this region. Those who die will be extremely numerous. I will leave some gold for you, mother and father, so that you can move your household to Yi Province [Sichuan] in order to avoid the baleful year.

Then she left several cakes of gold and departed by ascending to heaven. Her father and mother followed her instructions and moved their household to the Shu commandary. That year an epidemic poisoned the black-haired people. In the territory of Ya, it was especially severe. They mourned three or four out of every ten [people]. [9b] The year in question occurred during the Qilin Virtue period [664-666].

Now the common folk call her Huang Guanfo [Capped Buddha]. This is probably because they do not recognize her image as a Daoist heavenly honored one. And it is also a case of the name Huang Guanfu changing to Huang Guanfo through an error of transmission.[175]

---

[174] The three serving girls are usually attendants to the three high gods of the three heavens of Shangqing Daoism: the Supreme, Jade, and Grand Clarities.

[175] Clearly Buddhists and Daoists both claim Huang as a saint. Each group gives her a name in accordance with their tradition. She is known to Buddhists as "Crowned Buddha" and to Daoists as "Fortune of the Belvedere." The fact that they fought over her suggests

24. Yangping Zhi

Yangping Zhi 陽平治 (Government of Mount Yangping) is another southerner and another center of a popular local cult whom Du Guangting adopts. Her name comes from a divine mountain in Zhejiang with a grotto heaven underneath and a prosperous tea plantation on its sides. Her story joins the themes of banished immortals and magic with a lesson in the divine geography and bureaucracy of grotto heavens.

The story also contains elements of ancient animistic tree worship. In the previous entry, Du Guangting showed the power of a Daoist transcendent to save people from an epidemic; here he shows a Daoist deity using her arts to help people threatened by a flood. Du also asserts the authority of the institutional Daoist church over popular sacrificial cults, a claim of domination that goes back to the Celestial Masters. He portrays a female transcendent instructing a human male, as the great Shangqing goddesses taught male adepts. In addition, Yangping Zhi and her husband provide a rare example of marriage as a religious vocation. Du also describes women acting quite unladylike, according to the standards of propriety associated with traditional Chinese female roles. And he refers to minority ethnic groups, numerous in the south both in his day and now.

The entire story of Yangping Zhi takes place during one tea harvest. We know nothing about her surname, given name, family origins, or childhood. When Du first introduces her, she is already over twenty years old and working as a seasonal tea picker. She marries a banished immortal who appears in the guise of another young farm worker, an orphan adopted into the family of Zhang Shougui 張守珪, a wealthy landowner with estates located in present-day Sichuan and Zhejiang provinces. Admiring Yangping Zhi's virtue and propriety, Zhang Shougui gives her in marriage to his adopted son. Zhang's actions show that a landholder in Tang times had great power over his workers, extending even to their

---

that her cult and spirit shrine were very popular. Du Guangting claims that her Buddhist name and identity are simply mistakes, perhaps explained by the erroneous substitution of one near-homophone for another.

personal lives. Ms. Yangping Zhi rewards Zhang Shougui with revelations.

Both Yangping Zhi and her new husband possess magic arts. When floodwaters block the roads to market, Zhang Shougui misses his salt and koumiss. Koumiss, fermented mare's milk, is not a drink produced or appreciated by Han Chinese, but a favorite of several minorities, especially nomadic peoples. Yangping Zhi tells Zhang to offer money beneath a tree, strike the tree, and make his request. Whatever he asks for will be granted. The tree continues to fulfill the desires of Zhang and others.

Another time Yangping Zhi meets her married women friends at the market town. They purchase a single bowl of wine and keep drinking from it until all are intoxicated, yet the bowl remains full. News of the miracle spreads far and wide. This incident features women going far outside their domestic sphere into the public marketplace, congregating in non-familial groups without their husbands, and drinking excessive amounts of wine. According to custom and the classics, this is not proper behavior for good wives. It is, however, typical behavior of a type of male Daoist adept: the eccentric and drunken genius. Famous cases include the Seven Sages of the Bamboo Grove during the Six Dynasties era and the Tang poet Li Bo. Once again, Du Guangting shows his Daoist female subject transgressing normative gender barriers.

In the next episode, Zhang Shougui questions Yangping Zhi. She becomes his teacher, as Lady Wei and other goddesses taught the Shangqing patriarchs in the *Zhen'gao*. When asked about her powers and their origins, she reveals that she is a banished immortal from beneath Mount Yangping. Du Guangting takes advantage of this situation to deliver a lecture on the structure and functioning of the grotto heavens, describing them as perfect worlds in miniature, located inside holy mountains. They are caves inhabited by transcendents, places where the faithful can go to survive the devastation at the end of a world age.

When her benefactor Zhang Shougui wants to hear more about government in the grotto heavens, Yangping Zhi informs him that these caverns are complete microcosms, with bureaucracies that run pretty much like those of this world. Celestial transcendents descend from the heavens on the three great annual Daoist festivals known as the Three Primes, and join with grotto transcendents to plan events on the earth. Their meetings determine such things as human lifespan, weather, and crop fertility.

Du further claims that they control animal sacrifices to ancient local deities—a broad assertion of authority over local popular cults. This statement reminds readers of Celestial Masters school's attempts to reform the bloody practices of popular religion at the end of the Han dynasty, and recalls Du Guangting's repeated portrayal of his Shangqing school as descendents and heirs of the Celestial Masters tradition.

After delivering the lesson for Du Guangting, Yangping Zhi and her husband leave together, presumably returning to the grotto heaven beneath Mount Yangping. The previous biography views marriage as something to avoid even at the cost of one's life. But this couple's joint efforts and departure exemplify marriage as a religious vocation. Yangping Zhi verified her transcendence and proved her legitimacy as a Daoist saint by correctly predicting her own departure. From other biographies, we know that grotto transcendents are not as elevated in the Daoist hierarchy as heavenly transcendents, but that both groups communicate and work together.

Translation

[116.9b] Yangping Zhi [Government of Mount Yangping] was the wife of a banished immortal. We do not know her given name. Now, the household of Zhang Shougui, who lived in Jiulong [Sichuan], was extremely wealthy.[176] They had a tea garden at Mount Yangping [Zhejiang], where transformed transcendents lived inside the mountain. Every year they would summon a hundred men and women as laborers to pick the tea. They would hire the laborers, then scatter them throughout the garden. One youth hired to pick tea said he had no relatives or clan. His nature was very smart and diligent. He requested that Shougui pity him and take him as an adopted son. There was a woman over twenty years old, also without relatives, who was willing to become the adopted son's wife. She was filial, correct, refined, and respectful. Shougui appreciated her very much. [10a]

---

[176] I am unable to identify Zhang Shougui. Adoption was not easy in official circles in the Tang dynasty. For an account of adoption in later times that may give us some ideas about the practice in the medieval times, see Waltner 1990.

One morning run-off from the mountain caused floods. Because roads to the marketplace were severed, salt and koumiss became unavailable. Shougui was very depressed. The new wife told him: "You can buy these things. Take some money and go ten paces outside your gate, set the money beneath a tree, and then knock the tree with your staff." He obtained salt and koumiss, then returned home. Later, whenever someone needed something, she would have the person strike the tree and take it. It never happened that they did not obtain [what they wanted]. Her husband's arts were also like this.

Later she was together with ten of her woman neighbors in the Coral Mouth Market, where they met to buy a bowl of wine. She drank it together with the flock of wives. They all got drunk and yet the wine in the bowl was not emptied. Far and near they told this story and people all marveled at it.

When Shougui asked about her arts and from whom they had been received, she replied; "I am a transcendent from inside the grotto[-heaven] in [Mount] Yangping. Because of a small transgression, I was banished to dwell among people. After a short time I must depart."

Then Shougui said: "Are offices in the grottos more or less the same as our municipal ones?" She replied:

> There is one great grotto for each of twenty-four transformations. [10b] Some are about fifteen hundred or thirteen hundred *li* square. In the center of all of them are the sun and moon and flying essences, which we call the roots of concealed deities. The light they send down to illuminate the inside of the grottos is no different from that in the world. Within [the grottos] are transcendent kings, transcendent ministers, and transcendent officials who help and assist each other like officials in this world.

> Those who have attained the Way and have accumulated virtues so that they become transcended deities who return to life, all dwell [in the grottos'] midst as their populations. Every year on the great festivals of the three primes, supreme realized beings from the various heavens descend and travel among the grotto heavens to observe the place and to regulate good and evil. Such things in the human world as life and death, rising and falling, water and draught, wind and rain are

arranged in advance within the grottos. The management of all blood sacrifices at shrines and ancestral temples of dragons and deities is controlled by governing departments of the grottos.

Aside from the twenty-four transformations, [Mounts] Qing-cheng, Emei, Yideng, Cimu, Fanyang, and Bozhong all have grottos that are not numbered among the ten great grotto heavens or the thirty-six lesser grotto heavens.[177] The transcendent officials in the grottos are just like the flock of governing agents in human commandaries and counties. [11a] It is impossible to record each of them in detail.

Within ten days, husband and wife suddenly departed together.

---

[177] Mount Qingcheng is a Daoist holy mountain in present day Sichuan, linked with the first Celestial Masters Zhang Daoling and also the residence of Du Guangting in his later years. Mount E'mei, a Buddhist and Daoist holy mountain in modern Sichuan, is still an important pilgrimage site. Mount Cimu is located in Anhui, Mount Fanyang in Sichuan, and Mount Bozhong in Shanxi. Du Guangting's work on sacred Daoist sites and lucky places (DZ 599) includes many of the places mentioned here.

25. Shen Gu

Shen Gu 神姑 (Divine Maiden, 792–c. 820), Lu Meiniang 盧眉娘(Eyebrow Girl), is another southerner, associated with the Canton area. A "maiden" like the Flower Maiden, Transcendent Maiden Xu, and Transcendent Maiden Gou, she too possesses miraculous skills, wanders in solitude, and practices asceticism that includes fasting and celibacy. Like several of Du Guangting's subjects, she is connected to the imperial court. In fact, she has links with two courts: those of the Northern Wei (386-534) and the Tang.

Her connection to the later or Northern Wei dynasty (the earlier Wei, 220-265, was one of the Three Kingdoms) is through her ancestor Lu Jingzuo 盧景祚. Symptomatic of the religious complexity of the times, Master Lu's elder brother was a devout Buddhist, while Lu himself reportedly instructed an emperor known as "Northern Ancestor" (Beizu 北祖). The official histories record no such emperor, but the term "ancestor," regularly used to honor the father of the first emperor of a dynasty, suggests that he was the father of the dynasty's founder, Dao Wudi (r. 386-409). Lu probably belonged to the Northern Celestial Masters movement that culminated in a short-lived Northern Wei Daoist theocracy masterminded by Celestial Master Kou Qianzhi 寇謙之 (365-448).[178] Lu Jingzuo's family was prominent enough to merit a biography in the *Weishi* 魏史 (History of the Wei Dynasty).

Lu Meiniang was named for her iridescent black eyebrows, so shiny that they reflected green light, already present at her birth. Of her immediate family Du tells us nothing, but by 805 the Lus had moved south and must have fallen upon hard times. They were economically or politically vulnerable enough that, when the military governor of the region requisitioned their teenaged daughter as tribute for the imperial harem, they had to hand her over. (Later accounts reveal that families would do anything they could to avoid having their daughters impressed into service in the inner apartments of the palace.) Du's story here provides early

---

[178] On the theocracy, see Mather 1979

evidence of the objectification and commodification of women that increases in the following Song dynasty.

Lu Meiniang accordingly lived in the women's quarters of two Tang emperors: Shunzong (r. 805) and Xianzong (r. 805-820). Like Bian Dongxuan, she embodies the womanly discipline and craft of textile production, but Lu's works of art are marvels as well as commodities; her pieces are said to surpass Buddhist icons and temple décor. In addition, Lu is the only woman in Du Guangting's records who has an independent reputation as an author. Three of her poems appear in the great Qing dynasty compendium of Tang poetry known as the *Quan Tangshi* 全唐詩 (Complete Tang Poetry, 9756).

In one of them, she speaks in a male voice, choosing the famous poet Li Bo as her alter ego and indicating her predilection for the Daoist path:

> I studied to obtain [secrets of] cinnabar and blue-green [pigments] over many myriads of years,
>
> While, among people [in this world], how many times did the mulberry fields transform?
>
> Although the mulberry fields transform, cinnabar and blue-green are still here;
>
> Whoever can join cinnabar and blue-green will attain transcendence.

Cinnabar and blue-green refer to mineral pigments and also to the minerals the alchemist mixes to compound the elixir of immortality. Cosmic mulberry fields alternate with the world sea in an image of huge cycles of time favored by Daoists, while mulberry groves in ancient times were places where men and women could meet and where many a cautionary tale about sexual license was set. Stealing the voice of the male poet, Lu does the literary equivalent of cross-dressing, expressing her vision of the ultimate goal of transcendence.

Her other two poems are responses to the verses of another woman: Zhuo Yingying 桌英英, a native of Chengdu, who, like Lu, was chosen for the imperial harem in Chang'an. The two may have met in the women's apartments after Lu Meiniang was summoned there. Zhuo initiates the exchange. Homesick, in her poem she recalls her town's mild climate and scenic spots. But conjuring up visual images brings along disturbing sensual memories and languor.

Lu Meiniang replies by acknowledging the beauty of the world and the joys of spring and youth, but emphasizing the floating nature of the world and the ultimate goal of transcendence. She says:

> The silkworm market just opened; everywhere it's spring.
>
> At the nine crossroads, bright and seductive [young shoppers] raise fragrant dust.
>
> In this world, there are always affairs of floating flowers,
>
> This does not compare to the people in transcendent mountains who leave the world behind!

In contrast to the bustling silkworm market and the trysts of lovers in transient "floating flower affairs", Lu devotes herself to the solitary pursuit of transcendence. Speaking as an older instructress, she gently rebukes her correspondent who is seduced by remembered visions. The poems refer to many stages of silk production: silkworms, silk threads, the silk market, and silk city. Their words embodying silk making, the poems subversively suggest that poetry making is also womanly work.

The third poem responds to Zhuo's lament that her practice on the reed organ arouses distracting erotic feelings, so she cannot play music to please the immortal Jin: he whose play was so divine that phoenixes descended to dance for him. In answering, Lu Meiniang encourages her frustrated friend, assuring her that her playing is good enough to attract a transcendent companion, none less than the poet Li Bo, known as Taibo 太白, "Great White," after the planet Venus and Mount Taibo. Already a legend for his Daoism, drinking, and eccentricity even before Meiniang was born, Li Bo makes the perfect companion for a female poet or Daoist adept. Later Zhuo will fly through the heavens, yoking phoenixes, the preferred vehicles of the immortals. Being transcendent herself, what need would she have for Transcendent Jin?

> Just warm up and blow your reed organ in the secluded women's apartments,
>
> And the Realized Transcendent of Great White will naturally [respond with] passion.
>
> Another day, in the cinnabar empyrean, you'll team up white phoenixes,
>
> Why worry if young Jin can't hear your sounds?

With her accomplishments in weaving and literature, her amazing wisdom, spiritual accomplishment, and skills, Lu Meiniang was quite a prize for the imperial harem. Her textile work exemplified female virtue and tradition, and much more. The scenes of Daoist paradises that she constructed by hand out of dyed and knotted silk threads surpassed the most elaborate and fantastic representations of Buddhist paradises found in wall paintings in the cave temples of Dunhuang or the pages of the *Lotus Sutra* and *Pure Land Sutra*. Lu magically created three-dimensional microcosms in cloth, large but nearly weightless. As an (al-)chemist, she also concocted a preservative to conserve her creations. Emperor Shunzong was awed. In recognition of her miraculous craftsmanship and asceticism, the palace community called her Divine Maiden.

Apparently, the Divine Maiden never dwelt willingly in the palace women's quarters. After the succeeding emperor Xianzong took the throne, he allowed her ordination as a Daoist nun, gave her a bracelet shaped like a phoenix as a parting gift, and sent her home. Along with the gold bracelet, the emperor also gave her a new name: Xiaoyao 逍遙 or Fancy Free. This is a favorite Daoist term for free and easy wandering that goes back to chapter one of the *Zhuangzi*, implying she was released to roam far and wide. The name connects her with the ideal sages of that Daoist classic.

This is one of several cases of Tang women entering Daoist holy orders after leaving the imperial harem. Two others, Empress Wu Zetian (d. 705) and imperial consort Yang Guifei (d. 756), stayed for some time in Daoist convents after leaving the household of one member of the royal family and before entering the palace of another. In each case, entering holy orders meant leaving the old life behind and becoming ritually purified. The Divine Maiden reclaimed her celibacy if not her physical virginity, and was able to resume her ascetic practices fully. In addition to providing a temporary retreat and purification, the Daoist convent, like the Buddhist, served as a more permanent residence for women retiring from the household life or from a profession such as courtesan.

Lu came from the south and she returned to the south. In later years, her cult was associated with Mount Luofu, east of Canton in modern Guangdong province.[179] Mount Luofu had been the final home of Ge

---

[179] On Mount Luofu, see Schafer 1967, 88-89 and 107; Soymié 1943.

Hong, a Daoist ancestor claimed by both Shangqing and Lingbao schools, and was associated with other famous Daoist figures. Ge Hong also appears in the fourth entry of this text. Zhuming 朱明, "Vermilion Luminosity," the seventh of the ten major grotto heavens, was located directly under this mountain.

After returning south, the Divine Maiden fasted and received visits from deities. Like the other maidens, she was transformed into a feathered transcendent through liberation by means of the corpse. The fragrant clouds that filled her living quarters at the time of her departure, and the replacement of the cadaver in her coffin with a pair of shoes, verified her sainthood. The substitution of shoes for the woman's body prefigures the literary identification of shoes and women that takes place after the custom of foot-binding becomes widespread in later dynasties. Du Guangting mentions that later people saw her flying over the sea on a purple cloud, indicating that her cult continued after her departure. In closing he cites two biographies of the Divine Maiden, one of which survives today in a Song imperial encyclopedia, that provided material for his account.

Translation

[116.11a] The Divine Maiden was Lu Meiniang [Eyebrow Girl], a descendent of Lu Jingzuo,[180] teacher of the Later Wei thearch posthumously known as the Northern Ancestor. She was born with long black-green eyebrows, so she was named for them.

In the primal year of the Eternal Probity reign period [805], the Grand Protector of the South Seas [Canton] submitted her as tribute to the capital because of her outstanding craftsmanship and extraordinary spirituality. The Eyebrow Girl had been wise and perceptive since youth. She could divide a single thread into three filaments and dye them various colors in the palm of her hand. She would then knot them to make an umbrella-like canopy of five tiers. Inside it would be images of the ten continents, three islands, heavenly people, jade women, platforms and basilicas, *qilin* and phoenixes, while on the outside were arranged at least a thousand transcendent youths grasping

---

[180] This biography is translated in Schafer 1979. Her poetry is discussed in Cahill 2003. According to *Taiping guangji* 66, Lu Jingzuo was one of four brothers, the eldest of whom was a devout Buddhist with biographies in *Weishu* 84 and *Beishi* 30.

banners and holding insignia aloft. Although it was a yard wide, [the whole thing] weighed less than three ounces. She herself boiled a numinous aromatic that she transferred as an ointment to the cloth, making it so strong and firm that it would not tear. [11b] The Illustrious Thearch Shunzong gasped at the wonder of her craftsmanship. Within the two palaces she was called the Divine Maiden. When she entered palace [service], she was just fourteen. Every day she ate only two or three spoonfuls of sesame-flavored rice.

In the middle of the Primal Accord period [c. 813], the Illustrious Thearch Xianzong, appreciating her wit and wisdom, gave her a golden phoenix bracelet to encircle her wrist. For a long time she had been unwilling to dwell in the palace annex [women's quarters], so he had her ordained as a female Daoist Master and released her to return home to the South Seas, bestowing upon her the cognomen "Fancy Free."

[After this], for a number of years she did not eat, and divine people descended regularly to meet her. One morning she was transformed into a feathered transcendent. Fragrant vapors filled her apartment. When they lifted her coffin to begin her burial ceremony, it felt light. When they removed its cover, nothing was there but her old shoes. From time to time, people see her riding over the sea on a purple cloud. Li Xiangxian of Mount Luofu wrote "Transmissions Concerning Fancy-Free Lu" and Su E entered her case on his "Duyang Chapters."[181]

---

[181] Du Guangting bases his account on that of Su E, *Duyang zapian* (Scattered Chapters from Duyang) collected in the entry on Lu Meiniang in *Taiping guangji* 66.284-285, a source he follows closely. He also uses Li Xiangxian's now lost biography.

26. Wang Fengxian

Wang Fengxian 王奉仙 (Offering to the Transcendents; ca. 838-886) was born in the south to a poor peasant family. After struggling in adolescence with her parents over her religious eccentricities, she became a wandering ascetic and teacher of great popular renown. Through argument and magic, she narrowly escaped being sent as tribute (*gong* 貢) to the Tang imperial harem. She became a successful practitioner and famous teacher. Wang's biography contains the latest date in the book: 886.

Du Guangting makes Wang Fengxian's life another occasion to settle grievances with Chinese Buddhists. He identifies Wang as a purely Daoist saint, rejecting strong Buddhist claims on her. As he tells her story, Du explains what he believes is the proper relationship between Daoism, Confucianism, and Buddhism. He uses analogies to family relationships. Daoism is compared to the father in a household, Confucianism to the older brother, and Buddhism the mother. Du argues that Daoism and Confucianism, alike in dignity, are natural allies and should be recognized as sources of our deepest religious and social values. Buddhism may seem the most beloved and best known, but is ultimately least deserving of respect. This argument states Du's beliefs about the three teachings at the same time as it also expresses his ambivalence about motherhood and gender equality. Wang's life provides a powerful example of the gender hierarchy that is so deeply embedded in Chinese culture.

Wang Fengxian's poor family subsisted on farming and textile production. Her religious calling came suddenly when she was a young teenager. As she carried food to the workers in the fields, a flock of transcendent girls came to play with her. The goddesses then began visiting her at home at night, the whole group fitting easily by means of magic into her tiny room. They brought divine delicacies to put on a ritual feast, as in the case of the Queen Mother visiting the Martial Thearch of the Han. When Wang's worried parents spied on the noisy nocturnal parties, her guests simply vanished. Her parents, suspecting possession by malevolent spirits, interrogated her. Like any teenager, she lied. Their curiosity put an end to the all-night gatherings, but the celestial maidens could not stay away from Wang Fengxian. They came during the daylight hours, taking her on distant journeys, but always respecting her parents' curfew and bringing her back before dark.

Wang Fengxian began a severe regimen of fasting and became ever more eccentric. She learned to fly by leaping off the tops of tall bamboo plants growing in her family's courtyard. Her practice flights recall the lyrical sword fight above the bamboo grove in the film, "Crouching Tiger, Hidden Dragon." Wang's parents grew ever more alarmed at her apparently self-destructive behavior and kept asking her to explain herself. She finally told them the whole story. Divinities responded by descending suddenly and cutting her hair in a style called a pageboy today. This mini-tonsure and the fact that her hair did not grow back signified both her desire for Daoist ordination and the deities' approval.

After this event she fasted for a year, purifying her body so that she looked like a celestial being. She was renowned as knowledgeable and brilliant in debate. Du's emphasis on these abilities assumes that Wang was literate and spoke in public, unusual enough achievements among literati class women, and certainly rare among female peasants. Education and the chance to play a part in public life may have been motivations for Tang Daoist women to enter holy orders, as was also the case for Buddhist women. People revered Wang and called her Guanyin, after the Mahayana bodhisattva of compassion. Her skill in debate matched that deity's compassionate *upaya* or "skill-in-means," the ability to teach according to the level of the audience. She could compete with Buddhism at its own game. This identification also shows that the feminization of that Indian Buddhist deity, originally portrayed as a male, that was to become apparent in the Song dynasty, was already well underway by the late Tang dynasty.

When she was in her thirties, prominent officials stationed in the south asked to become her disciples. One upright local bureaucrat grew concerned that she might be fomenting a heterodox and dangerous cult. But when he investigated her, she treated him with respect. He asked why people called her Guanyin, and she replied in no uncertain terms that it was Daoism she was practicing and Daoist salvation she had attained. Common folk were simply mistaken in calling her after a bodhisattva. Quoting a famous Daoist forefather, Zhuangzi, Du suggests that a true saint is indifferent to such distinctions. This neutrality, also called "making things equal" after chapter two of the *Zhuangzi*, is the Daoist answer to the Buddhist notion of *sunyatā*, the emptiness that resolves all contradictions. But our Shangqing Daoist author, Du Guangting, does worry about distinctions. He takes care to set matters straight with the rival faith. To him, Wang Fengxian was a thoroughly Daoist saint who must never be confused with a Buddhist deity.

Apparently her accomplishments and popularity made her a desirable commodity, for Du Shenquan 杜審權, appointed military governor of the south in 859, planned to send her as tribute to the emperor. Unlike Lu Meiniang, Wang Fengxian entirely escaped harem life. First she tried to argue her way out of being dispatched northwards like a package of goods. Her usual skill in debate did not prevail, however, so she fled and hid in a Buddhist temple. While she stayed there, people revered her, offering her incense and cash. Du Guangting blames her accidental residence in a Buddhist temple during this incident for the mistaken identification of her as a Buddhist saint on the part of the common people. Du argues that her ascetic accomplishments were purely Daoist, as were the divinities who encouraged her. In addition, he claims that her own reported indifference to what people called her puts her above the debate. But Du protests too much. Mixing of elements of Daoism and Buddhism was common on the elite as well as the popular level. Du's insistence on her Daoist identity suggests that Wang was an important cult figure in both traditions.

Wang Fengxian's practice was evidently effective: she looked eighteen or nineteen in middle age and dressed like a Shangqing goddess. She possessed plants of magical potency. She had been entrusted with Daoist scriptures. She engaged in techniques designed to prolong her life and escape the world. She never tired as she wandered at will through earth and the heavens.

At the height of her career, she received a formal invitation to the celestial palace of a Heavenly Honored One, a title reserved for the highest Daoist deities such as the teacher of the Queen Mother of the West. Her trip may have taken place in a dream or visualization. The Heavenly Honored One's palace arrangements looked much like those of the Tang court. He gave Wang, as further evidence of her transcendence, a prediction that she would return to heaven after spending fifty years as a mortal. The Heavenly Honored One then gave her jade broth to drink and told her she must stop eating regular human foods, as that diet hastened death. After he gives Wang Fengxian her personal predictions and instructions, he gives her and the readers a lecture on the proper relations of the three teachings. Speaking through the Heavenly Honored One, Du allies Daoism with Confucianism as the father and elder brother of humanity, both superior to Buddhism as the mother. He also claims that the Buddhist images so ubiquitous in Tang material culture are in fact just copies of Daoist divinities. His evidence is that the images of the so-called Buddhist deities do not look like real monks and buddhas. That is: they do not look foreign. Resembling ethnic or Han Chinese rather than Indian or Central Asian people, he reasons, these icons must represent Daoism, the native religion of China. Since Chinese people had been entering Buddhist holy orders for over seven centuries when he wrote these words, Du's argument is unconvincing.

Upon her return, Wang fasted another twenty years. She traveled the south, preaching to the masses on matters dear to the hearts of Confucians and Daoists alike. The people revered and supported her. She even converted fierce military leaders into her disciples. Toward the end of her life she settled down at Mount Dongting in Jiangsu and finally received formal ordination as a Daoist nun. She lived there with two female disciples.

In 885, Wang Fengxian moved to Mount Qianqing in Zhejiang province, where followers had built her a small retreat. After a little over a year, she ascended to transcendence without even taking sick. The usual cranes and fragrant clouds accompanied her departure, signs that she was a true saint. Her body was youthful and pure from taking elixir drugs and meditating. Du uses a term specific to Daoist meditation, "sitting in forgetfulness." Du asserts that anyone who thinks she accomplished all this by means of Buddhist practice is sadly mistaken. As further proof of her purely Daoist authenticity, Du ends his account with the statement that she is now the equal of two great Daoist goddesses.

Translation

Wang Fengxian [Offering to the Transcendents] was the daughter of a peasant family from Dangtu county in Xuan prefecture [near Xuanzhou, Anhui].[182] Her household was poor. Her father and mother wove and spun to provide for themselves.

Once when Fengxian was about thirteen or fourteen, as she brought food to [her parents and other peasant] laborers in the fields, she suddenly saw ten or more young girls. After she played with them for a long time, they scattered and departed. Another day she saw them again, just as before. From that time on, whenever she brought meals to the fields, flocks [of young girls] coming to play became a regular thing. For over a month, various girls met at night in her house, talking and laughing the whole evening until dawn, when they would scatter. Some brought along strange fruits; others set out rare delicacies. None of it was anything we have in this world. Although her room was narrow and confined, and the flock who came was numerous, it did not seem too constrained.

Her father and mother, hearing the talk and laughter, became suspicious. So they spied upon the visitors in order to scrutinize them, whereupon [the flock of girls] just disappeared again. In addition, Wang's parents suspected that she was being misled by bewitching goblins, so they examined her in great detail. Of course she used other [evasive] words to answer them. From this time on, the various girls did not descend at night again.

Girls often came and went during the daylight hours. Sometimes they drew her along on prolonged and distant journeys. Skimming the void, drifting far and returning, there was no place they did not reach. By evening she would return home. [12b] In addition she never drank or ate. Day by day, she grew increasingly odd. One day towards evening, her mother saw her throwing herself to the ground from the tips of the bamboo plants growing in the corner of their courtyard. [She was learning to fly.] Growing more and more worried and anxious, her mother begged Wang to tell her why she did this. So she told her mother and father about the things she had encountered. But before she had finished explaining her experiences from start to finish, several divine girls [suddenly appeared and] cut Fengxian's hair.[183] They exposed her eyebrows in front and left just enough hair hanging down in back

---

182 An earlier version of this translation appeared in Cahill 2001. Another brief biography of Wang Fengxian is found in the *Sandong qunxian lu* (Records of the Hosts of Transcendents Versed in the Three Grottoes, DZ 1248), compiled in 1154 by Chen Baoguang.

183 Cutting the hair is a traditional part of Daoist and Buddhist ordination practices. Instead of shaving the head, Daoists left the hair long enough to replicate the fashions of immortals. On ordination of Daoist nuns in the Tang, see Despeux 1986; Benn 1991.

to reach the tops of her shoulders. From this time on for several years, her hair simply did not grow.

She did not eat for a year or more.[184] Her skin and flesh became rich and lustrous, as clean as ice or snow. With her cicada-shaped head and rounded [literally: "maggot"] neck, she seemed made of luminous matter with bright pupils. Her appearance was like that of a heavenly person. She was brilliant and perceptive in knowledge and argument. People south of the Yangzi River called her Guanyin [bodhisattva].[185]

At the end of the Total Comprehension reign period [860-874], the Official Who Assists the Nation [Prime Minister], Common-lord Du Shenquan, pacified Jinling [near Nanjing], while Common-lord Linghu Tao settled Weiyang [Yangzhou, Jiangsu].[186] Their reputation for writing poetry and making donations [to Wang Fengxian] was widespread south of the Yangzi River. Later Qin Yan requested that she stay in Jiangdu [near Yangzhou] and let him revere her as his master.[187]

---

[184] On fasting, an important Daoist ascetic practice, see Lévi 1983; Maspero 1981; Eskildsen 1998. On the significance of fasting in women's religious practice in medieval Europe, see Bynum 1987.

[185] Guanyin (Jap.: Kannon) is the Chinese name of the bodhisattva Avalokiteśvara. A male deity in India and Tibet and transformed into a female savior in China, Guanyin is the bodhisattva of compassion and the most popular Buddhist deity of the Far East. The key protagonist of chapter twenty-five of the *Lotus Sutra*, informally called the "Guanyin sutra," the deity was well known even to illiterate people of the Tang dynasty. For studies, see Chamberlayne 1962; Blofeld 1978; Yü 2001. Noting her similarity to Guanyin, Du Guangting implies that Wang possesses what *upaya* or "skill-in-means," the ability to teach each listener according to his or her own capacity. This miraculous skill in communication is demonstrated in the famous parable of the burning house (*Lotus Sutra*, ch. 3).

[186] Du Shenquan, an official who passed the imperial examinations and served as a minister under Xuanzong [846-859], was appointed military governor in the south under Yizong [859-873]. During the Pang Xun rebellion of 868-869, he was instrumental in restoring peace. Du Shenquan has official biographies in *Jiu Tangshu* 177 and *Xin Tangshu*. 96. Linghu Tao [802-879], another official who passed the imperial examination and served as a minister under Xuanzong, held a military post under Yizong and played a part in suppressing the Pang Xun rebellion. He has official biographies in *Jiu Tangshu* 172 and *Xin Tangshu* 166. The garrison revolt of Pang Xun (868-869) paved the way for the disastrous Huang Chao rebellion of 878-884. Both began in the south, with origins in popular unrest and lack of faith in the imperial government, and the Huang Chao rebellion spelled the beginning of the end for the Tang dynasty. See Twitchett 1979, 695-700.

[187] Qin Yan (d. 888) was a former thief who became a leader in the Huang Chao rebellion. He has official biographies in *Jiu Tangshu* 182 and *Xin Tangshu* 224. On the Huang Chao rebellion, see Levy 1961; Twitchett 1979, 723-47.

The lofty official, headman Li Huaigao, a man of natural and unrestrained uprightness and rectitude, suspected her of doing something heterodox.[188] So he visited and questioned Wang. [13a] Welcoming him, Wang treated him with reverence. She spoke of the Way for several days. The headman asked her: "The basic principles of what you have discussed are more or less in accordance with the basic essentials [of the Way], so why do you have the title [of the Buddhist deity] Guanyin?" Fengxian said: "What I have encountered is the Way. What I have gained is transcendence. Babbling common folk just flatter me with the name of Guanyin."

Some years passed and then Common-lord Du sought her [at her hermitage] between Penglai and Mount Mao, intending to offer her as tribute for the consorts' apartments inside the imperial palace. She tried to avoid this, using the excuse of having short hair. When he still would not allow her to return home to serve her parents, she remained inside a Buddhist temple. In the lanes and alleyways people did not really understand the situation, but they randomly gossiped and praised her. [Their adulation] reached the point where they lifted incense and held up candles [in reverence to her], contributing their treasures and giving her metal vessels [in donation]. Thus some years passed. Up to the present, nobody really understands that her hiding [in a Buddhist temple resulted in her false identification as a Buddhist deity].[189]

Now as for her being able to practice and nurture [her breaths] and her not being confined to the women's quarters of the imperial palace: these facts provide clear evidence that realized transcendents secretly protected her by cutting off her hair to neck length. Shouldn't everyone be satisfied and pleased with [the evidence of her Daoist identity]? Moreover, there is no obstacle between names [categories or designations] and the Way. [13b] As Master Zhuang said: "If people consider me an ox, then I will act like an ox; if they consider me a horse, then I'll act like a horse." Forgetting form and body, realized ones do not take the names of things as binding. Therefore they do not despise people.[190]

---

188 I have not been able to identify Li Huaiguo. Presumably he was a local official concerned with the possible dangers of an unauthorized cult.

189 This episode suggests that Wang lived and received homage for a time in a Buddhist temple, perhaps passing as a Buddhist nun. This supports the idea that both Buddhists and Daoists claimed her as a saint, and makes Du Guangting's perplexity disingenuous.

190 The quote attributed to the Warring States Daoist thinker, Zhuangzi, does not exist in any current recension of the *Zhuangzi*. Wang Fengxian's words suggest that the saint is unconcerned with how people identify her and only cares about the good of the people and

Moreover, whenever anyone saw her, she looked like a girl of eighteen or nineteen. Her face and appearance were different from those of ordinary people. She wore a garment with huge sleeves, made of damask and embroidered with patterns of clouds and auroral mists. What she held were transcendent flowers and numinous grasses. What she chanted and intoned were transcendent classics and chapters from the [Three] Caverns [i.e., the Daoist Canon]. What she spoke about were techniques pertaining to matters of the divine transcendents for prolonging life and escaping from this world. Consequently, whenever she went about she could ramble at leisure or rush in a hurry, but she never experienced fatigue. She went to heavenly palaces and transcendent watchtowers, golden storied buildings and jade audience halls, narrow corridors and broad courtyards, mushroom fields and cloud orchards, places full of divine birds, heavenly wild animals, gemstone trees, and numinous fragrant plants not seen in the mundane world.

Passing over the Starry Han River [Milky Way], going who knows how many thousands of myriads of *li*, she attended court to pay a formal visit to the Heavenly Honored One. Inside the broad basilica in the palace of the Heavenly Honored One, feathered guards were densely arrayed. The Heavenly Honored One declared to Fengxian: "After you have lodged your life in the human world for fifty years, then you will certainly return here." He ordered his attendants of the left and right to take a single cup of jade broth [elixir] and give it to her to drink. [14a] When she finished, he warned her: "As for the produce of the hundred grains or the fruits of the grasses and trees [on earth], eating them kills people and cuts short years of longevity. It is particularly important for you to cut them out." From this time on, she did not eat for twenty years.

Now the Heavenly Honored Ones perform their transformations in the heavens, teaching people by means of the Way, extending people by means of life, ruling and guiding all the myriad created things, protecting and nurturing universally on all sides: they are like fathers among the people of this world. [In contrast,] Shakyamuni [Buddha] performed transformations on earth, urging people to stop evil and inducing people to seek blessings; he was like a mother among the people of this world. The classics of the Confucian literati school now circulate among the people, showing [proper behavior] to them by means of the five constant [relationships], and instructing by means of a hundred courses of action. [Confucius] is like an older brother

---

her religious practice. The ideas suggest the chapter on "Making Things Equal." See Watson, 1968, 36-49.

among people of this world. A baby in this world recognizes only its mother; it does not know its father and older brother should be revered. Thus among ordinary people those who know the Way are few and those who respect Confucian [scholars] are scarce. This is nothing to wonder at.

In addition, among the people from above the heavens who have been seen, the males wear cloud caps and feathered clothing or tufted chignons and blue aprons, while the females have golden hairpins with kingfisher ornaments, and either three hair coils or a pair of horn-shaped chignons. [14b] In their hands they hold jade tablets; on their necks they wear round and radiant [jewels]. They fly along riding the void. No one can fathom their transformations. There are also riders on dragons, *qilin*, simurghs, and cranes, as well as stalwarts with feathered standards and rainbow tallies. They are like thearchs and rulers among humans. You will not see likenesses of Buddhas or Buddhist monks among them. In the meantime, images emerging from diagrams and paintings offered up [by the Buddhists] are extremely numerous. And they all actually look like the forms of heavenly people, thearchic kings, lords of the Way, and flying transcendents; they do not represent the real appearance of monks and Buddhas. [That is: they do not look Indian; they look Chinese.]

During the Broad Illumination [860-873] through the Radiant Disclosure [885-888] reign periods, altogether about forty years, [Wang Fengxian] wandered around the Wanling region of the Huai and Zhe Rivers [Anhui]. Whenever she arrived, spectators gathered like clouds. In her preaching to the masses, she often took up the Way of loyalty, filial piety, uprightness, and rectitude, the admonitions to be clear, clean, temperate, and simple, and the essentials of the secret [Daoist] practices for refining the body [self-cultivation]. Therefore everyone from far and near respected her, setting money and precious substances before her. Rejecting all the myriads of things she was given, she departed, never looking back. Although the rivers of the Three Huai Rivers region had rolling waves and billows, and the Four Wildernesses [beyond Chinese civilization] had mist and smoke, she always perched and stopped there naturally, unconcerned and unworried. [15a]

And then there were imposing tyrants such as Sun Ruo, Zhao Hongbei, and Shi Tuo, who led mobs, intending to annoy her with improper behavior and coerce her with white [metal] swords.[191] But once they glimpsed her divine appearance, without even knowing what they were doing, they would bow,

---

[191] Sun Ruo, a great military leader at the time of the Huang Chao rebellion, has an official biography in *Xin Tangshu*. 188. I have not been able to identify the other two men.

kneel, and extend to her the rites of disciples. Afterwards she lived at Mount Dongting [Jiangsu] and formally entered the Way in the company of two women disciples.[192]

At the beginning of the Radiant Disclosure reign period [885], she moved up to Mount Qianqing in the region of Yuhang [Zhejiang]. The people below the mountain built her a floriate cottage to dwell in. After over a year [886], she was transformed without ever getting sick. She was forty-eight years old. Auspicious tokens of cloud cranes and strange fragrances were present. This tallied precisely with the period of fifty years mentioned [by the Heavenly Honored One]. In addition, she had not eaten for thirty years. She had a youth's complexion and snowy flesh as if she had remained a virgin. If not the work of gold and cinnabar elixirs and jade fluid, how could she have reached this point? Also her spirits frequently wandered to the borders of heaven, and she could sit upright [in meditation] for over a month. Sometimes she descended to inspect the affairs of earthly bureaus or stygian passes, or she sat and looked to the eight extremities. She often spoke with people who possessed the Way. People in this world do not recognize that [her accomplishments were all achieved] by sitting in forgetfulness [meditation]. She is now a peer of the Primal Ruler of the Southern Pole and the Incomparable Mother of the Eastern Tumulus.[193]

---

[192] The Mount Dongting referred to here in a mountain in Jiangsu rather than the more famous one near Lake Dongting in modern Hunan.

[193] On sitting in forgetfulness, see Kohn 1987. The titles "Primal Ruler of the Southern Pole" and "Incomparable Mother of the Eastern Tumulus" designate two great goddesses of heaven and earth in the Shangqing tradition.

27. Xue Xuantong

The life of Xue Xuantong 薛玄同 (Dark Unity, ca. 828-882) is the last biography in Du Guangting's "Records of the Assembled Transcendents of the Fortified Walled City." It contains the second to last date recorded in that text, 883, and also contains Du's last words on the subject of female Daoist saints. He engages several of his familiar themes here. His subject is a southerner whose good works and rigorous practice allows her to achieve transcendence. The deities and texts Du mentions are closely associated with the Shangqing school of Daoism. Xue Xuantong's marriage is presented as an obstacle to her austerities, rather than as a religious vocation. Her achievements demonstrate the superiority of Daoism over Buddhism. Her undecaying and eventually disappearing body demonstrates that she has attained liberation by means of the corpse. Finally, her life and ascent testify to the glory of the Sichuan region and to the firm possession of the mandate of heaven by the Tang imperial line who can then pass it on to the Former Shu dynasty.

Du reports nothing of Xu Xuantong's place of origin, family, or childhood. Her apparent literacy suggests that she grew up in a wealthy and official class family. So does her marriage. She married Feng Hui 馮徽, an official in Shanxi province with landholdings in the south. Twenty years later, when she was probably in her mid-thirties, Xue suddenly informed her husband that she wanted to live in seclusion. She evidently thought that she could not achieve perfection as a Daoist adept while remaining within the confines of her marriage. This agrees with Du's generally negative view of conventional marriage as a fruitful ground for religious practice. Should friends and family inquire, Feng Hui could use illness as a face-saving excuse for her celibacy and even more important, for her failure to produce a male heir to the Feng lineage.

From this time on, Xue Xuantong's practice intensified. For the next thirteen years, she carried out devotions and repeatedly chanted the *Huang-ting jing* 黃庭經 (Scripture of the Yellow Courtyard, DZ 331, 332)--a classic of Shangqing Daoism, closely associated with Lady Wei Huacun, that contains detailed instructions for visualizing internal body gods. Chanting the text makes it probable but not irrefutable that Xue was literate, since she could have memorized it. As a result of this intense devotion, in 874, when Xue Xuantong must have been around forty-seven, Wei Huacun sent two divine maidens to visit her and prepare her for a visit from the goddess. They explain that Xue had already come to the attention of the celestial bureaucracy because of her good works.

In preparation for the goddess's visit, Xue purified herself and practiced the strictest asceticism for five days and nights. Then Lady Wei Huacun, attended by twenty-seven serving girls, descended into her room. Soon Lady Wei revealed esoteric techniques for visualizing, summoning, and controlling deities. She also gave Xue a grain of the famous nine-times recycled elixir, instructing her to take it eight years later. Before leaving, she predicted Xue's eventual ascent, and promised to send a heavenly host to accompany her to Marchmount Song, the holy mountain of the Center. As we have seen in other entries, such predictions verify sainthood.

From this time on, Xue Xuantong's religious practice escalated in intensity. She fasted and meditated. In response, deities visited, music sounded in empty space, and divine fragrances and light manifested. Her husband, angry at her distance, criticized her in public. Du editorializes that another female saint of the fourth century faced and triumphed over such defamation.

Xue Xuantong's liberation takes place against the background of the Huang Chao rebellion (878-884). Rebels attacked the capital cities, and the imperial court fled to Chengdu in Sichuan province. Officials either left the capitals or stayed and served the rebel leaders. During this time, in late 881, Xue Xuantong, her husband Feng Hui, and their entire household were traveling by boat in what is now Zhejiang province. They encountered a huge and imposing army. The family party shrank back in terror, believing that this was a rebel brigade. But Xue recognized the soldiers as a divine entourage coming to take her away to Mount Song. She scolded them and said she had no intention of departing at this time or from this place. She told them she would leave next spring from her own residence. Everyone present witnessed this event, but did not understand that they had seen Xue refuse to obey an improperly sent divine summons. The summons provides more evidence of her transcendence; her confident refusal indicates her superior position in the celestial hierarchy. This event underlines the bureaucratic nature of human relations with the divine in Daoism.

Early in 882, Xue Xuantong prepared herself for burial. The narrative of her death is especially rich with religious meanings. She took control of her own transformation, preparing her body for her funerary rites by washing her own face and hair—cleansing rituals that were usulaly performed after death by female relatives. Then she took the elixir Lady Wei had given her. Two transcendent girls came to accompany her on her trip to Mount Song. She became ill and passed away overnight at home. Thirty-six cranes, symbols of longevity and favorite ride of the transcendents, settled on her roof and stayed ten days. Her body remained light, warm, and lifelike. A spot of light appeared in the middle of her forehead, then changed into a purple vapor and disappeared, marking the moment of her passing. Preparing her body for burial, the mourners discovered that her hair had thickened and grown longer, a miraculous and paradoxical sign of health in a corpse. The next day, heavenly clouds filled her room, while lightning struck and thunder resounded. Her coffin flew open, revealing only her burial garments and bedding. Xue had already ascended to heaven through liberation by means of the corpse.

The military governor of the region (modern Zhejiang), Zhou Bao, heard of Xue Xuantong's holy life and divine departure. He sent a memorial to Emperor Yizong at his temporary residence in Chengdu, praising the saint and claiming that her career showed heaven's approval of the Tang imperial family. He flattered the emperor, referring to the imperial court's humiliating retreat to Chengdu as a purposeful strategy to expand government-held territory without the bother and bloodshed of war. He celebrated Xue Xuantong as a living auspicious omen, comparing her to famous transcendents of the past. He asserted that she never could have practiced so effectively and attained immortality had it not been for his majesty's charisma.

As proof of her sainthood, he offered the miraculous events surrounding her departure and funeral. The miraculous growth of her hair after death, the gathering of auspicious cranes, the music booming out from invisible sources in broad daylight, the fragrant clouds, the fierce storm that lifted the top off her coffin, and most of all the disappearance of her corpse from that coffin: all these proved beyond a reasonable doubt that she had attained perfection. Her achievement would bring blessings to the region and to the dynasty. Zhou suggested that even in this dark hour of decline, the Tang royal family still possessed the mandate of heaven. (And so they can transmit that mandate to the Wang family, rulers of Former Shu, at whose court Du Guangting served.)

Zhou Bao soon received a response from his majesty, dated 883 and sent from his temporary residence in Chengdu. The emperor acknowledged Xue Xuantong's sainthood and accepted her as an auspicious sign illuminating his reign and nation. He compared her to female saints and goddesses of earlier times, such as the Flower Maiden, number seventeen in this collection, and Lady Wei. The emperor instructed history officials at court to compile Xue's story, and officials at the local government level to fund Daoist institutions associated with her life. Zhou Bao's memorial and the emperor's response certainly served as primary sources for Du Guangting in writing this account. Du closes this biography and his whole book with these words from Emperor Yizong: "We respond to the highest mysteries and extend reverent feelings." This statement makes a suitable end for a work that commemorates holy women by linking them to the highest mysteries of the Dao on the one hand and the devotional responses of humans on the other.

Translation

[116.15b] Ms. Xue was the wife of Feng Hui, the Lesser Governor of Hezhong Province [Shanxi].[194] Her Daoist name was Xuantong [Dark Unity]. Twenty years after being sent in marriage to Feng Hui, she told him that she wanted to live chastely and used illness as her pretext for dwelling alone. Having vowed to burn incense and chant Daoist scriptures, she consistently chanted the "Scripture of the Yellow Courtyard" two or three times a day.[195]

Thirteen years later, two blue-clad jade girls [divine messengers] descended to her room one night. Just before they arrived, radiance like that of the moon illuminated her courtyard, and a fragrant wind breezed through. The season must have been early autumn. The scattering heat was still intense just then, but the clean cool void [the sky] acted as her parasol, while the wind breezed through as if the place were a grotto. The two girls announced:

---

[194] An earlier version of this translation appears in Wang 2003, 366-371. A later account may be found in *Taiping guangji* 296. I have no other information on Feng Hui.

[195] For studies of the *Huangting jing*, (DZ 331, 332) see Homann 1971; Schipper 1975; Kroll 1996.

The Primal Ruler of the Purple Barrens [Lady Wei Huacun] governs the registers concerning education of commoners in the southern quadrant. She has commanded all the various realized ones and great transcendents to descend and [search everywhere] outside the four seas and inside the six directions, in the famous mountains and great rivers. [They are to find all those adepts] who seek and desire long life, profundity of mind, and the veritable Way, and then to descend and instruct them. [16a] Because of Xuantong's skill in good works, she has been recommended repeatedly by the deities of the Earth Bureau. Their reports are already in the archives of the Purple Barrens. In addition, [Lady Wei] has heard that this woman has set her mind [on immortality]. She is especially delighted with your devotion. After a few days she will personally descend here.

It went on like this for five nights in all. Xuantong burned incense and increased the strictness of her practice as she waited for the Primal Ruler. And then, in the fifteenth year of the Total Comprehension reign period [874], on an A-horse [*jiawu*] day, the Primal Ruler descended to Xuantong's room together with a flock of twenty-seven serving girls and realized ones.[196] [Xuantong] bowed to welcome them at the gate. The Primal Ruler sat down and rested. After a good long while, she showed Xuantong the [esoteric] orders from the Yellow Courtyard for enrolling deities, visualizing, and doing religious practice. She gave her one grain of the nine-fold floriate elixir, ordering: "Swallow it after eight years. Then I will certainly send jade girls and a whirlwind chariot to welcome you to Marchmount Song." Saying their farewells, [the visitors] scattered and departed.

From this time on, Xuantong [engaged in Daoist practice to] deepen her mind and still her spirits. She hardly ate. Although realized transcendents descended to invite her with presents, although radiant phosphors lit up empty space while numinous winds [carried] strange fragrances and the harmonious music of cloud harps was performed in her room, [her husband] Feng Hui was not aware of any of this. [16b] Because Xuantong had a separate room, and because she became distant and refused intimacy when she practiced the Way, Feng Hui harbored ignorant and jealous feelings. He regularly slandered and ridiculed her. This was just like the suspicions [of an

---

[196] The Total Comprehension reign period (860-873) took place during the reign of Xianzong. It did not have a fifteenth year, but if it had, it would have been 874.

earlier angry husband that led local officials] to seize the Incomparable Mother of the Eastern Tumulus (Dongling shengmu).[197]

During the G-rat [*kengzi*] year of Broad Illumination [880], great thieves [Huang Chao rebels] penetrated the [capital] city watchtowers.[198] Those wearing the cap strings of office fled and escaped. The ones who remained made illegitimate peace [with the rebel leaders]. Feng and Xuantong sojourned at Jinling in Chang Province [Sichuan]. She was now visualizing deities ceaselessly, and growing in her practice of reverence and devotion.

In the tenth month of the primal year of the reign period Centered Accord [881], [Feng Hui and Xue Xuantong] traveled by boat to the mouth of the Zhi watercourse [Zhejiang]. Riding on the current with numerous family members, neighbors, and female companions, they were approaching their country villa. Suddenly they saw vermilion- and purple-clad official envoys along with armed and armored military officers, all standing on the riverbank in orderly array as if waiting for Xuantong's boat to row over to them. Now this was a region of many villains from all four borders, a place of marauders and thieves. When the people on the boat saw [the assembly on the riverbank], they were startled and alarmed, unwilling to draw closer. Xuantong said, "Don't be afraid," then moved her boat right up to them. The officers and envoys all saluted her. Xuantong commanded them, saying: "Not yet! I will only depart next spring from my private residence. Don't rush me!" Officers and envoys thereupon scattered and departed. [17a] The people sharing the boat with her all witnessed this event, but none understood its meaning.

The next year [882], an I-tiger [*renyin*] year, in the second month, Xuantong washed her hair and face [to prepare her own corpse for burial], then took out the tidbit of elixir that the Primal Ruler of the Purple Barrens had given her.[199] Two transcendent girls descended in secret to her room, urging her to

---

[197] The Incomparable Mother was a fourth-century Daoist saint who flew out a prison window after her husband had her jailed for neglecting her domestic duties in favor of religious practice. Her biography appears in the *Shenxian zhuan*, see *Campany*, 146. Compare entry twenty, the Tea Granny of Guangling.

[198] The Broad Illumination reign period of Xizong lasted only one year: 880. The Huang Chao rebellion lasted from 878 to 884. That rebellion destabilized the late Tang government and economy and caused the reigning emperor to flee to Chengdu in Sichuan province. See Levy 1961; Twitchett 1979.

[199] She is, in effect, preparing her own body for burial. The term "washing the face and hair," *muyu*, refers to bathing the whole body before dressing it in funerary garments. Female family members did the ritual washing of the body after death.

proceed to the heights of Marchmount Song. On the fourteenth day of that month she presented symptoms and passed away in a single evening at her private residence. Thirty-six wingspans of transcendent cranes gathered atop her room. Xuantong's form and substance were light and warm, her appearance like that of a living person. The center of her forehead looked misty, with a spot of white radiance that transformed after a good long time into purple vapor. In her [earlier] ritual washing of her own hair and face, her dark hair had increased in thickness and grown several feet in length.

On the night of the fifteenth day, clouds of variegated colors filled her room, and suddenly people heard sounds of thunder and lightning shaking and crashing. Her coffin lid flew up inside the courtyard. Her corpse had disappeared, leaving behind just her empty burial garments and quilt. Strange fragrances arose. The cloud cranes stayed ten days before departing.

The Regulating and Ordering Notary from Zhexi Province [western Zhejiang], Minister Zhou Bao memorialized:[200]

> This humble one has heard that on the day Lady Zhao ascended to distant regions, her jade appearance was like that of a living person.[201] And at the time when Prior-Born Tao tired of the world, strange fragrances were ceaseless.[202] These instances of feathered transformation [ascents to immortality] are both recorded in the transcendent classics. Might we say that in these brilliant times we are once again seeing such events?

> This humble one takes Feng Hui's wife, Ms. Xue, as someone who rejected dirt and vulgarity from early on, and practiced at the mysterious gate [of the Way] for a long time. As for texts containing the esoteric secrets of the divine transcendents, she was able to grasp their mysterious meanings. Women's [usual] affairs of floriate lead [make up] did not upset her equanimity. If she had not abstained from grains [fasted], eaten magic mushrooms, preserved the genuine [Way], observed a plain white [vegetarian diet], and if she had not entered the world during your incomparable highness's reign, which sets the

---

[200] Zhou Bao was a military governor from an elite family who served under Emperor Xizong during the Huang Chao rebellion.

[201] Lady Zhao was a second-century saint from an eminent Daoist family.

[202] Prior-Born Tao was the great editor, author, and Shangqing Daoist master Tao Hongjing (456-536).

standard for transformations of nonaction by the Mysterious Prime for preserving the one [Way]; if all this were not so, then how could she ever have obtained [elixir] recipes or meditated?

[Ritual] drums and basins along with numinous wild animals repeatedly descended [to her]. Right in the mirror with its image of a grieving simurgh, her hair mysteriously grew again. Thunder and lightning together with auspicious clouds and auroral haze manifested her difference. When she returned to heaven, stringed and wind instruments were heard in broad daylight. Her coffin was empty; only her clothes and quilt were there. She came in exile to dwell temporarily among humans. Becoming a transcendent, she returned to her home above the heavens. Her story transmits a thousand old beauties and raises up this singular time. Although she belongs among the blessings and auspicious omens of this commandary, her story is also a bountiful event for the nation and the dynasty.

Your servant respectfully divides the abundance, sending along this hastily completed memorial. Having heard with surpassing delight the news of our government's rushing heaven and extending our territory without the responsibility of combat, I offer my utmost congratulations.

The same year [883], on the fifteenth day of the second month, the temporary government in Chengdu issued an imperial memorial that read:

The Way of the teachings of heaven is manifested in the transcendent classics. Those of the highest virtue diligently practice hidden good works. After reading this memorial [from Zhou Bao], I realized [that Dongxuan's story] harmonizes different auspicious signs. Like Ms. Wei [Huacun's] ascent to transcendence or compared to the Flower Maiden's descent into our world, she adds comparable radiance to her commandary and county in addition to illuminating our nation and dynasty. It would be appropriate to instruct history officials to compile [her story] on tablets and fascicles. And I instruct officials from the circuit level on up to provide money for the purpose of repairing Daoist altars with their golden ordination registers in the places where she dwelt. Thereby we respond to the highest mysteries and extend reverent feelings. Written during the third year of residence at the imperial halting place in Chengdu [883].

Conclusions

In translating this set of biographies of Daoist holy women by Du Guangting, I had several intentions. I wanted to introduce the world and practice of medieval Daoist women to a wider audience, and for that purpose I have tried to let Du Guangting's work speak for itself, while clarifying it with relevant and detailed but not tedious annotations.

Beyond that, my most ambitious goal has been to return women to the Chinese historical world. Women were all over the place in Chinese history: in the family, in the fields, in the marketplace, in the harem, in the convent, and in the hermitage. Through Du Guangting's book, I have found women in all these locations.

Women were also present in the Chinese textual record. Scholars have often ignored texts about or by women as unreliable, uninteresting, or not appropriate for intellectual analysis. Poetry, material culture, and hagiography have especially been dismissed or treated with suspicion if not contempt. Until we discover a new set of documents that directly answers all our questions about gender and the lives of women in medieval China, we have to work with what survives. We can devise techniques to use whatever historical sources remain concerning women's lives and experiences. Hagiographical texts, such as the subject of the present study, make valuable primary sources.

Du Guangting's "Records of the Assembled Transcendents of the Fortified Walled City" provides a wealth of information about women in relation to Daoism, the state, and society during the Tang dynasty. If we read Du Guangting's hagiographical accounts with care, allowing for his beliefs and agendas as a male Daoist master and court official, they reveal a great deal about women in both private and public life. His accounts often draw from contemporary cult or family records, placing them close to their subjects. When we have a chance to verify a historical event or custom using reliable outside sources, Du's records invariably hold up. They contain numerous references to family, government, class, technology, work, material culture, and daily life.

The collection of biographies also deepens our understanding of Tang Daoist theory and practice. Most of this information appears in small lectures Du Guangting smuggles into individual biographies. In this manner he presents his teachings on meditation and elixirs, hierarchies of practice, stages of religious attainment, classes of transcendents, governments of the grotto heavens, and individual responsibility for attaining the Dao.

Du's "Records" complicates and enriches our picture of Tang society and thought. We see that neither the Daoist religion nor the Tang dynasty created social equality between men and women, but that Tang Daoism provided opportunities for some women that were quite extraordinary. Tension between the possibility of spiritual equality in religious practice along with the persistence of inequality between males and females in Tang society runs through the lives of the Daoist female saints. As presented here, they made their worlds, but they did not make them just as they pleased. Gender hierarchies, along with those of age and social class, profoundly affected their daily and religious lives.

In dwelling upon physical practices, the biographies also foreground the female body. Du exposes the body as both instrument and obstacle to his subjects' desires. His "Records" also document medieval Daoist beliefs about the body. These include the image of the body as a microcosm filled with deities, the efficacy of physical austerities such as fasting and sexual abstinence to purify and transform the body, and the transcendence of the adept's body at the end of a life of devoted practice. In addition, we see that Tang women Daoists carried out religious practices roughly identical to those of Tang men. This was not true in later periods, when men and women's paths and practices were rigorously separated.

We also see that medieval Daoists did not necessarily consider Confucian scholars the enemy. The Tang dynasty predates the triumph and institutional hegemony of the didactic Li-school, known in the West as Neo-Confucianism, that became characteristic of later imperial periods. With the special patronage of the Tang royal family, and the devotion of officials and merchants as well as farmers and craftsmen, Daoism played on a more equal field of ideas in the Tang than it would in later dynasties. In fact, Daoists competed most vigorously with Buddhists for imperial patronage and popular devotion. As a court official, Du aligns himself with the Confucian values and political interests of the imperial bureaucracy. As a Daoist master, he promotes the efficacy of Daoism as a means of self-cultivation and salvation and disparages Buddhism.

Most of the biographies of Chinese women that have been studied and translated previously, with the notable exception of accounts of Buddhist nuns, follow Confucian models. They depict women in situations that exemplify virtues related to family obligation, such as hard-working and self-denying mothers, dutiful daughters-in-law, devoted wives, faithful widows, and occasionally filial daughters. Du Guangting's biographies stand outside the Confucian norms, and offer a dramatically different view of the possibilities available for women. The stories do not always contest traditional norms, but they always adjust or complicate our picture. The lives of the Daoist holy women are a useful corrective to the more one-dimensional portrayal of women in most other sources.

Du Guangting narrates the different stories in different styles, from poetic to dramatic to humorous, depending on the content and probably on his sources. The author's language can be quite lush and colorful, describing scenes of rituals and heavens with enough detail for us to visualize them. Du's word pictures have an intense and hypnotic attraction that become part of the message he is trying to convey. The text itself can express sublime spirituality in beautiful words that must have influenced readers then and later, and certainly had an effect on women's spirituality in later periods of Chinese history. Traces of Du's stories appear in women's (and men's) poetry and accounts of visionary experiences of later periods. If we know these stories, we can interpret the later texts that refer to them.

I hope that the small group of biographies translated here will provide useful comparative material for scholars investigating women in other religions in Asia, such as Buddhism, Hinduism, and Islam. The women Du chronicles also share points of similarity and contrast with women of other times and places, such as medieval to early modern Christian nuns. Future pursuit of these commonalities and differences can certainly shed light on religion, culture, and gender as well as on their interactions.

Du Guangting's writing, quite vivid and detailed at times, preserves many elements of Tang dynasty material culture. Read in conjunction with the archaeological record and with textual material preserved in official and unofficial sources, his records of the Daoist holy women provide rich descriptions of clothing, hairstyles, utensils, means of transportation, sacred and secular architecture, crops, foods, diseases, weaving and textiles, and animals both real and imaginary.

Finally, I think the stories themselves, even without any commentary, are fascinating, entertaining, and sometimes inspiring. If I have fulfilled my intentions, they will provide pleasure and diversion as well as instruction and stimulation to further inquiry.

Bibliography

Adshead, S. A. M. 2004. *T'ang China: The Rise of the East in World History*. New York: Palgrave McMillan.

Anderson, Poul. 1994. "On Reaching the Gate of Heaven Together: Equality and Inequality of the Sexes in Early Daoism." Paper presented at the Association for Asian Studies, Boston.

Barrett, T. H. 1996. *Taoism under the T'ang: Religion and Empire during the Golden Age of Chinese History*. London: Wellsweep Press.

Bell, Catherine. 1987. "Tu Kuang-t'ing." In *Encyclopedia of Religion*, edited by Mircea Eliade. New York: Macmillan.

_____.1992. *Ritual Theory, Ritual Practice*. Oxford: Oxford University Press.

Bell, Rudolph M. 1985. *Holy Anorexia*. Chicago: University of Chicago Press.

Benn, Charles. 1991. *The Cavern-Mystery Transmission: A Taoist Ordination Rite of A.D. 711*. Honolulu: University of Hawai'i Press.

_____. 2002. *China's Golden Age: Everyday Life in the Tang Dynasty*. New York: Oxford University Press.

Birch Cyril. 1965. "The Curly-Bearded Hero." In *Anthology of Chinese Literature*, edited by Cyril Birch, 1:314-22. New York: Grove Press.

_____, ed. 1974. *Studies in Chinese Literary Genres*. Berkeley: University of California Press.

Birrell, Anne. 1993a. *Popular Songs and Ballads of Han China*. Honolulu: University of Hawai'i Press.

_____. 1993b. *Chinese Mythology: An Introduction*. Baltimore: Johns Hopkins University Press.

_____. 1999. *The Classic of Mountains and Seas*. London: Penguin Books.

Blofeld, John. 1978. *Bodhisattva of Compassion: The Mystical Tradition of Kuan Yin*. Boulder: Shambhala.

Bokenkamp, Stephen R. 1986. "The Peach Flower Font and the Grotto Passage." *Journal of the American Oriental Society* 106:65-79.

_____. 1997. *Early Daoist Scriptures*. With a contribution by Peter Nickerson. Berkeley: University of California Press.

Boltz, Judith M. 1987. *A Survey of Taoist Literature: Tenth to Seventeenth Centuries.* Berkeley: University of California Press.

Bray, Francesca. 1997. *Technology and Gender: Fabrics of Power in Late Imperial China.* Berkeley: University of California Press.

Brown, Peter. 1981. *The Cult of the Saints: Its Rise and Function in Latin Christianity.* Chicago: University of Chicago Press.

Bumbacher, Stephan Peter. 2000. *The Fragments of the Daoxue zhuan.* Frankfurt: Peter Lang.

Bynum, Caroline Walker. 1987. *Holy Feast and Holy Fast: The Religious Significance of Food To Medieval Women.* Berkeley: University of California Press.

Cahill, Suzanne E. 1985. "Sex and the Supernatural in Medieval China: Cantos on the Transcendent Who Presides Over the River." *Journal of the American Oriental Society* 105:197-220.

_____. 1990. "Practice Makes Perfect: Paths to Transcendence for Women in Medieval China." *Taoist Resources* 2.2:23-42.

_____. 1992. "Sublimation in Medieval China: The Case of the Mysterious Woman of the Nine Heavens." *Journal of Chinese Religions* 20:91-102.

_____. 1993. *Transcendence and Divine Passion: The Queen Mother of the West in Medieval China.* Stanford: Stanford University Press.

_____. 1999. "Smell Good and Get a Job: How Daoist Women Saints Were Verified and Legitimized During the Tang Dynasty." In *Presence and Presentation: Women in the Chinese Literati Tradition,* edited by Sherry Mou, 171-86. New York: St Martin's Press.

_____. 2000. "Pien Tung-hsüan: A Taoist Woman Saint of the T'ang Dynasty (618-906). In *Women Saints in World Religions,* edited by Arvind Sharma, 205-20. Albany: State University of New York Press.

_____. 2001. "Biography of the Daoist Saint, Wang Fengxian, by Du Guangting (850-933)." In *Under Confucian Eyes: Writings on Gender in Chinese History,* edited by in Susan Mann and Yu-yin Cheng, 16-28. Berkeley, University of California Press.

_____. 2002. "Material Culture and the Dao: Textiles, Boats, and Zithers in the Poetry of Yu Xuanji (844-868)." In *Daoist Identity: History, Lineage, and Ritual,* edited by Livia Kohn and Harold D. Roth, 102-26. Honolulu: University of Hawai'i Press.

_____. 2003a. "Discipline and Transformation: Body and Practice in the Lives of Daoist Holy Women of Tang China." In *Women and Confucian Cultures in Premodern China, Korea, and Japan,* edited by Dorothy Ko et al., 251-78. Berkeley: University of California Press.

_____. 2003b. "Resenting the Silk Robes that Hide Their Poems: Female Voices in the Poetry of Tang Dynasty Daoist Nuns." In *Tang Song nüxing yu shehui* [Women and Society in the Tang and Song Dynasties], edited by Deng Xiaonan, 1:519-67. Shanghai: Cishu chubanshe.

Campany, Robert Ford. 1996. *Strange Writing: Anomaly Accounts in Early Medieval China*. Albany: State University of New York Press.

_____. 2002. *To Live as Long as Heaven and Earth: A Translation and Study of Ge Hong's Traditions of the Divine Transcendents*. Berkeley: University of California Press.

Cass, Victoria. 1999. *Dangerous Women: Warriors, Grannies, and Geishas of the Ming*. Lanham, Md: Rowman and Littlefield.

Cedzich, Ursula-Angelika. 1993. "Ghosts and Demons, Law and Order: Grave Quelling Texts and Early Taoist Liturgy." *Taoist Resources* 4.2:23-35.

_____. 2001. "Corpse Deliverance, Substitute Bodies, Name Change, and Feigned Death: Aspects of Metamorphosis and Immortality in Early Medieval China." *Journal of Chinese Religions* 29:1-68.

Chamberlayne, J. H. 1962. "The Development of Kuan Yin: Chinese Goddess of Mercy." *Numen* 9:45-52.

Chavannes, Edouard. 1910. *Le T'ai chan: Essai de monographie d'un culte chinois*. Paris: Annales de Muset Guimet.

Ch'en, Kenneth. 1964. *Buddhism in China: A Historical Survey*. Princeton: Princeton University Press.

Cutler, Robert Joe, and William Gordon Crowell. 1999. *Empresses and Consorts: Selections from Cheng Shou's Records of the Three States with Pei Congzhi's Commentary*. Honolulu: University of Hawai'i Press.

DeBary, Wm Theodore, and Irene Bloom, 1999. *Sources of Chinese Tradition*. New York: Columbia University Press.

DeMeyer, Ian A. M. 1998. "A Daoist Master's Justification of Reclusion: Wu Yun's Poems on 'Investigating the Past'." *Sanjiao wenxian* 2:9-40.

_____. 1999. "Mountainhopping: The Life of Wu Yun." *T'ang Studies* 17:171-211.

Deng Xiaonan, ed. 2003. *Tang Song nüxing yu shehui* [Women and Society in the Tang and Song Dynasties]. 2 vols. Shanghai: Cishu chubanshe.

Despeux, Catherine. 1986. "L'ordination des femmes taoïstes sous les T'ang." *Etudes chinoises* 5:53-100.

_____, and Livia Kohn. 2003. *Women in Daoism*. Cambridge: Three Pines Press.

DeWoskin, Kenneth. 1983. *Doctors, Diviners, and Magicians of Ancient China: Biographies of Fang-shih*. New York: Columbia University Press.

_____, and J. I. Crump. 1996. *In Search of the Supernatural: The Written Record*. Stanford: Stanford University Press.

Duby, Georges. 1978. *Medieval Marriage: Two Models from Twelfth-Century France*, transl. *Elborg Forster*. Baltimore: Johns Hopkins University Press.

Ebrey, Patricia B. 1993. *The Inner Quarters: Marriage and the Lives of Chinese Women During the Sung Dynasty*. Berkeley: University of California Press.

_____. 2003. "The Book of Filial Piety and The Book of Filial Piety for Women." In *Images of Women in Chinese thought and Culture: Writings from the Pre-Qin Period Through the Song Dynasty*, edited by Robin R. Wang, 372-90. Indianapolis: Hackett Publishing.

Eskildsen, Stephen. 1998. *Asceticism in Early Chinese Religion*. Albany: State University of New York Press.

Furth, Charlotte. 1999. *A Flourishing Yin: Gender in China's Medical History, 960 - 1665*. Berkeley: University of California Press.

Gomez, Louis O. 1996. *The Land of Bliss: The Paradise of the Buddha of Measureless Light*. Honolulu: University of Hawai'i Press.

Graham, A.C. 1990. *The Book of Lieh-tzu*. New York: Columbia University Press.

Grant, Beata. 1995. "Patterns of Female Religious Experience in Qing Dynasty Popular Literature." *Journal of Chinese Religions* 23:29-58.

Guisso, R. W. L. 1978. *Wu Tse-t'ien and the Politics of Legitimation in T'ang China*. Bellingham: Western Washington State Press.

Hahn, Thomas H. 1988. "The Standard Taoist Mountain and Related Features of Religious Geography." *Cahiers d'Extrême-Asie* 4:145-56.

_____. 2000. "Daoist Sacred Sites." In *Daoism Handbook*, edited by Livia Kohn, 683-707. Leiden: E. Brill.

Harper, Donald. 1994. "Resurrection in Warring States Popular Religion." *Taoist Resources* 5.2:13-28.

Hawkes, David. 1959. *Ch'u-Tz'u: The Songs of the South*. Boston: Beacon.

_____. 1974. "The Quest for the Goddess." In *Studies in Chinese Literary Genres*, edited by Cyril Birch, 42-68. Berkeley: University of California Press.

Hightower, J. R. 2000. "The Peach Blossom Spring." In *Classical Chinese Literature: An Anthology of Translations*, edited by John Mitford and Joseph S. M. Lau, 1: 515-17. New York: Columbia University Press.

Hinsch, Bret. 2002. *Women in Early Imperial China*. Lanham, Maryland: Rowman and Littlefield.

Homann, Rolf. 1971. *Die wichtigsten Körpergottheiten im Huang-t'ing-ching*. Göppingen: Alfred Kümmerle.

_____. 1976. *Pai Wen Pien*. Leiden: Brill Academic Publishers.

Hurvitz, Leon. 1976. *Scripture of the Lotus Blossom of the Fine Dharma*. New York: Columbia University Press.

Hyland, Elizabeth Watts. 1984. "The Oracles of the True Ones, Scroll One." Ph. D. Diss., University of California Press, Berkeley.

Idema, Wilt, and Beata Grant. 2004. *The Red Brush: Writing Women of Imperial China*. Cambridge: Harvard University Press.

Jamison, Kay Redfield. 1999. *Night Falls Fast: Understanding Suicide*. New York: Albert A. Knopf.

Ji Yougong. 1962. *Tangshi jishi* [Recorded Anecdotes Concerning Tang Poetry]. Hong Kong: Zhonghua.

Johnson, Wallace. 1979. *The T'ang Code: Volume I, General Principles*. Princeton: Princeton University Press.

_____. 1997. *The T'ang Code: Volume II, Specific Articles*. Princeton: Princeton University Press.

Jordan, David K. and Daniel Overmyer. 1986. *The Flying Phoenix: Aspects of Chinese Sectarianism in Taiwan*. Princeton: Princeton University Press.

Kaltenmark, Maxime. 1953. *Le Lie-sien tchouan*. Peking: Universitaire de Paris.

Katz, Paul. 1999. *Images of the Immortal: The Cult of Lü Dongbin at the Palace of Eternal Joy*. Honolulu: University of Hawai'i Press.

Kelly, Jeanne. 1978. "The Poetess Yü Hsüan-chi." In. *Traditional Chinese Stories: Themes and Variations*, edited by Y. W. Ma and Joseph S. M. Lau, 305-06. New York: Columbia University Press.

Kieschnick, John. 2003. *The Impact of Buddhism on Chinese Material Culture*. Princeton: Princeton University Press.

Kinney, Anne Behnke, ed. 1995. *Chinese Views of Childhood*. Honolulu: University of Hawai'i Press.

_____. 2004. *Representations of Childhood and Youth in Early China*. Stanford: Stanford University Press.

Kirkland, Russell. 1986. "The Last Daoist Grand Master at the T'ang Imperial Court: Li Huan-kuang and T'ang Hsüan-tsung." *T'ang Studies* 4:43-67.

_____. 1991. "A Taoist Priestess in T'ang China." *Journal of Chinese Religions* 19:47-73.

_____. 1992. "Tales of Thaumaturgy: T'ang Accounts of the Wonderworker Ye Fashan." *Monumenta Serica* 40:47-86.

_____. 1997. "Dimensions of Tang Taoism: The State of the Field at the End of the Millenium." *T'ang Studies* 15/16:79-123.

_____. 2004. *Taoism: The Enduring Tradition.* New York: Routledge.

Ko, Dorothy. 1994. *Teachers of the Inner Chambers: Women and Culture in Seventeenth Century China.* Stanford: Stanford University Press.

_____. 2001. *Every Step A Lotus: Shoes for Bound Feet.* Berkeley: University of California Press.

_____, JaHyun Kim Haboush, and Joan Piggot, eds. 2003. *Women and Confucian Cultures in Premodern China, Korea, and Japan.* Berkeley: University of California Press.

Kohn, Livia. 1987. *Seven Steps to the Tao: Sima Chengzhen's Zuowang lun.* St. Augustin/Nettetal: Steyler Verlag.

_____, ed. 1989. *Taoist Meditation and Longevity Techniques.* Ann Arbor: University of Michigan.

_____. 1995a. *Laughing at the Dao: Debates among Buddhists and Taoists in Medieval China.* Princeton: Princeton University Press.

_____. 1995b. "Kôshin: A Taoist Cult in Japan. Part II: Historical Development." *Japanese Religions* 20.1:34-55.

_____. 1997. "Yin Xi: The Master at the Beginning of the Scripture." *Journal of Chinese Religions* 25:83-139.

_____. 2003. *Monastic Life in Medieval Daoism: A Cross-Cultural Perspective.* Honolulu: University of Hawai'i Press.

_____, and Russell Kirkland. 2000. "Daoism in the Tang (618-907)." In *Daoism Handbook*, edited by Livia Kohn, 339-83. Leiden: E. Brill.

Kominami Ichirō. 1974. "*Seiōbo to shichi seki denshō*" [The Queen Mother of the West and traditions about the Sevenths Night]. *Tōhō gakuhō* 46:33-81.

Komjathy, Louis. 2002. *Title Index to Daoist Collections.* Cambridge, Mass.: Three Pines Press.

Kroll, Paul. 1984. "True Dates of the Reigns and Reign Periods of the T'ang." *T'ang Studies* 2:25-30.

_____. 1985. "In the Halls of the Azure Lad." *Journal of the American Oriental Society* 105:75-94.

_____. 1996. "Body Gods and Inner Vision: *The Scripture of the Yellow Court*. In *Religions of China in Practice*, edited by Donald S. Lopez Jr., 149-55. Princeton: Princeton University Press.

Lai, Sophia Sufen. 1999. "Father in Heaven, Mother in Hell: Gender Politics in the Creation and Transformations of Mulian's Mother." In *Presence and Presentation: Women in the Chinese Literati Tradition*, edited by Sherry Mou, 187-214. New York: St Martin's Press.

Lagerwey, John. 1987. *Taoist Ritual in Chinese Society and History*. New York: Macmillan.

Lee, Pauline C. 2003. "Biographies of Women." In *Images of Women in Chinese Thought and Culture: Writings from the Pre-Qin Period Through the Song Dynasty*, edited by Robin R. Wang, 149-61. Indianapolis: Hackett Publishing.

Levering, Miriam. 1989. "Studies of Enlightened Women in Ch'an and the Chinese Buddhist Female Bodhisattva/Goddess Tradition." In *Women and Goddess Traditions in Antiquity and Today*, edited by Karen L. King, 137-76. Minneapolis: Fortress Press.

Lévi, Jean. 1983. "L'abstinance des céréales chez les taoïstes." *Etudes chinoises* 1:3-47.

Levy, Howard. 1961. *Biography of Huang Ch'ao*. Berkeley: University of California Press.

Lewis, Mark E. 1990. *Sanctioned Violence in Early China*. Albany: State University of New York Press.

Liang Boquan. 1999. "Shi *sheng*" [Explaining the term *sheng*]. *Xin'gen* [Root Exploration] 8:41-44.

Lin, Yuan-huei. 1990. "The Weight of Mt. T'ai: Patterns of Suicide in Traditional Chinese History and Culture." Ph. D. Diss., University of Wisconsin, Madison.

Little, Stephen, and Shawn Eichman. 2000. *Taoism and the Arts of China*. Berkeley: University of California Press.

Loewe, Michael. 1979. *Ways to Paradise: The Chinese Quest for Immortality*. London: George Allen and Unwin.

Luo Chengming. 2003a. "*Guanyu Du Guangting shengping jige wenti de kaochang*" [An Examination of Several Problems in the Life of Du Guangting]. *Wenxue yichang*, 5:39-46.

_____. 2003b. "*Yongchengliexian zhuan caizi Liexianzhuan pianmu tanxi: Jianlun Du Guangting dui Fanzhongshu zhi taidu*" [Comparison of the Material in 'Transmissions of the Arrayed Transcendents of the Fortified Walled City' and 'Transmissions of the Arrayed Transcendents': A Discussion of Du Guangting's Attitude to Manuals about the Arts of the Bedchamber]. *Guji zhangli yanjiu xuekan* 3:38-42.

Ma, Y.W., and Joseph S.M. Lau, ed. 1978. *Traditional Chinese Stories: Themes and Variations*. New York: Columbia University.

Mair, Victor. 1989. *T'ang Transformation Texts*. Cambridge: Harvard University Press.

_____, ed. 1994a. *The Columbia Anthology of Traditional Chinese Literature*. New York: Columbia University Press.

_____. 1994b. "Transformation Text on Maudgalyayana Rescuing his Mother from the Underworld, with Pictures, One Scroll, with Preface." In *The Columbia Anthology of Traditional Chinese Literature*, edited by Victor Mair, 1093-1127. New York: Columbia University Press, 1093-1127.

Mann, Susan. 1997. *Precious Records: Women in China's Long Eighteenth Century*. Stanford: Stanford University Press.

_____, and Yu-yin Cheng, eds. 2001. *Under Confucian Eyes: Writings on Gender in Chinese History*. Berkeley: University of California Press.

Maspero, Henri. 1981. *Taoism and Chinese Religion*. Translated by Frank Kierman. Amherst: University of Massachusetts Press.

Mather, Richard . 1979. "K'ou Ch'ien-chih and the Taoist Theocracy at the Northern Wei Court 425-451." In *Facets of Taoism*, edited by Holmes Welch and Anna Seidel, 103-22. New Haven, Conn.: Yale University Press.

Mathieu, Rémi. 1978. *Le Mu tianzi zhuan: Traduction annotée, étude critique*. Paris: Institut des Hautes Etudes Chinoises.

_____. 1983. *Etude sur la mythologie et l'ethnologie de la Chine ancienne*. 2 vols. Paris: Collège du France.

McNair, Amy. 1998. *The Upright Brush: Yan Zhengqing's Calligraphy and Song Literati Politics*. Honolulu: University of Hawai'i Press.

McNamara, Jo Ann Kay. 1996. *Sisters in Arms: Catholic Nuns Through Two Millennia*. Cambridge: Harvard University Press.

Mitford, John, and Joseph S. M. Lau, eds. 2000. *Chinese Classical Literature: An Anthology of Translations*, 1. New York: Columbia University Press.

Mori Ogai. 1951. *Gogenki* [Yu Xuanji]. In *Ogai zenshū* [Complete Works of Ogai]. Tokyo: Iwanami.

Mou, Sherry E., ed. 1999. *Presence and Presentation: Women in the Chinese Literati Tradition*. New York: St Martin's Press.

_____. 2004. *Gentlemen's Prescriptions for Women's Lives: A Thousand Years of Biographies of Chinese Women*. Armonk, New York: M.E. Sharpe.

Needham, Joseph, et al. 1954-2005. *Science and Civilisation in China*. Cambridge: Cambridge University Press.

Nienhauser, William H., Jr. 1986. *The Indiana Companion to Traditional Chinese Literature*. Bloomington: Indiana University Press.

O'Hara, Albert Richard. 1971. *The Position of Woman in Early China: According to the Lieh Nü Chuan*. Taipei: Meiya.

Owen, Stephen. 1996. *An Anthology of Chinese Literature*. New York: Norton.

Paul, Diana. 1985. *Women in Buddhism: Images of the Feminine in Mahayana Tradition*. Stanford: Stanford University Press.

Penny, Benjamin. 2000. "Immortality and Transcendence." In *Daoism Handbook*, edited by Livia Kohn, 109-33. Leiden: E. Brill.

Percy, Walker. 1979. *Lost in the Cosmos*. New York: Washington Square Press.

Raphals, Lisa. 1998. *Sharing the Light: Representations of Women and Virtue in Early China*. Albany: State University of New York Press.

Robinet, Isabelle. 1979a. "Metamorphosis and Deliverance from the Corpse in Taoism." *History of Religions* 19:37-70.

_____. 1979b. "A Study of the Relationship between the Shangqing Movement and the Traditions of Fang shih and the Seekers of Immortality." Paper presented at the Third International Daoist Studies Conference, Unterägeri, Switzerland.

_____. 1984. *La révélation du Shangqing dans l'histoire du taoïsme*, 2 vols. Paris: Ecole Française d'Extrême-Orient.

_____. 1990. "The Place and Meaning of the Notion of *Taiji* in Taoist Sources Prior to the Ming Dynasty." *History of Religions* 29:373-411.

_____. 1993. *Taoist Meditation: The Mao-shan Tradition of Great Purity*. Translated by Julien Pas and Norman Girardot. Albany: State University of New York Press.

_____. 1997. *Taoism: Growth of a Religion*. Translated by Phyllis Brooks. Stanford: Stanford University Press.

Robinson, Richard H., and Willard L. Johnson. 1982. *The Buddhist Religion: A Historical Introduction*. Belmont, Calif: Wadsworth.

Robson, James. 1995a. "The Polymorphous Space of the Southern Marchmount (*Nanyue*)." *Cahiers d'Extrême-Asie* 8:221-64.

_____. 1995b. "The Marchmount System." In *The Sacred Mountains of Asia*, edited by John Einarsen, 16-17. Boston: Shambhala.

_____. 1995c. "Polymorphous Space: the Contested Space of Nanyue." In *The Sacred Mountains of Asia*, edited by John Einarsen, 121-24. Boston: Shambhala.

Rong Xinjiang et al., eds 1995-2005. *Tang yanjiu* [Tang Studies]. Beijing: Beijing daxue.

Saso, Michael. 1972. *Taoism and the Rite of Cosmic Renewal*. Bellingham: Western Washington University.

Schafer, Edward H. 1967. *The Vermilion Bird: T'ang Images of the South*. Berkeley: University of California Press.

_____. 1977a. *Pacing the Void: T'ang Approaches to the Stars*. Berkeley: University of California Press.

_____. 1977b. "The Restoration of the Shrine of Wei Hua-ts'un at Lin-ch'uan in the Eighth Century." *Journal of Oriental Studies* 15:124-37.

_____. 1978. "The Jade Woman of Greatest Mystery." *History of Religions* 17:387-98.

_____. 1979. "Three Divine Women of Ancient China." *CLEAR* 1:31-42.

_____. 1980. *Mao Shan in T'ang Times*. Boulder, Col.: Society for the Study of Chinese Religions.

_____. 1981. "Wu Yün's 'Cantos on Pacing the Void'." *Harvard Journal of Asiatic Studies* 41:377-415.

_____. 1982. "Wu Yün's 'Stanzas on Saunters in Sylphdom'." *Monumenta Serica* 35: 1-37.

_____. 1985. "The Princess Realized in Jade." *T'ang Studies* 3:1-23.

Schipper, Kristofer M. 1965. *L'empereur Wou des Han dans la legende taoiste*. Paris: Ecole Française d'Extrême-Orient.

_____. 1975. *Concordance du Houang-t'ing king*. Paris: Publications de l'Ecole Française d'Extrême-Orient.

_____. 1978. "The Taoist Body." *History of Religions* 17:355-86.

_____. 1979. "Le Calendrier de jade-note sur le *Laozi zhongjing*." *Nachrichten der deutschen Gesellschaft fur Natur- und Völkerkunde Ostasiaens* 125:75-79.

_____. 1994. *The Taoist Body*. Translated by Karen C. Duval Berkeley: University of California Press.

_____, and Franciscus Verellen, eds. 2004. *The Taoist Canon: A Historical Companion to the Daozang*. 3 vols. Chicago: University of Chicago Press.

Sharma, Arvind, ed. 2000. *Women Saints in World Religions*. Albany: State University of New York Press.

Sivin, Nathan. 1968. *Chinese Alchemy: Preliminary Studies*. Cambridge: Harvard University Press.

_____. 1980. "The Theoretical Basis of Elixir Alchemy." In *Science and Civilisation in China*, by Joseph Needham et al, 5.4:210-323. Cambridge: Cambridge University Press.

Smith, Thomas E. 1992. "Ritual and the Shaping of Narrative: The Legend of the Han Emperor Wu." Ph. D. Diss., University of Michigan, Ann Arbor.

Soymié, Michel. 1943. "Le Lo-feou chan: étude de geographie religieuse." *Bulletin de l'Ecole Française d'Extrême-Orient* 42:1-104.

Strasberg, Richard I. 2002. *A Chinese Bestiary: Strange Creatures from the Guideways through Mountains and Streams*. Berkeley: University of California Press.

Strickmann, Michel. 1978. "The Mao-shan Revelations: Taoism and the Aristocracy." *T'oung Pao* 63:1-63.

_____. 1979. "On the Alchemy of T'ao Hung-jing." In *Facets of Taoism*, edited by Holmes Welch and Anna Seidel, 123-92. New Haven, Conn.: Yale University Press.

_____. 1981. *Le taoïsme du Mao chan: chronique d'une révélation*. Paris: Collège du France, Institut des Hautes Etudes Chinoises.

Strong, Marilee. 1998. *A Bright Red Scream: Self-Mutilation and the Language of Pain*. New York: Viking.

Styron, William. 1990. *Darkness Visible: A Memoir of Madness*. New York: Random House.

Swann, Nancy Lee. 2001 [1932]. *Pan Chao: Foremost Woman Scholar of China*. Ann Arbor: University of Michigan, Center for Chinese Studies.

Teiser, Stephen F. 1988. *The Yü-lan-p'en Festival in Medieval Chinese Religion*. Princeton: Princeton University Press.

Thich, Nhat Hanh. 1988. *The Heart of Understanding: Commentaries on the Prajna-paramita Heart Sutra*. Berkeley: Parallax Press.

_____. 1992. *The Diamond that Cuts Through Illusion: Commentaries on the Prajna-paramita Diamond Sutra*. Berkeley: Parallax Press.

Tsai, Kathryn Ann. 1994. *Lives of the Nuns: Biographies of Chinese Buddhist Nuns from the Fourth to Sixth Centuries*. Honolulu: University of Hawai'i Press.

Tung, Jowen R. 2000. *Fables for the Patriarchs: Gender Politics in Tang Discourse*. Lanham, Md: Rowen and Litlefield.

Twitchett, Denis, ed. 1979. *The Cambridge History of China Volume 3: Sui and T'ang China, 589-906*. Cambridge: Cambridge University Press.

_____, and Michael Loewe. 1986. *The Cambridge History of China, Volume I: The Ch'in and Han Empires, 221 B.C- A.D. 220*. Cambridge: Cambridge University Press.

Van Gulik, Robert H. 1961. *Sexual Life in Ancient China*. Leiden: Brill Academic Publishers.

_____. 1968. *Poets and Murder*. Chicago: University of Chicago Press.

Vauchez, Andre. 1997. *Sainthood in the Later Middle Ages*. Translated by By Jean Birrell. Cambridge: Cambridge University Press.

Verellen, Franciscus. 1989. *Du Guangting (850-933): taoïste de cour à la fin de la Chine médiévale*. Paris: Collège du France, Institut des Hautes Etudes Chinoises.

_____. 1995. "The Beyond Within: Grotto-Heavens (*dongtian*) in Taoist Ritual and Cosmology." *Cahiers d'Extrême-Asie* 8:265-90.

Waltner, Ann. 1987. "T'an Yang-tzu and Wang Shih-chen: Visionary and Bureaucrat in the Late Ming." *Late Imperial China* 8:105-33.

_____. 1990. *Getting an Heir: Adoption and the Construction of Kinship in Late Imperial China*. Honolulu: University of Hawai'i Press.

Wang, Robin. 2003. *Women in Chinese Thought and Culture: Writings from the Pre-Qin Period through the Song Dynasty*. Cambridge, Mass: Hackett Publishing.

Ware, James R. 1966. *Alchemy, Medicine & Religion in the China of A.D. 320: The Nei P'ien of Ko Hung*. Cambridge: MIT Press.

Watson, Burton. 1963. *The Complete Writings of Chuang-tzu*. New York: Columbia University Press.

_____. 1971. *Chinese Rhyme-Prose: Poems in the Fu Form from the Han and the Six Dynasties Periods*. New York: Columbia University Press.

_____. 1974. *Courtier and Commoner in Ancient China: Selections from the History of the Former Han Dynasty by Pan Ku*. New York: Columbia University Press.

_____. 1993. *The Lotus Sutra*. New York: Columbia University Press.

Wile, Douglas. 1992. *Art of the Bedchamber: The Chinese Sexual Yoga Classics Including Women's Solo Meditation Texts*. Albany: State University of New York Press.

Woodward, Kenneth L. 1990. *Making Saints: How the Catholic Church Determines Who Becomes a Saint, Who Doesn't, and Why*. New York: Simon & Schuster.

Wright, Arthur. 1964. *Buddhism in Chinese History*. Stanford: Stanford University Press.

Xiong, Victor Cunrui. 2000. *Sui-Tang Chang'an: A Study in the Urban History of Medieval China*. Ann Arbor: University of Michigan, Center for Chinese Studies.

Yamada, Toshiaki. 2000. "The Lingbao School." In *Daoism Handbook*, edited by Livia Kohn, 225-55. Leiden: E. Brill.

Yang Jialuo. 1965. *Tangren xiaoshuo* [Fiction by Tang Dynasty Authors]. Taipei: Shijie shuju.

Yang Li. 2000. "Daojiao nü shenxian 'Yongcheng jixian lu' yanjiu" [A Study of the Biographies of Daoist Female Transcendents in the "Records of the Assembled Transcendents of the Fortified Walled City"]. Ph. D. Diss., Chinese University of Hong Kong, Hong Kong.

Yao Ping. 2004. *Tangdai nüfu de shenghuo licheng* [The History and Lives of Tang Dynasty Women]. Shanghai: Wenji chubanshe.

Young, Ed, and A-Ling Louie. 1982. *Yeh-shen, A Cinderella Story from China*. New York: Sandcastle.

Yü, Chün-fang. 2001. *Kuan-yin: The Chinese Transformation of Avalokitesvara*. New York: Columbia University Press.

Yuan He, ed. 1980. *Shanhai jing jiaoju* [The Classic of Mountains and Seas, with Commentary]. Shanghai: Wenji chubanshe.

Zhou Yuru. 2004. *"Tangdai Chang'an nüguan."* [Daoist Nuns in Chang'an in the Tang Dynasty]. Paper presented at the International Conference on Daoism and the Contemporary World, Mount Qingcheng, Sichuan.

Zürcher, Erik. 1959. *The Buddhist Conquest of China*. Leiden: Brill Academic Publishers.

_____. 1980. "Buddhist Influence on Early Daoism." *T'oung Pao* 66:84-147.

Index